Resounding Afro Asia

AMERICAN MUSICSPHERES

Series Editor
Mark Slobin

RESOUNDING AFRO ASIA

Interracial Music and the Politics of Collaboration

Tamara Roberts

OXFORD
UNIVERSITY PRESS

Oxford University Press is a department of the University of Oxford. It furthers the University's objective of excellence in research, scholarship, and education by publishing worldwide. Oxford is a registered trade mark of Oxford University Press in the UK and certain other countries.

Published in the United States of America by Oxford University Press
198 Madison Avenue, New York, NY 10016, United States of America.

© Oxford University Press 2016

Library of Congress Cataloging-in-Publication Data
Names: Roberts, Tamara.
Title: Resounding Afro Asia : interracial music and the politics of collaboration / Tamara Roberts.
Description: Oxford ; New York : Oxford University Press, [2016] | Includes bibliographical references and index.
Identifiers: LCCN 2015028851| ISBN 978–0–19–937740–4 (hardcover : alk. paper) | ISBN 978–0–19–937741–1 (pbk. : alk. paper)
Subjects: LCSH: Music and race—United States. | Asian Americans—Music—History and criticism. | African Americans—Music—History and criticism.
Classification: LCC ML3917.U6 R63 2016 | DDC 780.89/0596095—dc23
LC record available at http://lccn.loc.gov/2015028851

1 3 5 7 9 8 6 4 2
Printed by Webcom, Canada

Publication of this book was supported by the Dragan Plamenac Endowment of the American Musicological Society, funded in part by the National Endowment for the Humanities and the Andrew W. Mellon Foundation.

*For G'mommy
and
Grandpa Bob*

Contents

Contents

Acknowledgments

I will begin where most typically end, by thanking my family. My love and appreciation go out to the entire interrelated web of Roberts, Doak, Paradiso, and Fields members. You all have taught me firsthand the ins and outs, highs and lows, wonders and difficulties of building relationships across multiple lines of difference. I am grateful for your unending support and confidence in my abilities, even when I doubt them myself. As the newest addition to my family, Melissa Reyes has been the bedrock of my final years with this project. You have listened as I talked through my argument again and again (and again), offered invaluable suggestions, tolerated for way too long the dishes I left piled in the sink and the clothes I left crumpled on the floor, and continually reminded me that there is life outside of and beyond this book. I could not have done this without you, mi amor.

Like many first books, this one began as a dissertation project. I am indebted to my committee—Inna Naroditskaya, Micaela di Leonardo, and E. Patrick Johnson—for their investment in my scholarly training and continued support in the years since graduation. As my graduate (life?) advisor, Patrick, you deserve special praise. You have been there from the very beginning to the very end and I only hope to pay forward to my own students the time and energy you have expended on me. I would also like to thank other teachers, mentors, and colleagues (as the years pass, the roles shift) that supported my work in its formative stages and more fully realized forms, including Jennifer Brody, Susan Manning, Sandra Richards, Margaret Thompson Drewal, Paul Edwards, Dwight Conquergood, Stephen Hill, Ramón Rivera-Servera, Nitasha Sharma, and Alexander Weheliye.

Many thanks to my colleagues at the University of California, Berkeley. The faculty and staff of the Department of Music have provided needed support as I developed my work, especially Bonnie Wade, Jocelyne Guilbault, Benjamin Brinner, and James Davies. Conversations with graduate students in my Readings in American Musical Cultures and Topics in Performance Studies seminars have also been generative, as well as ongoing engagement with and research assistance from Beezer de Martelly. I have also been greatly aided by fantastic colleagues from across the university, including Brandi Catanese, Cecilia Lucas, Michael Omi, Juana María Rodríguez, Shannon Steen, Scott Saul, and Bryan Wagner.

A network of other scholars has been influential and indispensable in my completion of this book. My gratitude goes to Rashida Braggs, Tracy McMullen, Pattie Hsu, Jayson Beaster-Jones, Marcia Ochoa, Ellie Hisama, Ryan Bañagale, Ronald Radano, Victoria Levine, Kevin Fellezs, Deborah Wong, Kristin McGee, Öykü Potuoğlu-Cook, Fred Lieberman, the Northwestern University performance dissertation working group, and the staff and faculty of the University of Connecticut Asian and Asian American Studies Institute. For technical assistance in research, I would like to recognize the staff of the University of Connecticut Thomas J. Dodd Research Center, especially Kristin Eshelman. And for their excellent guidance through the publication process, I would like to thank Mark Slobin, Suzanne Ryan, the various Assistant Editors at Oxford University Press, and the anonymous readers from OUP whose comments greatly impacted the final manuscript. Domini Dragoone created the wonderful figures throughout the book. Ann T. Greene was graciously helpful in my quest for permission to use some of Fred Ho's works and Sonoko Kawahara offered invaluable access to production photos from *Deadly She-Wolf Assassin at Armageddon!*

I have been enriched by engagements with Marguerite Horberg, Ashraf Manji, Maya Kronfeld, Rafael Maya, Pablo Luis Rivera, Daisy Simmons, Kirbie Crowe, Jenny Holland, and Candice Hoyes. In addition, ongoing creative endeavors with Las Bomberas de la Bahía, The Crane and the Crow, The Singing Bois, and Ragged Wing Ensemble kept me grounded and mindful of the concrete realities of doing artistic work.

In its various phases, this project has been supported by a Ford Foundation Predoctoral Fellowship; University of Connecticut Asian and Asian American Studies Institute Fred Ho Fellowship; Northwestern University Presidential Fellowship and Graduate Research Grant; and University of California, Berkeley Humanities Research Fellowship, Faculty Research Grant, Institute of International Studies Manuscript Mini-Conference Grant, and Townsend Center for the Humanities Faculty Fellowship.

Last but certainly not least, I would like to thank the artists and other cultural workers that appear in this book. Exploring your propositions for bettering the world through music has inspired me, challenged me, shifted some of my long-held beliefs, and affirmed others. I am forever grateful for the time you took to speak with me, your willingness to share your thoughts and desires, the numerous invitations to rehearsals, performances, meals, and gatherings, and—always—your brilliant music.

Resounding Afro Asia

Introduction
Echoes of the Future

R ed Barock//The White House//04.02.12. A Facebook photo album is the only known documentation of New York–based Red Baraat's debut performance in the nation's capital (Red Baraat 2012b). Posted on the band's page, the twenty images hint at what appears to have been an electrifying performance. Blending an Indian wedding (*baraat*) band format, *bhangra* rhythms, New Orleans jazz, funk, and hip hop, the group entertained a predominantly Asian crowd in the Indian Treaty Room. Recounting the event, leader Sunny Jain added, "Not us, the other kind [of Indian]," highlighting the irony of his band appearing in a room by that name.[1] Indeed, this event was part of redefining what "Indian" means in the White House and the United States. The performance was staged for a philanthropic briefing as part of the White House's Initiative on Asian Americans and Pacific Islanders (AAPI). This working group—created by Clinton, dormant under Bush, and revived by Obama—is charged with improving "the quality of life of AAPIs through increased participation in Federal programs in which such persons may be underserved" (Obama 2009, 3). According to the band's website, the audience was expecting a string quartet (Red Baraat 2012a), but the band surprised and delighted listeners with its celebratory and participatory vibe. Blurry photos show a swirl of motion conjured by the group's glistening horns, listeners' smiles and outstretched hands, and Jain leaping into the air with his *dhol*.

Red Baraat is a perfect reflection of the commission's goals. With members who are Indian, Japanese, Middle Eastern, and Pacific Islander—not to mention black and white—they represent the diversity of Asian America. The group also highlights a shifting conception of Asian Americanness in which South and Southeast Asians are included alongside historically represented East Asians and their descendants. While the Asian population grew faster than any other racial group in the United States between 2000 and 2010, the Asian Indian population grew the fastest among the national and cultural groups within that category (Hoeffel, Rastogi, Kim, and Shahid 2012, 1, 16). With this growth has come a larger domestic audience for South Asian folk and popular culture like *bhangra* and *baraats*, which has spilled over into mainstream U.S. culture.

1

Yet Red Baraat's music is not wholly Indian. Jain had already made a name for himself as a jazz drummer, releasing three albums before founding Red Baraat in 2008. After purchasing a *dhol* on a whim while traveling in India, he took lessons and was inspired by the "whole other animal" that was unleashed in him when he played the drum. Jain says he created Red Baraat as a vehicle to play the *dhol* and experiment with the wedding band format that had impressed him when visiting India as a child. He funneled this music he found to be "exotic" through a jazz aesthetic, creating space for improvisation and developing music that he believed reflected his Indian and U.S. American heritage. He also wished to counter an elitism he saw rampant in the jazz world. While appreciating the music, Jain felt the scene had lost touch with its audience, attracting fewer listeners and being caught in esoteric inside jokes that alienated rather than embraced them. With Red Baraat, he aimed to create what he calls "community music" with an ensemble that is equally capable of playing onstage in a traditional venue or offstage in a local event, like it did at the nascent Occupy protests. Merging traditions, Jain sought to reinvigorate the performative and political potential for all of them.

Red Baraat was invited to bring this Afro Asian musical dialogue to the White House. Exceeding the bounds of the Asian American frame, it presented a group identity that was intercultural and interracial. While the full weight of "Red Barock" was not realized (the president did not attend the event), the band showcased a vision of U.S. Americanness that rivaled Obama's own variegated identity. Performing music from multiple cultural and, more importantly, racial demarcations, the band's work could not be reduced to a singular label any more than Obama's pedigree is accurately rendered as "black."[2]

Red Baraat is not the only "fusion" band to represent the nation in recent years. In 2007, under the administration of George W. Bush, Los Angeles–based Ozomatli began a series of world tours as U.S. State Department Cultural Ambassadors (Medina 2014, 9–10). The group was an odd choice, given its outspoken leftist and antiwar politics. Yet in light of the administration's challenges with immigration reform and the internationally unpopular War on Terror, the band's multihued faces and blend of North African, South Asian, Middle Eastern, Caribbean, Latin, and African American sounds were deemed a perfect emblem of supposedly progressive U.S. values. Like the jazz ambassadors of the mid-twentieth century, Ozomatli and Red Baraat were chosen to represent the United States as a country that tolerates and celebrates racial and cultural difference.[3] Fusion has become, so to speak, the new black.

In fashion jargon, the "new black" refers to the season's color that will unseat black as the paragon of sophistication and elegance (while never fully casting off the original as the quintessence). I use this phrase euphemistically to refer to a moment of cultural shift signaled by multicultural fusion music's vexed embrace by the Bush and Obama administrations as an emblem of Americanness. But I also use this phrase literally to indicate how a nation long invested in signs of blackness as evidence of egalitarianism has slowly given way to embrace broader evocations of brownness to signal the same thing. Red Baraat's appearance in Washington, D.C. evidences what Jeff Chang calls the "colorization" of the United States: the increased presence of people of color and their culture in mainstream discourse (Chang 2014). Not only has this process resulted in more visible diversity in media and other social realms, it has productively worked to unseat the black–white dichotomy as the paradigm of racial conversation.[4] At the same time, it begs questions about the continued role for and significance of blackness in conceptions of U.S. nationhood.

This book examines interracial music as a window onto interminority racial politics. I focus on Afro Asian performances: physical and/or sonic spaces in which blackness and Asianness coincide, through the juxtaposition of musical traditions, visual representations, and the identities of the artists that perform them. In the past decade, a number of "world fusion" bands like Red Baraat, Ozomatli, Dengue Fever, Balkan Beat Box, Antibalas, and Yerba Buena came to prominence in U.S. popular music, billed as sonic evidence of the intersection of people of color in the demographically shifting First World.[5] While heralded as new, I suggest these ensembles are instead the latest manifestation of musical relationships, aesthetic strategies, and political visions with a much longer—and at times more radical—history. To historicize the greater mainstream circulation of these world fusion groups, I examine Afro Asian projects that set the stage for them: Yoko Noge and her Jazz Me Blues and Japanesque ensembles (blues and Japanese folk), Funkadesi (Indian folk/classical, reggae, and funk), Fred Ho and the Afro Asian Music Ensemble (jazz and world music), and the unintended Afro Asian reception of Truth Hurts's 2003 hit "Addictive" (hip hop and Bollywood). Detailing histories of artists who began their careers in the 1980s and 1990s and incorporating ethnographic research I did in the mid-2000s, I ask what they can tell us about changes in the U.S. racial terrain from the late twentieth to early twenty-first century.

Discourses of cultural hybridity are prevalent in discussions of U.S. American music.[6] But when hybrid music is discussed in racial terms, prevailing racial assumptions and the structures of the music industry paint them as mono-racial (e.g., jazz as black or country as white). I claim that Afro Asian music is *interracial*, meaning its creators, audiences, and/or marketers explicitly acknowledge racial mixture in ways that co-opt and obfuscate industry structures based on racial segregation. By foregrounding multiply raced bodies and sounds, Afro Asian ensembles perform group identities and aesthetic utterances that cannot be collapsed into one officially sanctioned racial category. The latter half of the twentieth century brought increasing opportunities for the expression of identities that do not neatly fit into a "one-box" racial system.[7] Afro Asian music can help us think through the stakes of interracial identity formation, especially between multiple nonwhite categories or groups. Querying the im/possibilities of racial flexibility—both as mandated by institutional structures and as a progressive political strategy—provides insight into U.S. racial discourse that, unlike the majority of the Americas, has not sanctioned official frameworks for marking racial mixture (Pacini Hernandez 2010, 5–6). I explore the creation, performance, and consumption of Afro Asian music to reveal strategies that artists have developed to push against dominant racial divisions, as well as the longstanding racist structures that ignore, obscure, or challenge their success.

I highlight Afro Asian music because it displays in heightened relief the dominant perceptions of U.S. interminority relations. Media coverage of events like the 1992 uprisings in Los Angeles often portrays blacks and Asian/Americans in a state of conflict.[8] In racial discourse, Asians are labeled the "model minority" in comparison to the black "underclass." Similarly, popular representations of "Asian" music valorize it as high culture with complex, spiritual, exotic sounds. By contrast, "black" music is embraced as national culture yet often depicted as simple, hypersexual, or violent. Despite dominant conceptions of black–Asian enmity, this is not the full story. There has been a long history of joint labor organizing, antiracist mobilization, and urban cultural confluence, most notably the U.S. arms of the mid-twentieth-century global Third World (or Afro Asian) movement.[9] Music has been a key component of these allegiances and there is a rich history of black–Asian mutual influence and cooperation in multiple genres that span the twentieth century.[10] I present here stories that recognize complexity in how Afro Asian relationships are lived, often overlooked in typical narratives.

Music becomes "black" or "Asian" through a process I call *sono-racialization*: the organization of sound into taxonomies based on racialized conceptions of bodies.[11] Sounds are produced by bodies (for my purposes here, human) but once emitted can carry social and political meanings of their own.[12] Yet because race is assumed to be of the body, racialized sound retains a link to its attributed producer or whom it is supposed to represent, even if it has nothing to do with the actual cultural expressions of those bodies. Anyone, regardless of their race, can participate in the production of sonic blackness or Asianness for they are discursive signifiers that can be deployed or consumed toward the production or maintenance of racial structures. Of course, race is not a politically neutral phenomenon; its very foundation is predicated on maintaining unequal distributions of power. Thus, sono-racialization refers specifically to the incorporation of sound into a racial hierarchy: that is, it is both a *racial* and *racist* enterprise.[13]

Popular music is a potent site for understanding how blackness and Asianness have been jointly constructed in U.S. racial discourse and policy. This book reveals that representations and tangible structures of the culture industry have long operated with what Claire Jean Kim refers to as "racial triangulation." Racial triangulation is a geometric model for understanding the co-construction of whiteness, blackness, and Asianness along axes of "superior/inferior" and "insider/foreigner" (C. J. Kim 1999, 107). Asian Americans, Kim argues, have been valorized over blacks while simultaneously ostracized from U.S. civic life. In various iterations, this arrangement has permeated the nation's racial taxonomy for the past 150 years. As I will show in Chapter 1, you can see the imprint of racial triangulation on tropes of musical blackness and Asianness and how African American and Asian/American artists are incorporated into the culture industry. But music does not simply reflect these racial dynamics. One of my major claims is that popular music has also been a space for the production of racial triangulation and is a powerful mechanism through which it continues to play out in the U.S. racial landscape.[14]

Yet popular music is also a site in which musicians challenge these essentializing and segregating structures. Most of the artists in this book consciously attempt to produce images of blackness and Asianness that counter stereotypical or monolithic representations. Fred Ho, for example, actively resisted representations of Asian/Americans as docile and apolitical in his highly politicized messaging and performance of a range of Asian/American traditions (see Chapter 4). The artists I analyze also engage in music and community making across racial lines in ways that struggle with and against their construction, meaning, or fixity. They perform multiple racialized genres in tandem, suggesting an affinity between sounds that are deemed incompatible in standard racial logic. Their ensemble memberships also include artists from multiple racial backgrounds and thus afford expressive spaces for the performance of interracial identities and the active negotiation of racial difference. Finally, their projects sometimes serve to promote audiences and venues that defy the still segregated arts scenes of the nation's "global cities." In all, Afro Asian artists perform racial possibilities that confound dominant offerings, even as they draw on its constitutive elements. The potential for sound to replicate or counter the extant racial system is a tension I tease out over the course of this book.

Sound is my starting point, but my goal is to illuminate the gestures artists make toward one another in order to create interracial music. Much of the scholarship on black-Asian musical interaction focuses on Asian/Americans performing black traditions[15] or blacks performing stereotyped Asian imagery.[16] Both of these streams focus on unidirectional, crossracial appropriations. Only a few studies deal with interactions between black and Asian artists, a lacuna I aim to fill.[17] I illuminate spaces in which black and Asian performers engage "black" and "Asian sounds," offering a chance to hear from participants from multiple racial positions. Reading accounts of Asian/Americans performing black music, I often find myself wondering what black artists have to say, and how black music might function as something more than a tool for nonblack expression. And while discussions of black musical Orientalism are important, I want to explore what it means for black artists to perform actual Asian traditions with Asian people. I document endeavors that arise from the choices artists make to step outside of their extant communities, often against great odds. In the process, Afro Asian musicians forge new musical networks based on their shared desire to cross racial lines rather than the commonality of race, culture, musical style, or geography. At the same time, they model the differences, frustrations, and tension that manifest in interracial sites, as well as strategies they have tried in order to deal with them.

Rather than a fixed aesthetic or identity category, "Afro Asian" (or "interracial" more broadly) marks artistic and social processes through which race is dialectically constructed and deconstructed. I argue that the cases presented here are sites of *sono-racial collaboration*: intentional engagements in which artists employ racialized sound to form and perform interracial rapport. Sono-racial collaboration occurs in multiple ways in Afro Asian projects. First, artists forge relationships with artists of other racial or cultural backgrounds, employing sound as a medium for interracial communication and bonding. Artists also collaborate with racialized sounds in order to express born or chosen identities or understand themselves in relation to broader racial categories. Most surprisingly, racialized sounds themselves collaborate, working in tandem to construct interracial discourses even when bodies are not present (although always implied). Between these three dynamics, we can see that while often spoken about in the singular, collaborations are inherently plural and each site is a web of negotiations across multiple lines of difference. The musicians I discuss often come together with a desire for interracial engagement, but amidst mixed and sometimes competing goals, collaboration and coalition seldom make for a neat and tidy end result. Collaboration, in short, takes work, and often includes moments of both cooperation and discord.

Sono-racial collaboration is a dynamic praxis that contrasts with the static and bounded presentation of difference in multicultural spaces of the culture industry. Analyzing Afro Asian performance can thus provide opportunity to appraise the history of "multiculturalism" and its segregating discourses that persist in the culture industry. Born out of the hard-won gains of the social movements of the 1960s and 1970s, "radical" multiculturalism was meant to give voice to the unique concerns of people of color in the United States through the insertion of their histories and experiences into dominant institutions.[18] As Vijay Prashad details, for example: "In the aftermath of the civil rights movement, students of color fought against the assumption that American culture can be entirely grasped by a study of Europeanized high cultural artifacts" (2001, 59). In the arts, "pre-multicultural" performance—live and recorded—was primarily based on the white performance or framing of nonwhite music and people. Radical multicultural artists pushed for space to present themselves in dominant spaces.[19] The performance of marginalized identities was mobilized as a tool for political action, and artists and activists wielded images of racial and cultural Otherness as part of broader strategies for social and economic enfranchisement. These efforts slowly resulted in increased representation of people of color in mainstream media, and the greater circulation of diverse practices led many artists of color to work increasingly across racial and cultural lines.

In the 1970s and 1980s, however, these diversifying strategies were co-opted by dominant institutions as a tool for racial management.[20] Initially, "liberal" multiculturalism appeared to be a triumph: the official acknowledgment of the value of racial and ethnic diversity by elite socio-political institutions. As it unfolded, however, this policy bounded and contained difference, requiring marginalized subjects to assimilate into dominant classifications.[21] Liberal multiculturalism mandated how people of various backgrounds should be organized within U.S. social institutions such as health-care systems, voting configurations, education, jobs, and demographic analyses such as the census.[22] Pluralism, one manifestation of liberal multiculturalism, was promoted as an antidote to earlier assimilationist policies (Goldberg 1994, 6). But while these gestures invited the incorporation of diverse people and cultures into the national body, it was through a "leveling" of inter- and intraracial/cultural distinctions and the continued privileging of dominant culture (Lowe 1996, 90). In this era, "identity" became one's key to accessing social and economic capital, and artists of marginalized identities struggled to work against these structures and/or make themselves legible within them.

In the 1990s, "corporate" multiculturalism promoted the use of images of multihued bodies to sell products. The "mainstreaming" of multiculturalism (Chang 2014) suggested the goals of radical multiculturalists had been met: society was wildly brown and all had purported access to socioeconomic advancement through capitalist consumption. Identity was employed as a way to target niche markets and enfold diverse people and cultures into a neoliberal economy (Taylor 2007). During this same time, majority voices also strengthened their use of "color-blind" discourses that claimed all citizens had universal access to civic power and thereby removed support for the material enfranchisement of people of color.[23] In response to these dynamics, scholars grew critical of claims of multicultural harmony and desires for transcending racial boundaries grew suspect.[24] Representations of marginalized people and cultures in arts programming, advertising, and popular media, scholars argued, had become what Joseph Roach refers to as "effigies"—surrogates that stand in for the absence of an original and help perpetuate the status quo (1996, 36). It seemed the "hegemonic" forms of multiculturalism (liberal and corporate) had eroded the possibility that the multiculturalist ideology could ever again serve progressive political agendas.

All of the multicultural projects I have laid out—progressive and conservative—rely on a politics tying singularly raced bodies to a particular cultural output. This *body–culture determinism*, as I call it, is based on the belief that culture is the inevitable result of race: that when a particularly raced body is present, it will perform certain types of culture.[25] In the projects I chronicle, individuals collaborate with racially marked sounds that do not "match" their racial identity and bands create collective utterances that do not stand in one-to-one correlation with the racial makeup of their membership. They thus resist body–culture determinism and illuminate the performative nature of sono-racial expression. The groups I engage rely on the multicultural marking of difference in their music, staging, and costuming in order to make their interracial dialogues legible. Yet they also surprise in actualizing more complex versions of race and culture that exceed multicultural frameworks erected by the markets they engage. Thus, while the multiple multiculturalisms created a space for these artists to fill, I suggest that listening more closely reveals how they grapple with and against the limits of these discourses.

Instead of demonstrating a sharp break between radical and hegemonic multiculturalism, I argue that Afro Asian artists demonstrate how the revolutionary spirit of the former was kept alive through the culture wars of the 1980s and 1990s—when governing bodies attempted to silence more progressive multicultural voices by refusing them funding (Catanese 2012)—and into the 2000s. In this sense, my investigation shares common ground with Robin D. G. Kelley and Vijay Prashad's notion of "polyculturalism," a "provisional concept grounded in antiracism rather than in diversity" (Prashad 2001, xi).[26] Kelley and Prashad pose this term as an antidote to multiculturalism, to more accurately render the engagements between people of color in the United States and abroad as dynamic and counterhegemonic. I build on this conception by showing that, despite mainstream diversity parades, there is real interracial and intercultural activity that happens between people of color even when obscured in multicultural spaces. Afro Asian sites can thus present what Cruz Medina calls "subversive complicity" by working within dominant systems while simultaneously expressing counterdominant messages or actions that speak against those systems (Medina 2014). Because of this dual nature, however, I will show that even the most progressive Afro Asian performances are contested and provisional.

Criticizing multiculturalism has been a major scholarly project and, while some may now see this work as passé, I am reviving and refreshing this line of analysis for several reasons.[27] First, my research makes clear that it is still the governing paradigm for civic, nonprofit, and many for-profit arts spaces, as well as a term artists themselves use to refer to their work. Second, I believe the rush to discredit liberal and corporate multiculturalism inadvertently threw into question the radical project. I argue that we should not throw the baby out with the bathwater, especially as the experience of "cross-racial" and "cross-cultural" engagement is a reality for many people of color. Further, in a scholarly economy in which ethnic studies must fight to keep from being expunged from our institutions of higher education—and in some cases has lost this battle—it serves contemporary race theorists well to continue to build on this legacy. Third, especially in the so-called postracial era, I am intrigued by questions of what comes "next," especially as scholarly theorizations relate or do not relate to racial discussions in communities outside of the academy. If multiculturalism is indeed old news, how might interracial music propose new paradigms?[28]

To answer this question, I focus on key examples of sono-racial collaboration as opposed to delineating a historical lineage of Afro Asian music. Each chapter describes a particular impetus toward this action: shared oppression, personal affinity, community building, antiracist politics, and shared aesthetic pleasure. These motives are not mutually exclusive and most operate to various degrees across the case studies. But I have chosen to concentrate my analysis of each in one site in which they are central to the artists' mission. Each chapter also exposes how racial triangulation unfolds in the culture industry through discursive representation, city arts programming, venue spatialization, multicultural discourses, and music journalism. Each case highlights how artists mediate these dynamics by building interracial solidarity, nurturing intimate relationships, building interracial audiences, resisting identity politics, and interpreting texts in nonhegemonic ways. Examining a mix of individual biographies, ensemble histories, and interactions, I reveal commonalities across Afro Asian musical endeavors, including the deep exploration of root cultures, performance of these forms across musical/racial lines, and active engagement in the culture economy.

My goal, at the disciplinary level, is to complicate conversations about music and social identity by bringing them together with theory addressing joint racialization and mixed race identity. I thus engage literature from ethnomusicology, popular music studies, ethnic studies, American studies, and performance studies. Race is, of course, only one possible angle from which to approach my case studies. I have chosen it because of the power that this category of sociopolitical organization holds in the realm of popular music. While some voices declare the declining relevance of studies of identity, I believe this is, in part, a response to the limited sense in which identity has often been explored in relation to music.[29] *Resounding Afro Asia* argues for the continued relevance of studying identity conception and interpretation while suggesting ways to enliven this discussion. In a society still bent on defining for people of color who they are, identity matters. It is also political; not in the narrow identity politics of multiculturalism, but by the very fact that identities continue to shape how individuals engage with the social, political, and economic institutions around them.

In the remainder of this introduction, I will lay out some of the key theoretical issues I engage in this book and consider how analyzing Afro Asian music can help us think more deeply about them. In particular, I will discuss how this music helps us to understand the im/possibilities of sonoracial mixture and multiplicity, the racializing structures of the culture industry, and theorizations that attempt to frame race beyond standard black–white dichotomies.

Mixing Music

Black and Asian American music have provided powerful spaces for the performance of racial identity and articulation of counterdominant politics. Numerous studies detail the histories of black popular music in the United States and examine musical expressions of blackness as political interventions.[30] Because of the ubiquitous presence of black music in U.S. popular culture, scholarship on black musical politics has focused on differentiating it from a white "mainstream" and illuminating the racially inflected histories that inform even the most popular styles. Following in this stead, a number of scholars have similarly documented the musical production of Asian Americans in relation to racial politics in the United States.[31] These works began to emerge at a critical moment in the study of music and race, answering calls to "diversify" racial conversation in music studies and move past the equation of "race" with "black" (Radano and Bohlman 2000). In contrast to black music studies, these texts note the lack of mainstream representation of Asian American musical voices and jointly make a case for the presence of these forms in U.S. national culture, a point I make strongly with this study. But whereas it is seen as a given that black music is a homegrown expression, recent Asian American music has had to contend with the fact that, in the words of Deborah Wong, "Americans are definitely not at all sure what the difference is between Asians and Asian Americans and thus have no idea what Asian American music might be" (2004, 13). A major theme in this literature is that there has been no operative category of "Asian American" music in U.S. popular music discourse precisely because Asian/Americans are consistently racially constructed as outsiders to the nation.[32]

The best writings from both of these literatures trouble predominant assumptions of what constitutes black or Asian/American music by illuminating the heterogeneity of material performed by individuals of these racial backgrounds. My analysis of Afro Asian music expands on this intention, further querying the rigid boundaries of what constitutes black or Asian sonic identity. While scholarship has tended to treat these subjects separately, there are many ways in which blacks and Asians have used music associated with the other as part of their own expressive formations. Reading scholarship on black and Asian musical identities together reveals this mutual influence and works against mono-racially delimited conversations that pose either group solely against a white mainstream. Instead, I investigate the complex racial terrain and multiple power differentials at play when blackness, Asianness, whiteness, and other racial identities intersect in music, especially when nondominant bodies crossracially perform.

Afro Asian music creates a space similar to what Kevin Fellezs—borrowing from Isobel Armstrong—calls a "broken middle," a space between musical and racial categories that causes one to question their boundaries by remaining between them (2011, 9, 5). Fellezs uses this term in his study of jazz–rock–funk fusions in the late 1960s and 1970s, troubling how we understand genre as connected to racialized bodies. He argues that the "inability to be articulated by dominant discourse or to be pinned down to a particular set of musical characteristics" means these fusions hold the potential to reframe racial discourses, allow for more holistic self-expression, and speak to "individuals ... whose disheveled fit between categories allows them to challenge the displacements, misrecognitions, and histories that seek to silence them" (Fellezs 2011, 226, 228). My account of Afro Asian music similarly explores the flows between racial conceptions, cultural spaces, and individual experiences. Its creators hold multiple spaces in the "broken middle" that satisfy the culture industry and defy its parameters, playing the racial game while troubling it from the inside.

At the same time, artists operating in these interstitial spaces can also fall into what Christopher Waterman calls the "excluded middle" (2000). In his whirlwind analysis of the history of the song "Corrine Corrina" (first recorded in 1928), Waterman identifies multiple racial significations the song and those that performed it held. He argues that the song accumulated many racial meanings due to its origin in the hands of a racially mixed musician, Bo Chatmon, who worked across the black–white color line in the 1920s South. Waterman claims that Chatmon has been ignored in music studies because he does not fit into a racially segregated version of Southern music history. I build on Fellezs and Waterman's work as they argue for the recognition of people and sounds that do not sit neatly within existing sono-racial demarcations and the need for scholarship that accounts for their histories. While neither says so, they both implicitly call for work on race and popular music that does not reproduce racist structures. I heed this important call by accenting musical and social spaces—the "middles"—and the processes that produce and sustain them. In reality, to draw from Homi Bhabha, there is no single "third space" (1990). Rather, interracial music perpetually forms broken and excluded middles that are multiple and shifting.

An emerging conversation on racial mixing and passing in popular music has begun the important work of showing how sono-racial flexibility can destabilize racial structures—tangible and discursive.[33] At the group level, the urban confluence of people of color has provided opportunities for what Gaye Theresa Johnson calls "spatial entitlements," reclamations of space through the formation of interracial political and artistic coalitions (2013). In many cases, these alliances of, typically, working-class communities have resulted in a sharing of cultural material between racial groups and the joint production of existing and new forms. On a smaller scale, individual artists also articulate the conjunction of racial identities in their self-identification and presentation. In his work on Jero, an African American *enka* singer who is also part Japanese, Fellezs suggests Jero makes conscious musical, costume, and gestural choices from a variety of cultural possibilities available to him, rather than his music simply reflecting a mixed heritage (2012). In both of these examples, sono-racial collaboration is an agent toward aesthetic and/or political self-determination.

The ability for artists to change sono-racial identities further illuminates the extremes and limits of sono-racial collaborations formed between artists, sounds, and listeners. Examining the cases of musicians who successfully changed their racial identities over the course of their careers alongside some who were received as mono-racial despite their mixed backgrounds, George Lipsitz argues that the ability of these artists to "fool" the public "underscores the constructed and artificial nature of racial categories in a way that might lead us to new and productive ways of thinking" (2007, 190). Most important to my work here is Lipsitz's call to allow for self-definition to be considered a legitimate form of identity expression. Especially when these identifications cross boundaries enacted by a racist structure, they can function as acts of defiance that might empower the individual even if not altering the system. However, while Lipsitz claims that the power of mixed raceness is available for anyone to use as an antiracist tool, I argue for a more critical politics around how this identity is employed and question, in particular, the limits of self-naming.

Afro Asian and other interracial music propose that musical identity can be both a product of, in Lipsitz's words, "blood and bone" as well as "branching out," strategically connecting to other racial or cultural groups in order "to create new identities without having to surrender the historical consciousness and situated knowledges specific to their group" (2007, 205–206).[34] Rather than structuring a study around single racially demarcated "communities," I look for ways to theorize both heritage and affiliation as authentic claims to musical sound. Along these same lines, I argue against geography as a sole determinant of musical expression and identity formation. Rather than a result of populations in proximity, the interracial exchanges I chronicle are based on intentional crossing of physical and discursive spaces demarcated by race.

By resisting simple equations of race and sound, I ultimately seek to give credence to the aesthetic choices artists of color make, something deterministic race-based studies inadvertently deny. In his classic *Omni-Americans: Black Experience and American Culture* (1970), Albert Murray argues that the blues was no plain result of or response to racial and economic hardship. Instead, he says, the blues aesthetic is about meaning making and a particular approach to engaging with the world (1970, 58). While white artists have long been afforded the freedom to make music as a result of *who* they are and *what* they want to create, people of color are often seen as producing the by-product of their racial existence: a black person makes black music because they are black versus a white person who chooses to engage a particular aesthetic.[35] In this book, I show that Afro Asian music is a result of both impetuses, often in surprising ways. Much scholarship on music and race remains invested in the notion that music is defined solely by who makes it. Instead, I propose that music is also defined by what it does rather than what it is. The resulting interracial spaces and sounds are as myriad as the people who create them and vary in their success. Nevertheless, they provide a record of the ways in which differently raced people choose to interact in order to shift the terms on which they do so.

Mixing Race

To better theorize the production of collective interracial identities, I engage scholarly discussions of mixed-race identity. Starting in the

1990s but significantly increasing in the 2000s, this conversation consists of interrogations that link mixed-race identity formation to larger racial discourses,[36] consideration of mixed-race figures in the literary and other arts,[37] and popular fiction and nonfiction that chronicle the lives of mixed-race people, especially children.[38] From a variety of perspectives, these conversations use mixed-race personhood as a way to reveal the historic underpinnings of racial structures in the United States and abroad, and pose strategies for disrupting this legacy.

As an aesthetic analog to mixed-race identity, interracial music forces us to revise basic assumptions at the center of many of these projects. By exploring race mixing between people and sounds, I wish to challenge scholarly presentations of mixed-race identity that focus only on the level of the individual. A claim at the heart of mixed-race advocacy is that people have a right to be their true selves and have their identities that cross racial lines validated.[39] But "mixed race" is an oxymoron: the point of race is that it is bounded even as culture cuts across. Naomi Zack says, "The term 'mixed race' seems self-contradictory once it becomes clear that the term 'race' always connotes purity" (Zack 1995, 300). Mixed status is often proven by cultural evidence or a notion of blended blood that maintains the very biological fixity that mixed race is supposed to work against. The focus on individuals also preserves a notion of race mixing based on heteronormative relationships and familial structures. Mixed children are the supposed result of reproductive sex between a man and a woman, reifying the race-as-biology position.

This concentration on mixed individuals confuses the biological with the social. And the locus of political action remains buried somewhere deep within a mixed person's body and psyche. I contend mixed raceness is better understood at the level of the communal. To me, the most interesting thing about interracial couples is not their progeny, but the relationships that developed to get them to that point. It is in interracial families, communities, organizations, and artistic encounters that new racial meanings and alliances are generated. A group or sound can do more productive work in destabilizing racial discourses than the mere existence of a mixed-race person because it is an externalized process. Interracial music makes audible the workings of mixed groups that identify with multiple racial positions. When this music is performed, artists and audiences tangibly participate in the experience of racial confrontation and negotiation.

While denaturalizing race, examining Afro Asian music also shows that what we often take for the substance of race is something different: culture. Mixed race is frequently taken as evidence of cultural hybridity and the results of mixed raceness are generally described in cultural terms (e.g., being caught between two worlds). But this notion is false, especially in the United States in which the hybrid nature of mainstream culture means that differently raced bodies can come into contact holding the exact same cultural material. How does one talk about the music created by rocker Lenny Kravitz, for example? His mixed black and white Jewish parentage is indeed reflected in the musical mix of European and

African elements but not because of his lineage.[40] To assume race and culture stand in for each other is to miss large parts of the story. We will see self-described mixed-race individuals in this book, but at no point will I suggest that this identity alone gives rise to the music they make. Further, nonblack and non-Asian artists appear, because these actors also have a hand in building Afro Asian spaces.

Music is a potent site for these explorations given the presence of aesthetic performances of race and culture and the "everyday" performance of identity.[41] It is especially useful to engage in relation to mixed-race studies as race and vision have long been conjoined as indexes for one another. Michele Elam claims that the desire to see race is a "flawed search for ontological gratification," but that while "the visible does not reveal biological or metaphysical truths, it most certainly indexes social realities" (2011, 25). The fetishization of mixed-race phenotypes, Elam argues, ends up disavowing those who do not appear racially ambiguous from serving as spokespersons. Music can challenge the reliance on a politics of visibility as the means toward mobilization and enfranchisement, providing a flexible space in which to resignify racially marked sounds. Music is both embodied and ephemeral. This double phenomenology means that it provides a medium through which to consider how bodies produce and disrupt racial meaning. Even more, as an experience that must unfold through time, music provides an important way into understanding the construction of race as a process.

I draw on performance theory throughout this text to provide a framework to understand how interracial performance can be both emergent and historically situated. The foundation of this work builds on Judith Butler's formulation of performativity—that identities are "tenuously constituted in time" through "stylized repetition of acts" (1990, 179). For example, E. Patrick Johnson suggests that "blackness" is a discursive combination of shifting signifiers and that "individuals or groups *appropriate* this complex and nuanced racial signifier in order to circumscribe its boundaries or to exclude other individuals or groups" (2003, 2–3). It is through performative acts that these signifiers cement into identity at any given moment. Similarly, Dorinne Kondo suggests that by viewing race as performative, "one necessarily engages recent social constructivist, poststructuralist, and deconstructive approaches to identity formation that subvert fixed, essentialist notions of identity—a critically important political move if one's goal is to effect social transformation" (1997, 7). Musical performance is a means through which bodies are racialized, but also a means through which individuals express identities counter to dominant norms. But, as Johnson reminds readers, "The consequences of its [blackness's] signification vary materially, politically, socially, and culturally depending on the body on which it settles" (2003, 218). My research plumbs the interstitial space between fixed notions of race and shifting identity performances.

As I try to distinguish between race and culture, I also recognize that they are deeply intertwined in their manifestation. While practically difficult to fully disengage how racial and cultural identities and institutions feed into one another, it is theoretically necessary to do so for culture has in many instances been used as a code word for race in hegemonic multicultural discourse. Claire Jean Kim suggests that the "field of racial positions has undergone one salient change in response to the post-civil rights context: it is now elaborated in nonracial terms ... talk about a group's culture often serves to disguise what are fundamentally racial claims" (2000, 53). This elision of race and culture has resulted in the conflation of lived practices and experiences with state-determined identity boxes, often simplifying or misrepresenting the former. Even more, the guise of cultural diversity has cloaked numerous "color-blind" projects that have neglected or attacked tangible racial redress, such as assaults on affirmative action. My system of separation is not foolproof, however, a fact that reveals the deeply ingrained confusion between race and culture in contemporary sociopolitical discourses. Afro Asian, for instance, is neither simply a racial nor cultural formation. Instead, it highlights the impossibility of ever separating the two: culture produces racial structures and race gives rise to culture.

I intentionally say "interracial" rather than "mixed race" because "inter-" indicates a moving, building, or space between categories. Key to my investigation is the notion that the mixing of race occurs at the level of the social. There are many collectives that are not served by mono-racial labeling. Can a musical community be defined by efforts toward inter-racialism rather than a fixed identity label? Are these categories that can hold meaning in our current racial system? Is it possible to speak about a cohesive community that is not simply black and Asian together but Afro Asian? Johnson argues that the performative essence of race allows it to circulate and be taken up by individuals regardless of heritage or phenotype (2003). It is no great leap, then, to propose that a group can perform multiple racial categories together. They do not combine into a new "body," however; they become a network of bodies, discursive categories, and sociopolitical meanings with varied consequences for their appropriations. I will thus explore the work of individual artists and ensembles as webs of relationships in process.

Racializing Sound

Despite the lived experience of racial redefinition found in this book's case studies, these projects also reveal the intensely segregated structures through which music is produced and consumed in the U.S. culture industry. Several studies have detailed the intentional ways racial separation was built into the music industry at the turn of the twentieth century.[42] Jim Crow laws colored musical reception, but the notion that music could express racial information was an emerging paradigm fostered by the industry's hand. While Southern black and white musicians shared a body of songs and techniques up until this period, Karl Hagstrom

Miller shows how industry actors—recording engineers, musicians, consumers, and scholars—sutured distinct sounds to different racial groups through a process he calls "segregating sound" (2010). Key to this process is that racially marked sounds were given meaning in their contrast to other sounds, instituting what Jennifer Stoever-Ackerman calls the "sonic color-line" (2010).

I argue that the sonic color-line ghettoized Asian/American music, segregating it both from white and black music. I add this sono-racial category to the conversation by incorporating literature on Asian racialization in popular music. In its messy unwieldiness that has historically encompassed everything from xenophobic send-ups of Chinese immigrants to exoticized tales of "Hindoo" princesses, "Asian music" is a perfectly poised example of the machinations it takes to solidify cultural practices into racial categories. Several studies have done much to illuminate how sonic depictions of Asianness corroborated conflicting racial notions of Asians in the United States: they were exotic and intriguing from afar but, once on "our" shores, become a dirty threat.[43]

This understanding of Asian music is thrown into greater relief when compared with "black music," which is typically claimed as uniquely U.S. American. Looking at the racialization of both categories together, I am able to show how the construction of one reinforces the other's profile. I also show how actual African American practices have been able to hold space in popular discourse, even if its representations are not completely controlled by black people. By contrast, very little of the Asian music that was purveyed in the early 1900s had anything to do with actual Asian/American traditions. Still, Ronald Radano has shown that many sonic tropes that define black music are less about properties that exist in African/American music and more about colonial notions of sono-racial difference that were perpetuated by creators and consumers of multiple races (2003). In this sense, sono-racial conceptions are frequently based on larger racial discourses rather than simply cultural differences between various populations.

Miller suggests that the early 1900s brought a shift from "minstrel" to "folklore" authenticity in the hearing of racialized sound (2010). Minstrel authenticity was based on the idea that race is performative and "genuine" black music could come from white bodies. This notion of sono-racialization shifted to folklore authenticity claiming that there are scientific racial essences embedded in musical practices and, for example, "real" black music could only come from black bodies. Jon Cruz corroborates Miller's account of the evolution of sono-racial thinking in his work on early African American religious music (1999). He notes how folklorists, clergy, and abolitionists jointly defined the "spiritual," crystallizing varied practices into an entity that could be studied and sold as evidence of essential blackness—toward conservative and progressive ends. While the move to folklore authenticity was partly a rejection of dominant stereotypes of African American practices, creating a definitive link between "black," "Asian," or "Latin" music and bodies marked by these labels often meant that people of a given race were required to enact bounded images of themselves in order to fit into a mainstream portrait of their musical identities.

This same linking of race and culture forms the basis for multiculturalism, especially as it adheres to body–culture determinism. The performances I analyze, however, show there is the possibility that racialized sound can legitimately come from differently raced bodies, although these gestures must be matched with other aesthetic and political work to avoid replicating a minstrel dynamic. First, artists might operate with a desire to build relationships with those of other racial backgrounds through performing their music, versus the goal of separation documented in studies of historic minstrelsy.[44] Second, rather than perpetuating racial stereotypes, cross-racial performances can honor cultural histories and work toward producing accurate portrayal versus stereotypes. Finally, there are ways in which artists can be cognizant of power differentials between participants and work toward mitigating them. Many of the artists in this book are quite savvy about larger questions of race and power and have battled with the institutions that present them to do so in antiracist ways. Ultimately, I propose that the "one-can-do-whatever" minstrel model and the "one-can-only-do-their-own" folklore model are not the only options for racial performance.

In the 1990s, discourses of hybridity, or "fusion," offered new language to discuss musical authenticity, resulting in continued sono-racial segregation (Taylor 2007). As a marketing term, "fusion" was (and continues to be) attached to everything from cars, fashion, exercise programs, disposable razors, haute cuisine, and Pop-Tarts. In music, in addition to world fusion bands, there have been a host of one-time projects that have attempted to capitalize on this fad. For example, British record company owner Nick Gold—the mastermind behind the *Buena Vista Social Club*—orchestrated a collaboration between musicians from Mali and Cuba, resulting in the 2010 album *AfroCubism* (Hudson 2010). As is often the case in one-off fusions, this recording merges styles due to the producer's curiosity, rather than the musicians' impetus. At the fringe of the fusion trend are artists such as M.I.A. who, despite not actively drawing on hybridity discourse themselves, have been analyzed as such in popular media.[45]

"Fusion" is one of several terms used in a similar manner: east-meets-west, mash-up, hybrid, and global. John Hutnyk claims that for contemporary scholars, "Hybridity, diaspora and postcoloniality are now fashionable and eminently marketable terms," and Timothy Taylor has argued much the same for popular culture at the turn of the twenty-first century (Hutnyk 2000, 31; Taylor 2007). As these labels are overused, they become inadequate to signify distinct lived realities or cultural dynamics (after all, isn't everything a fusion?). Hutnyk and Taylor criticize discourses that treat hybridity as an inherently radical state or as the merging of cultures that are not themselves already hybrid. Most importantly, they both expose how this discourse has become a way to stereotype and marginalize people of color by emphasizing exoticism, essentialism, or the separation of hybrids from the dominant culture, in effect "identifying, commodifying, and selling what on the surface is a new form of difference, but one that reproduces old prejudices and hegemonies" (Taylor 2007, 143).[46]

"Fusion" and "hybrid" are terms rarely used by the artists in this book, yet this sono-racial framework is frequently applied to their work. By reading their creations alongside this discourse, I am able to place race more squarely into these conversations that too frequently are figured only as "cultural." I am interested in exploring how hybrid aesthetics might intervene in discourses of racial essentialism, as well as how discussions of fusion support or counter sono-racial taxonomies. I also wish to unveil the ways in which "fusion" rarely results in a single finished product, following Falu Bakrania's claim that "multiple forms of 're-fusing' are at the heart of what is generally considered fusion" (2013, 10). Finally, since my center of attention is on minority–minority mergers, I expand existing conceptions of fusion music beyond white-nonwhite or West-non-West models.[47] By the 1990s, "collaboration" was a key trope used for discussing and marketing musical encounters between Western and non-Western artists. Exploring sono-racial collaboration between non-dominant parties, I intend to complicate scholarly narratives of appropriation and seek out instances of "cross-racial affiliative potential" in musical performance (Taylor 2007, 158).

Performing Afro Asia

Music made in tandem by multiple nonwhite people asks us to hear race beyond the black–white paradigm that has marked U.S. racial logic and popular culture for centuries. I concentrate on black–Asian sites as a potent racial combination that is often invoked as a symbol of interminority interaction. The turning of the twenty-first century brought interest in the ways these communities intersect. Journalists dissect mixed black–Asian celebrities such as Kimora Lee Simmons, Tiger Woods, and R&B singer Amerie. Restaurants like Hip-hop Chow and Sushi Blues serving African American soul food and various Asian cuisines crop up increasingly in cities like New York, Chicago, and Miami. And movies such as *Mississippi Masala* (1991), *Romeo Must Die* (2000), and the *Rush Hour* comedies (1998, 2001, 2007) use heteronormative romance or "buddy duos" to stand in for large-scale relationships between the two groups. This interest is predicated on the notion that blacks and Asians are a sociocultural odd couple. They are frequently figured as the most distant racial positions from one another—in valuation, citizenship status, and perceptions of cultural difference.

Galvanized by these popular currents, comparative ethnic studies scholars have responded with their own black–Asian explorations. These studies are meant to counteract the "ne'r the twain shall meet" discourse, posing black and Asian as mutually constructed racial categories and detailing nuanced encounters in the United States and abroad. Theorists plumb the depths of interminority tensions, arguing for their root in immigration laws[48] and domestic economies.[49] These texts do excellent work uncovering tangible factors that give rise to interracial struggles, revealing the longstanding hand the government has had in structuring these dynamics through programs that have engineered the nation's demographics. In some, though, the connections between the social and political are stated too deterministically and do not allow for the full agency of black and Asian actors to recognize or change their relationships. I aim to add to these works by showcasing examples of black–Asian encounters that occur due to the power of Afro Asian artists. Rather than being thrown together, I detail cases in which blacks and Asians choose to be in each other's company, allowing me to ask why and how they do so despite political-economic barriers.

Another stream of Afro Asian scholarship has focused on how the two racial groups have been jointly constructed, either in dominant discourse or more delimited black and Asian conversations.[50] Helen Jun, for example, shows that both racial groups have had to negotiate each other's exclusion in their own quests for national inclusion, while Vijay Prashad documents how representations of South Asian immigrants have been used as an antiblack "weapon" in dominant racial discourse and policy (Prashad 2000). While I focus more on the auspices of the culture industry, Jun and Prashad's theorizations are helpful for my understanding of the ways in which artists' impressions of each other become foils for their own racial and cultural expression. My book differs from these projects, however, in that the artists in my case studies, rather than desiring to ascend the racial ladder over one another, are more interested in raising their status together, and not simply toward whiteness. Shannon Steen's *Racial Geometries of the Black Atlantic, Asian Pacific and American Theatre* (2010) has proved useful in this regard, as she details alliances and misrecognitions between black and Asian artists in the mid-twentieth century. Steen's book draws connections between U.S. racial policy and international relations with nations of the Pacific Rim, arguing that race can function as an analytic to translate across multiple axes of space and power. She places performance at the center of her analysis, suggesting that "the most important reason to turn to performance ... is the way performers themselves function as representations of racial hierarchies but are also subject to them in their offstage lives" (2010, 20). In this respect, I build on Steen's project in examining the intersections between aesthetic and everyday Afro Asian performances.

Other scholars focus on solidarities built between blacks and Asian/ Americans through culture and politics.[51] These texts have inspired my work in the range of productive relationships that they chronicle, especially forged through art making and joint political actions. Of particular note are the anthologies *Afro Asia: Revolutionary Political and Cultural Connections Between African Americans and Asian Americans* (Ho and Mullen 2008) and *AfroAsian Encounters: Culture, History, Politics*

(Raphael-Hernandez and Steen 2006), which feature analyses of black–Asian exchanges that span location and era. A primary intervention I make into these studies is the postulation that this conglomeration can represent a community. Most of the previous studies are framed around the meeting of the two racial groups as separate entities. My research, on the other hand, suggests that new collectives are formed out of these encounters that exist as their own holistic unit, distinct from both black and Asian. Looking across my cases, I find continuity in that they are in some way framed as Afro Asian expressions, even when encompassing more than those two. This book posits Afro Asian as an entity unto itself and contributes to understanding what common dynamics flow across these varied interracial networks.

Of course, black–Asian is not the only interminority relationship worth exploring, and studies of black–Latino and Asian–Latino relationships have complicated this discussion.[52] Like Afro Asian studies, these publications similarly detail interracial tensions and/or shared racial experiences, although these elements may unfold quite differently than in black–Asian cases. Latinos are currently the largest minority population in the United States—while Asians are the fastest-growing—indicating the importance of these projects that focus on their connections to other marginalized groups (United States Census Bureau 2013). As such, I do not suggest that blackness and Asianness cover the full extent of the U.S. racial terrain, nor are they a stand-in for the particularities of other cross-racial engagements. When applicable, I discuss Latino people or Latin music here. Afro-Caribbean practices, in particular, are important in understanding how blackness exists outside of only African American contexts.

I am conscious of the pitfalls of comparative ethnic studies work that can too easily make equivalent categories or populations with significantly different access to power and ability to speak within interracial discussions. For example, Traise Yamamoto makes such dangers clear when she discusses the ways in which blacks suffer greater consequences than Asians when whites decide to shut down their "crosstalk" (2002). Likewise, as I detail in Chapter 5, critics of Afro Asian encounters frequently denigrate blackness as part of their analyses. Reading black, Asian, and other bodies together provides access to understanding how Afro Asian endeavors are marked by differences in power and privilege. A major theme running throughout this book is that blacks and blackness function in ways distinct from other nonwhite races in interracial formations. Marion Kilson argues that biracial people who are part black face a unique set of challenges compared to other mixed-race people in that they are less likely to be seen as something other than solely black (2001).[53] Black music, in a sense, faces the opposite problem: rather than being all-encompassing, it can very easily be erased in black–Asian settings in which jazz, blues, or other styles are simply viewed as "American." This predicament contrasts with the exoticizing of Asian musical practices and mixed Asian people.

Afro Asian scholarship has gone far to uncover a history of interracial convergence and coalition that refigures the U.S. racial taxonomy and cultural landscape as harboring people and experiences beyond a black–white binary. But I follow Julia H. Lee in contending, "The claim that Asians and Africans have a kinship based on intersecting histories of commerce and oppression operates with the same logic as the notion, propagated in the past forty years, that African Americans and Asians feel an implacable animosity toward each other" (2011, 3–4). Rather than posing my cases as indications of one or the other stream of black–Asian discourse, I suggest they present a range of projects that can exhibit both dynamics. As such, I highlight how blackness and Asianness are co-constructed as well as how antiracist actions for one group have the potential to support the other.

Afro Asian performances sound a history of black–Asian entanglements. They resonate with the cultural and affective politics of Afro Asian history, in which nonwhite people sought to determine their own identifications rather than remain slave to dominant representations. What emerges is the incompatibility of our existing racial and cultural language. On several occasions when discussing my work, I have been asked "which Asia?" At face value, this is a fair question. Asia is a vast continent with numerous people and cultures, and distinctive histories of how such varied populations end up in the United States. Thus, in this book, I take pains to point out distinctive East and South Asian stories and the ways in which people of these populations have not necessarily considered themselves akin to one another. But as I will show, there are many ways in which multiple Asian cultures have been racialized in similar positions in U.S. popular media—thus my decision to include both East and South in this study. I want my work to call out and critique the ways in which racial structures place varied groups into the Asian category through the same exoticizing gestures.

But why hasn't anyone asked me "which black?" The black people and forms represented in this study are from the African diaspora on multiple continents. Why can we talk about a supposedly unified African diaspora but not an Asian diaspora? Why do we say "black" and "Asian" when one refers to color and another a continent? I am not suggesting they are the same thing, but that we clarify why they are distinct and what factors have led to the differences between them. Nitasha Sharma discusses how African Americans express themselves in racial terms, while South Asian immigrants and their descendants speak more in a discourse of culture or ethnicity (2010). The difference between these social categories reduces the ability for communication and understanding. It also leads to scholarship that feels constricted because of the lack of terminology to speak across difference. I seek to stimulate new vocabularies that can translate between varied lives and experiences.

Instead of asking "which black?" or "which Asia?" or the implicit "which Afro Asia?," a more consequential question is "why Afro Asia?" Why pay attention to these crossings? What can they teach us? And why is music critical to these conversations? In this book, I show how cultural production is a key element that structures racial thought. There is a conscious and unconscious investment in maintaining sono-racial separation because there is a larger national and international investment in maintaining racial segregation. The culture industry operates by capitalizing on what is popular and familiar. Consuming culture that replicates existing structures works to perpetuate them; yet the creation and consumption of culture that resists these structures can work to unseat them. Afro Asian formations have the potential to do both. In what follows, I wish to show how crossed discourses of blackness and Asianness help us to better comprehend racial systems as a whole.

Moving Forward

What you will find in the chapters to come is born of an interdisciplinary methodology, including ethnography, critical theory, and music and performance analysis. From 2005 to 2010, I conducted field research on Yoko Noge's groups and Funkadesi in Chicago, and Fred Ho and the Afro Asian Music Ensemble in New York City. After this period, I did multiple follow-up and supplementary interviews, including one with Sunny Jain of Red Baraat. In total, I interviewed approximately thirty musicians, venue staff, audience members, and promoters. I also sat in on rehearsals and performances, analyzed recordings and scores, and worked on the stage crew for Ho's theatrical production of *Deadly She-Wolf Assassin at Armageddon!* Unless otherwise stated, all artist quotes in this book are taken from interviews I conducted, casual conversations, or stage patter from public performances.

I do not view this project as a strict ethnographic study of Afro Asian performance. In some cases, you will find that I focus more on texts than on social data. I view the ethnographic components as a jumping-off point, a means to ground my analysis of these projects in how they play to other people and to their creators. In addition to fieldwork, starting in 2003, I documented the Truth Hurts case in the media (Internet articles, radio, blogs), in social spaces, and through email exchanges with several of the participants. In subsequent years, I conducted research on Paul Robeson and Liu Liangmo, including analyzing audio and film recordings of their work. I also investigated Bob Cole and Billy Johnson's *A Trip to Coontown*, including analyzing the sheet music of "The Wedding of the Chinee and the Coon" and enlisting a pianist to do a performative reconstruction of the song. Finally, over the span of my entire project, I have consistently examined and reexamined the websites, e-blasts, and other online promotional materials of the contemporary artists in my case studies.

In Chapter 1, I begin my analysis with an investigation of how sonic blackness and Asianness have historically been depicted in mainstream U.S. popular culture, as well as Afro Asian projects that have reflected and countered these currents. Using "The Wedding of the Chinee and the

Coon" (1898) as a central case, and drawing evidence from other early-twentieth-century popular songs, I show how these texts evidence the ways in which "sono-racialization" sutures sound to singular racial meaning and how "sono-racial triangulation" has been solidified into the overarching structure of the popular music industry. I then turn to examples of Afro Asian engagements that troubled this system by disrupting links between bodies and sound, as well as the industry separation of "black" and "Asian" music. I offer an extended example of Paul Robeson's performance of Chinese folksongs on the 1941 album *Chee Lai* as part of a larger leftist endeavor to locate commonalities between world folk traditions and highlight cultural and political connections between African Americans and various Asian nations. I finish by detailing the rise of mid-twentieth-century Afro Asian political mobilizations and survey a number of Afro Asian musical projects that emerged in its wake. I pose the concept of "music of color" as a theoretical means to understand the types of inter- racial musical affinities explored in numerous later-twentieth-century Afro Asian explorations, precursors to the contemporary case studies in the book.

In Chapter 2, I expose the ways in which sono-racial triangulation and resistance to it play out in the musical life of Yoko Noge, a blues artist who moved from Japan to Chicago in the early 1980s. Noge came to the United States to get closer to the blues she was already performing and recording in Japan, an indication that the Afro Asian process can begin even before artists set foot on U.S. soil. Yet her move was also founded on a search for authenticity in Chicago blues communities. I lay out the ways in which Noge's understanding of her place within the blues tradition—and relationship to blackness and Japaneseness—shifted as she became more ensconced in the Chicago scene and through collaborations with black artists. I also examine narratives of national assimilation and question their applicability to immigrant artists of color. Since African American culture is such an important component of U.S. culture, Asian and Asian American musicians would be hard pressed to avoid being influenced by black forms. Reading several of Noge's compositions that merge her Japanese identity with African American history, I explore why people of color are drawn to participate in each other's traditions and the political grounding this requires. I argue that Noge and her multiracial collaborators jointly produce African American and Japanese culture illuminating alternative criteria for interracial authenticity in experience, participation, and advocacy.

In Chapter 3, I illuminate the ways in which Afro Asian artists merge traditions, communities, and sectors of the culture industry in ways distinct from mono-racial or mono-cultural bands. I focus on Chicago-based Funkadesi in order to discuss how sono-racialization articulates through space, arguing that mixing racialized music has the potential to engender racially mixed audiences. The physicalization of Funkadesi's musical blend is aided by certain kinds of spaces that provide a temporary relaxation of the strict racial boundaries of the culture industry. The performance of interracial camaraderie has the potential to bring about such dynamics within a physical space, pointing "toward a corrective vision of social life in the 'doing' of certain elements of performance" (Dolan 2002, 496). Jill Dolan's theorization of the "performative utopia"—when participants are able to see a glimpse of the "what if" rather than the "as is"—provides an important undercurrent to this chapter (2002, 515). I consider the ways in which interracial sounds become embodied in individual music practice, ensemble relationships, and audience engagements. I also query the potential for artists to mobilize these dynamics outside of the performance space, explore what challenges this transfer produces, and uncover how the culture industry contributes to discouraging social action by using these works to promote "consumer-friendly multiculturalism" with little tangible effect (Feld 2001, 213).

In Chapter 4, I focus on Chinese American jazz artist Fred Ho's use of racially marked sounds to explore the contemporary musical ramifications of identity politics. Ho's "radical interracialism" counters hegemonic multiculturalism by historicizing and repoliticizing music of color, rejecting static racial labels. Yet by favoring instruments, melodies, and narratives for their supposed cultural and sonic difference, he also runs the risk of participating in "sonic identity politics," a rendering of culture that results in the re-inscription of simplified racial markers. Due to longstanding sonic stereotypes, the work of someone like Ho remains bound between these two polarities. Artists who wish to challenge the current racial system must actively work to not only have their creations heard in the mainstream but also rebuild the signification system through which they are heard.

In Chapter 5, I stretch beyond the local scope of the previous chapters and consider the inter/national case of "Addictive," a song that was at the center of a copyright infringement suit between U.S. hip hop producers and a Bollywood composer. I illustrate how sono-racial assumptions factored into the monetary skirmish, despite the piece's popularity with a multiracial and multinational audience. I continue lines of argument from Chapters 2 and 4 in which I discuss Afro Asianness as a performative or critical stance. By turning the lens on a creation process that is not clearly collaborative, I argue that radical interracial political possibility resides in unintended places and requires a sono-racial collaboration between text and listener. Reading the "Addictive" affair as such, I ask what we can learn about all black–Asian musical encounters by analyzing their progressive and conservative potential.

Afro Asian and other interracial music are spaces of sono-racial collaboration in which cross-racial allegiances, solidarities, and frustrations are modeled and explored—echoes of the future that reverberate into the present. *Resounding Afro Asia* signals this intimate connection between sound and politics as artists draw on Afro Asian cultural and political histories in their work. It also calls out the continual resounding of black–Asian dynamics in music and the new Afro Asian formations that might emerge. The following chapters illuminate the true quandary of our era: how to express and understand complex identities within simpler, existing racial formations, without reducing the former to the latter. The work of the artists I chronicle suggests that there are ways to step beyond the confines of racial categories that do not dissolve into color-blindness or universalism and that carry forward the embrace of diversity and antiracism engendered in the 1960s. Afro Asian music illuminates the complex ways that people of color come together and how this shapes current artistic practice. At the same time, the ways in which these artists move within the culture industry illuminate the long shadow the racial system of the twentieth century will cast into the twenty-first.

1

This Strange Amalgamation
Afro Asian Roots

I magine it is 1907. You and your family gather in the parlor of your home for a bit of entertainment, circling the piano that holds a copy of the song "The Wedding of the Chinee and the Coon" by Billy Johnson and Bob Cole. The cover of the sheet music features the enticing combination of a big-lipped black man holding hands with a stocky China Doll, eyes pinched so tight she seems incapable of seeing her groom. Both have dressed for the occasion: the man wears a striped suit accessorized with oversized bowtie and a pompom lapel·flower, the woman a pantsuit embroidered with cherry blossoms, holding a fan and perched in tiny platform shoes that hold her, surely, bound feet. Folding back the cover, you start to play an opening figure in C minor, a line that sounds exotic thanks to a snaky chromatic combination of sixteenth notes laid over open fifths in the left hand. Someone starts to sing along: "I heard there's gwine to be / A mighty jubilee / Way down in Chinatown tomorrow morning." Numerous grace notes ornament the accompaniment, bringing us squarely to some "Chinatown" with a piercing cymballike chirp in the high register of the piano. But "gwine" signals an unexpected narrator is telling the story. In fact, even though it draws on racist stereotypes of blacks alongside those of Asians, the song is sung from the point of view of a black onlooker. Oxymoronically, "Wedding" appears to be an Orientalist coon song.

The first verse ends with the crux of the scene: "Of all things beneath the skies / This will be a great surprise / For a pretty Chinese girl will wed a coon." With this revelation, the piano launches into a texture that feels more familiar, like a vaudeville or ragtime number. Everyone joins in to sing the chorus: "This strange amalgamation twixt these two funny nations gwine to cause an awful jumble soon / Twill cause a great sensation over the whole creation / The wedding of the Chinee and the coon." This celebration of an unusual union inspires a shift to E-flat major and simple syncopation provides rhythmic play easily realized even by pianists not grounded in an African American musical aesthetic.

As the story unfolds, the song continues to move back and forth between these two tonalities, textures, and arsenals of sono-racial signifiers. A final verse takes you to the wedding day, when "coons and chinese all mingle

Figure 1.1. Front cover of "The Wedding of the Chinee and the Coon."
Courtesy of the Library of Congress, Music Division.

together" [sic] until an argument arises over whether a black or Chinese
spiritual head will wed the pair. The coons brandish their ever-present
razors, one cuts off the queue of the Chinese "priest," and ultimately the
black parson marries the couple—the moment depicted on the sheet
music cover. The final rousing chorus is both comical and foreshadows
the real possibilities for societal change through the monstrously hybrid
union of these two disparate races. While in one sense a lighthearted love
song, it also poses temporally relevant questions about how the black–
Asian couple will actually move through the world. Ultimately, it suggests

their relationship and the implied mixed-race children that will come of it will change the entirety of "creation" with their "awful jumble."

"The Wedding of the Chinee and the Coon" is one of several turn-of-the-century popular songs that bring together stories of black and Asian people with visual and sonic images of blackness and Asianness.[1] The piece is a cornucopia of racial stereotypes drawn from the legacy of the nineteenth-century minstrel show. The lyrics feature slurs like "coon" and "heathen chinamen" [sic], along with references to a "Joss-house Priest," "Parson chicken feather," and "Chop-suey." The mocking of black and Chinese people and cultural formations in words is supported by sonic tropes that respectively signal the included racialized subjects. Black music forms the foundation of the piece; its cadences, chord progressions, and rhythms resonate with minstrel songs as well as emerging ragtime and jazz idioms. This sonic framework forms the cultural norm into which the "Chinese" elements are added, a familiar gesture in the longstanding use of Asian images as "fantastical ornamentation" on U.S. stages (Steen 2010, 44). The particular miscegenation of "Wedding" is deemed funny because of the supposed absurdity of black and Asian people ever coming together in marriage and community. But to listeners familiar with the popular songs of that era, it would have also been humorous as it weaved together audio images usually found separately in coon or "Chinese" songs. Throughout the song, tropes of blackness and Asianness serve to solidify each other through contrast.

"Black" and "Asian" sounds served as sono-racial gestures through which professional and amateur performers could play with embodying racial difference. Despite its unfamiliarity today, the scene I painted above would have been quite common among middle- and upper-class whites (and smaller numbers from other races) in the early-twentieth-century United States, consumers with enough income to support owning and studying the piano. "Wedding" would likely have sat in a stack of sheet music with other ethnic novelty songs depicting various marginalized groups, each cementing racial misrepresentations into their owners' daily vocabularies. These performances were ways to work out a moment of significant racial concern for white U.S. Americans and the unique roles blacks and Asians held in this equation. The slow dissolution of the slave economy propelled by the end of the Civil War in 1865 was met by the instantiation of Jim Crow laws to tame blacks as they entered the realm of full citizenship. At the same time, growing concern over an influx of Asian immigrants led to Asian exclusion laws that barred Asians from this very status, despite a continued reliance on their labor. On a global scale, Japan defeated Russia in the Russo-Japanese War in 1905, the first time an Asian nation triumphed over a European one in modern warfare. The twin fears of the dark entity within and foreign threat from without were captured in minstrel-like depictions of subhuman blackness and nostalgia for a slave past, along with a flurry of anti-Chinese songs that expressed xenophobic sentiments toward Asian immigrants.

Understanding the origination of "Wedding," however, speaks to more complicated engagements of people of color with each other and in the burgeoning popular culture industry in this era. The song was written for *A Trip to Coontown*, the first full-length musical comedy entirely created, performed, and produced by blacks (Riis 1989, 28).[2] The show featured several actors performing cross-racially: composer Cole as a white hobo and Tom Brown as a Chinese man.[3] By 1898, when *Coontown* debuted, the visual and sonic racial tropes employed were an integral part of the popular lexicon used by industry artists of all races. But, as David Krasner argues, black performance of other races was notable in that it showed that cross-racial performance was not solely the province of white artists (1997). Cole and Johnson's production illustrated that blacks could participate in the performative production of supposed racial authenticity, even if drawing on problematic images. What is more, they actively engaged in an emerging representational economy of ethnicity: race was a hot topic, and Cole and Johnson used categories and colors as entities to entice audiences, sometimes without even referring to humans (Krasner 1997).[4] The pair ultimately challenged the white-stated terms under which sono-racial images of blackness, Asianness, and whiteness could be used, while never fully disavowing the stereotypes they perpetuated.

"Wedding" and *Coontown* have been examined as the simultaneous debasement of blacks and Asians (Tsou 1997), black reproductions of black and Asian stereotypes (Moon 2005), a space for blacks to parody the minstrel tradition (Krasner 1997), a radical celebration of the inevitable future of mixed-raced marriage (Moon, Krasner, and Riis 2011), and a means for its creators to work through the conflicted ways in which larger societal relationships between black and Asians were figured at the time (Lee 2011). While seemingly contradictory, I believe the myriad sono-racial collaborations present in Cole and Johnson's work meant that the song and production likely did all of this work simultaneously. In addition, I assert that "Wedding" reveals the ways in which a song might have a distinctive sono-racial life when coupled with variously raced bodies; when performed by black or white (or Asian) people, the collaboration between performing body and sound offers the possibility for different types of interracial conversation and power negotiations to emerge. Especially once the sheet music circulated apart from the black bodies of the production, the song took on its own sono-racial life. We cannot know now how much of the larger context of the *Coontown* production an average home player would have. But it is clear that the song carried with it vivid sono-racial images that communicated racial meaning on their own, allowing players and listeners to engage blackness and Asianness through their performances.

I start this chapter with "Wedding" because it showcases, in various permutations, the ways in which racialized sounds and people collaborate. The longer history of "Wedding" also reveals the ways in which racial representations correlated to actual structural engagement of blacks and Asians—and black and Asian sound—within the culture industry. While blacks were marginalized in the white-dominated industry, they gained increasing ground as performers in the first decades of the twentieth century. Chinese and other Asian/American popular performers existed, but they were frequently faced with industry workers and audiences who were dubious as to their ability to speak and sing in English and render U.S. American popular styles (Moon 2005, 144). Further, while the aping of blackness by whites prevalent in the minstrel tradition grew to be considered less "authentic" as black performers stepped into these roles, the prevalence of whites in yellowface persisted for decades more (Steen 2010). Scholars have shown how sonic distinctions between race records and hillbilly (or old-time) records shaped the opportunities for blacks and whites in the industry.[5] What were tangible ways music performed by or associated with Asians did or did not factor into this schema? How did the presence of black or Asian representations and people shape how the other fared in songs, advertisements, and recording deals? And how have these dynamics shifted or endured in subsequent decades?

Answering these questions requires an examination of the historically segregated terrain of U.S. popular music and racial discourse, which I will examine specifically in regard to these two racial positions. My argument is twofold: I first contend that racial triangulation (C. J. Kim 1999) is present in longstanding sono-racial representations as well as in the tangible structures of the music industry. Racial beliefs shaped how creators and consumers interacted with recording engineers, label owners, and marketers and these solidified into recurring patterns and infrastructure that perpetuated the same dynamics. In contrast, I claim, there is a counterhistory of Afro Asian performances that challenges these racial, musical, and economic systems. To complicate matters, sometimes the same performances or recordings work in both directions; therefore, I push on Kim's formulation to suggest it is not quite as fixed as it may first appear. There are ruptures to the triangle when it maps onto sound, although not necessarily always in progressive directions. To understand the connections of the sonic and social, I will move back and forth between historical political detail and coterminous musical expressions. In doing so, I hope to show that the interaction of these two realms is a chicken-or-egg scenario in that they are both part of an ever-unfolding, self-referential, and self-fulfilling system.

I begin by laying out how racial triangulation operates in racial policy and show how this has manifested in popular music from the turn-of-the-century forward. In doing so, I illuminate how, what I call, *sono-racialization* sutures phenotypic racial notions to cultural expressions, establishing a representational economy that limits how people of color can be seen and heard. I then analyze *Chee Lai: Songs of New China*, a 1941 collaboration between African American vocalist Paul Robeson and Chinese composer and conductor Liu Liangmo. This production demonstrated an alternative to separation between black and Asian people and sound in the culture industry and a growing cross-racial and transnational political consciousness that fomented in the early twentieth century. I finish with a brief account of Afro Asian political and musical history in the second half of the twentieth century and show how the notion of a collective "people of color" inspired what I propose as *music of color*, a shared body of traditions that could be performed across racial and cultural lines to showcase affinities between nonwhite or non-Western people. Throughout the chapter, I continue to trace the ways in which Afro Asian musical engagements reveal tensions between race as performative or embodied, as well as the ways in which these collaborations resist and reproduce sono-racial structures.

Sono-Racial Triangulation

What circulate as "black" and "Asian" music are socio-politically constructed categories shaped by broader racial dynamics in the United States and the West. Since the mid-1800s, the two racial categories have been depicted as mutually exclusive and in diametric opposition to one another. This joint racialization process was built on longstanding European compartmentalization of colonial holdings and colonized people, "divide and conquer" strategies meant to deter rebellion. In many colonies, enslaved people and other laborers were segregated by race through polarizing racial discourse, spatial segregation, and emerging class differences, serving to discourage joint uprisings by producing interracial animosity (Prashad 2001, 74–79). In addition, colonial infrastructures were built so that colonies could only communicate and do trade with the metropole rather than each other, impeding consciousness of shared oppression across national and racial boundaries (Kimche 1973, 2). In the post-Emancipation United States, lawmakers manipulated the immigration process for economic means, further exacerbating social and economic distinctions between racial populations. Immigrant groups— notably Asian and Latino populations—were brought into the country to perform certain jobs and, frequently, forced out when their labor was no longer needed.[6] Animosities grew between races as they vied for limited economic resources and state and media agents generated discourse to perpetuate these divisions.[7]

The results are longstanding distinctions between blackness and Asianness that continue to support a racist economy. In dominant U.S. racial discourse, Asian immigrants and Asian Americans have been constructed in seemingly contradictory ways, depending on national origin, historical moment, and region. When the first major population of Chinese immigrants began to coalesce on the West Coast in the mid-1800s, newspapers, popular songs, and theatrical pieces lampooned them as a source of physical and moral pollution (Lee 1999). Local and federal legislation was created in order to prevent this foreign threat from lingering beyond the usefulness of its labor. When the 1870 naturalization law was passed to give blacks the right to citizenship, it was silent about Chinese and other East Asian populations. Several Asian exclusion acts followed, beginning with the Chinese Exclusion Act of 1882, which barred Chinese immigrants from citizenship. Blacks were thus symbolically incorporated into the civic fabric of the nation, albeit unequally, while East Asians were kept in the status of alien.

South Asians had a varying but analogous immigration history. The first major wave of Indians came later than East Asians, primarily Sikh workers in the late nineteenth and early twentieth century (Sharma 2010, 302). South Asian immigration was not barred with the Asian exclusion acts, but was outlawed separately in 1917. In 1923 the Supreme Court ruled Indians could not become citizens, which was overturned in 1946. After the 1965 Immigration and Naturalization Act, a second wave of Indian professionals came to the States, followed by a third in the 1980s (Sharma 2010, 302). Despite particularities, however, the overarching contours of South Asians are similar to those of East Asian immigrants and they have factored into the racial imaginary in similar ways at different historical moments. The post-9/11 Islamaphobic vilification of South Asian/Americans, for example, stands distinct from coterminous views of East Asians. The linking of a domestic Asian population to a perceived enemy nation, however, is a historically familiar gesture: the same exoticizing conflation occurred during the World War II when Japanese/Americans were interned as potential threats to national security.

When needed as racial leverage, Asians have also been embraced into dominant discourse in more positive terms. Claire Jean Kim argues that in several eras Asians were racially triangulated in relation to blacks and whites: unable to fully assimilate as U.S. Americans, they were nevertheless strategically valorized over blacks (1999, 106–107). Racial triangulation is based on the idea that race is a multidimensional field of positions that merges relative value and civic inclusion (see Figure 1.2). The first major instance of this triangulation occurred when Chinese laborers were imported to avoid hiring newly freed blacks in the Reconstruction era (C. J. Kim 1999, 108–109; Jung 2006). Chinese and, later, Japanese immigrants were praised for their supposedly superior culture, work ethic, and intelligence in contrast to lazy blacks. While Kim talks about the construction of this field from a dominant white perspective, Helen Jun furthers this project by detailing how blacks and Asians perpetuate these dynamics through discourses of black Orientalism and Asian uplift. Black Orientalism refers, in part, to the use of exoticizing images by blacks, but, more importantly, Jun says it illuminates the larger ways in which black national inclusion was tied to Asian exclusion (Jun 2011, 6).

Likewise, Asian uplift narratives can perpetuate antiblack racism, but also showcase the ways in which Asian national subjectivity was bound to notions of black racialization that characterized this group as degenerate (Jun 2011, 7). This notion of Asianness as superior to blackness persisted as the "model minority" stereotype. Since the second half of the twentieth century, Asian/Americans have been discussed as hard workers, docile citizens, and people who value family and education. By the 1990s, South Asians were included into this category, especially as they surpassed other

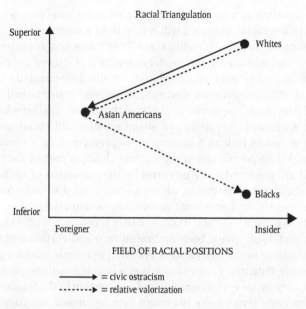

Figure 1.2. Racial triangulation. Graphic re-created by Domini Dragoone. Courtesy of Claire Jean Kim.

racial/ethnic groups in income and education level (Sharma 2010, 14). Model minority traits supposedly arise from Asians' "ancient" and "exotic" cultures, belief systems like Confucianism, modern grooming to be efficient workers, and asexual or tightly controlled sexual behavior. Despite seeming benevolence, this stereotype conflates all Asians in the United States into one identity, overlooks the structural disenfranchisement of many Asian/Americans, and elides the difference between native and foreigner.[8]

South and East Asian success has been used in government discourse to vilify black people and justify their political-economic disenfranchisement (Prashad 2000). The foils to the model minority are a host of black "underclass" figures that appear in different historical moments: the lazy or violent coon, the hypersexual Buck and Jezebel, the simpleminded Mammy, and more recent equivalents like the hip hop gangsta and oversexed welfare mother. These images are based on assumptions of cultural deficiency or, when munificent, as symptoms of racial oppression. Unlike Asians, however, whites have begrudgingly considered blacks to be part of the national body. Black people and African American culture have historically served as evidence of the United States as an egalitarian nation. Take, for example, the ways in which black jazz artists toured as State Department ambassadors during the Cold War. These musicians were featured internationally in order to paint the United States as antifascist in contrast to the Soviet bloc (Von Eschen 2004). While dominant racial discourse paints blackness as an inferior racial position, black cultural production—such as jazz—is often treasured as national property, a complication to the racial triangle I will return to in a moment.

In this racial taxonomy, whites are "the unspoken overclass to the underclass and majority to the model minority ... factored out of the picture as if they were neutral, colorblind, wholly disinterested observers" (Kim 2000, 20). In dominant discourse, whiteness is unmarked and thus unbound from racial expectation. It is also the default against which other races are measured. Regardless of social position, all racial groups are locked in a system in which betterment is predicated on a move toward whiteness. White people and whiteness are clearly a part of the racial triangle, but are rendered more powerful by the consensus of silence. More importantly, as Jun illuminates, whites are not needed in order for the system to propagate. Its hegemonic nature means that all social actors have the ability to consciously and unconsciously reproduce it (2011).

Blacks and Asians have been embraced into and reviled within dominant U.S. culture in respective ways, reflected in representations purveyed in the culture industry. Performance was a key means through which the contemporary racial system was worked out starting in the Reconstruction era. In the early part of the twentieth century, music industry workers drew on racial perceptions as a means to distinguish new markets and get recordings into the hands of nonwhite consumers. Carefully crafted representations of "black" and "Asian" music also fed back into racial discourse, cementing the post-bellum racial taxonomy of the nation.[9] In order for this process to occur, concerted effort had to be made to link racial categorization to cultural production, especially in an industry drawing on folk culture that had previously been produced and consumed widely across racial and cultural lines (Miller 2010).

Black and Asian racial categories are crystallized into sounds, music genres, and the structure of the music industry through *sono-racializaton*. Sono-racialization is a process of racial definition that sutures sound to racial meaning within a larger system. By selecting certain artists to record and promote, using racialized visuals in conjunction with recordings, or manufacturing discourse that presents traditions as the province of one racial group, industry actors put tremendous effort into binding racial labels to cultural practices. In the early days of popular Asian musical representations, they were depicted with similar sounds to blacks in a general sonic haze of Otherness (Moon 2005). As the industry developed, singular attachments between race and sound were key: a sonic signifier could only relate to one racial category. Horkheimer and Adorno have shown that capitalism thrives on predictability and the culture industry mass-produces repetitive products to keep the masses oblivious to their actual political-economic circumstances (2002 [1944]). In the context I am describing, a direct sound–race correlation was a means to clearly market and sell music to racially segregated populations in a manner that could be endlessly replicated.

The early days of recording exacerbated extant tensions between body and sound in the minstrel tradition. White performers were believed to performatively produce authentic blackness (or other sono-racial Otherness), yet some viewers were so convinced by their performances that they mistook their bodies for black. Thus, promotional materials were crafted to reinforce that, beneath their makeup, performers' bodies were still white (Lott 1995, 20). But while a performer's body and gestures were packaged together onstage, recording created situations in which sounds circulated free of bodies once they were produced. Lisa Gitelman suggests that this dynamic resulted in the early days of sound recording offering the potential for "colorblind" music consumption, but that this was quickly closed down by extra-musical gestures (1999, 133–137). In a moment when a white singer could sound black and vice versa, industry workers decided it was important that a listener know the racial identity of a performer and clearly interpret the racial identity a performer might choose to put on in performance as something Other than what they *were*. Thus, a fixed relationship was resinscribed between racialized bodies and cultural production "naturally" linked to them. This *body-culture determinism* was not only enforced by the industry but also grew to be embraced—or at least played out—by musicians of all races working within it.

It is no wonder that the sono-racial taxonomy developed in the Reconstruction era, the same moment in which the broader racial system grew increasingly segregated and policed. In the late 1800s, Karl Hagstrom Miller suggests, "performers regularly *employed* racialized sounds," but by the 1920s "most listeners expected artists to *embody* them" (Miller 2010, 4; my emphasis). While it took place over decades, Miller says this shift from "minstrel" to "folklore" authenticity resulted in a foreclosure of the types of sounds differently raced artists were allowed to produce in industry spaces. Cross-racial performance continued but it was increasingly framed as "unnatural" and part of the performative spectacle. This was more than just the division of sound into categories, but the continued performative investment in upholding these categories in what artists recorded and in the populations to which they were marketed. The sono-racialization process was built on the industry's recognition of people of color as consumers, but required them to be handled separately from whites and each other. White industry workers, scholars, and folklorists created the earliest sono-racial designations and they were often used to stigmatize and distance minorities. But as people of color joined in their use, they became a means to claim racial and cultural uniqueness. While the merger of bodies and racialized sounds was restricted for people of color, however, this process was never as strict for white artists who continued to have more freedom to perform traditions from across racial lines.

Sono-racial categories, like race overall, are distinct from cultural traditions and shift over time. When I say "Asian" music, I am referring to a set of aesthetic assumptions based on perceptions of Asians in dominant racial discourse, not the music's substantive origins in Asia. "Black" music is similarly a constructed category founded on racial expectations of blackness rather than actual African American cultural practices (although there is certainly overlap between them). Sono-racial labels are placed onto cultural expressions and in the process multiple traditions can end up with the same racial label. This is especially clear in the case of Asian music, in which a variety of South Asian, East Asian, and sometimes Middle Eastern styles all fall into the same sono-racial category. The racial definition of black and Asian music in U.S. popular culture has resulted in recurrent sonic stereotypes that often stand in for Asian/American and African American cultures in mainstream venues.

Asian music is racially constructed as sophisticated, spiritual, melodic, ancient, and foreign, providing sustenance for the academy, high-culture consumers, and new age hippies. This vision of Asian music is positive, but like the model minority myth, it misrepresents varied musical practices, homogenizes Asian cultural and musical differences, and ignores Asian pop and folk genres. Further, while Asian music is valorized as possessing high cultural and spiritual value, it is at the same time rendered geographically and temporally distant. Even music made by Asian Americans, Deborah Wong suggests, is often treated as a mere preservation of "authentic" and foreign Asian practices (2004, 12). Before the advent of sound recording technology, the first sonic images of Asia in U.S. mass culture were imported from Europe via sheet music. These pieces often featured romantic stories of Indian princesses and pseudo-transcribed "ancient" Hindu melodies, reflecting an interest in Indian culture inspired by the British Raj. With the appearance of Chinese immigrants in the mid-nineteenth century, U.S. composers started to write about characters such as John Chinaman, Chong from Hong Kong, "The Heathen Chinee," "Chinky Chinee Bogie Man," and female China Dolls. These songs were sung in salons and onstage, including minstrel shows (Tsou 1997). Sheet music covers were illustrated with ornate Oriental fans, lanterns, and umbrellas, men with slit eyes sporting queues, and women swathed in embroidered robes.

By the heyday of Tin Pan Alley in the 1920s, sonic tropes for indicating Asianness solidified into a standardized toolkit songwriters used to add exotic color to a tune. These included the use of chromaticism and/or dissonance, pentatonic scales, drones, patterns of repeating 16th notes, grace notes, and parallel 4ths and 5ths, all painting Asian music as possessing foreign melodies and harmonies, excessive ornamentation, and unusual sonorities (Moon 2005, 94–95). Songs frequently contained words such as "talkee" and "workee" to represent English spoken with an accent or, in the case of a song like "Ching Chong," nonsensical lyrics to mimic the sound of speaking Chinese. These racial signifiers have persisted in film, theater, and popular music into the twenty-first century, joined by the use of the gong, *sitar*, flutes, and the ever-present "Oriental riff" found in songs like Carl Douglas's "Everybody Was Kung Fu Fighting."

While representations of Asianness circulated in popular music, actual Asian traditions and Asian/American artists were virtually ignored by the industry throughout much of the twentieth century. This shifted with the emergence of the world music genre and Asian music—albeit only particular styles—was finally incorporated into the mainstream. A group of music executives created the "world music" genre in 1987 as a way to direct consumers to underselling merchandise including old ethnographic folk recordings, contemporary Latin American groups, Celtic ensembles, Afropop, Eastern European choirs, and Western-based new age experiments (Stokes 2004, 52). Asian musical styles were not initially central to the genre, but soon some of its biggest stars were artists such as Pakistani vocalist Nusrat Fateh Ali Khan (Farrell 1999, 14). World music discourse often cites these recordings as traditional Eastern music mixed with modern or Western recording technology, asserting the performers and styles as antithetical to the West and stuck in the past. Thus, when finally marketed in the mainstream, Asian music remained troped as foreign and known primarily through classical and religious genres such as Hindustani, Karnatic, or Sufi *qawwali*. *Bhangra*, as a popular form, emerged as an exception in the late 1990s; however, it retained the stamp of exoticism despite its primary producers and consumers being diasporic South Asians in the West.

In contrast to the singular exoticizing narrative of Asian sono-racialization, conceptions of black music have been polarized between competing narratives of valorization and degradation, thus occupying multiple positions in Kim's racial triangle (see Figure 1.3). In the antebellum and Reconstruction eras, black music was considered primitive, savage, sexual, violent, and a potential agent for infecting white society with the same qualities. Drawings on the covers of coon songs depicted banjo-picking Toms wearing ragged clothes or their urban counterpart Zip Coon, a faux-sophisticate who would turn on whites with his razor.

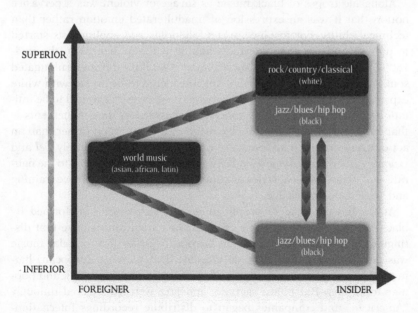

Figure 1.3. Sono-racial triangulation. Graphic by Domini Dragoone.

Minstrel shows featured derogatory characters such as Coon and Jim Crow who would speak imitations of black dialect such as "dem," "dat," and "brudder." These representations of blackness were taken so literally by white consumers that they assumed, for example, the coon songs of Stephen Foster were transcribed from slaves in the South as opposed to original compositions (Phinney 2005, 50).

Rhythm and drumming were early musical tropes used to indicate a savage and aggressive black sound. Many accounts of black music written by white observers from the 1600s to the 1800s emphasize the use of drums, often shrouded in fear, disgust, and intrigue. Drums—their volume ("noise"), power, and ability to communicate—were such a source of colonial anxiety that they were banned in the British colonies in the mid-1700s. The notion of rhythm as the heart of black music remained, however, and metric difference, particularly syncopation, solidified as its reigning trope. By the turn-of-the-century, as Ronald Radano notes, the "hot rhythm" of black music "perpetuated the same racial myths while providing a means of affirming positive identities in an egregiously racist, national environment" (2000, 459). White Tin Pan Alley composers used syncopated rhythms to represent black Otherness in their imitations of ragtime and jazz, retaining their "infectious" quality while removing its savageness. "This exalted hotness, in turn, supplied the creative and economic basis of an emerging urban subculture of black professional musicians, whose traditional proclivities toward performance were soon marketed as expressions of a racially inherited rhythmic gift" (Radano 2000, 459). Again, as in A Trip to Coontown, black artists used the existing racial lexicon to leverage their success.

Alongside tropes of black music as savage or violent was a pervasive notion that it was an expression of unadulterated emotion rather than technical ability. For instance, when folklorists and abolitionists started to publish and circulate spirituals among white audiences in the mid-1800s, they branded them as sacred music that flowed from a subjugated soul (Cruz 1999). The songs were not considered to be on par with white expressions, however, and in some instances were even claimed to be imitations of white hymns. The underlying message to these statements is that black music is an involuntary reaction to oppression rather than an act of agency. Black musicians are unskilled beings who simply *feel* and *express*, rather than *compose* and *create*. This stands in contrast to the figuration of Asian classical styles as complex and based on intensive training and systematic knowledge.

At the dawn of the recording industry, black music—performed by blacks, whites, or others—was celebrated as a cultural feature that distinguished the United States from Europe.[10] Earlier U.S. popular music was primarily based in classical Western (i.e., Western European) harmonic structures and verse and melodic forms from Anglo folk and popular traditions. But blues, ragtime, and jazz were considered uniquely "American" and companies began to distribute recordings internationally as U.S. national culture. As this music grew into the backbone of the music industry, "black" and "American" were elided. In the rock explosion of the 1950s and 1960s, quintessential pop artists such as Elvis and the Beatles gained popularity by performing music considered to be black, capitalizing on its supposed rebellious qualities while commodifying and taming this potential.[11] Further complicating sono-racial triangulation, then, are these exhibits of blackness by nonblack people, in which person and sound can occupy separate positions.

Hip hop—a genre forged in the de-industrialized urban spaces of New York City and Los Angeles in the mid-1970s—is now populated with base imagery and consumers have met it with both lust and ire. Illuminating the continuity of dominant attitudes toward black music, Timothy Brennan claims:

> The U.S. mainstream media's grasp of the genre known as "rap" is as distant from the source and often as hostile as much of the imperial travel narratives from earlier centuries—viewing events within their own country with the confusion and distaste usually reserved for reporting on antique lands. This reporting—which for at least a decade has been part of an unofficial public consensus—partakes of the same tropes as those found in the discourses of colonialism, even if it is a domestic issue by and about Americans. (Brennan 2001, 51–52)

Popular media describes hip hop music and culture as the rebellious voice of inner-city youth, telling tales of crime, poverty, and violence. Despite the presence of artists from multiple class backgrounds, the involvement of nonblacks and non-Americans since its beginning, and personal artistic license, hip hop was sono-racially constructed as black and male. The less-spoken reality of the genre is that as it moved to the center of the pop industry by the 1990s, music companies began to market it to young, white men who became its largest consumers (Rose 2008). Thus, throughout the historical evolution of black music, the tangible presence of blacks and their socio-political realities was erased, while musical blackness was consumed for the "underclass" qualities allegedly caused by these material circumstances.

In the 1910s and 1920s, black and Asian music were differently coded representations of Otherness incorporated into the white mainstream in a zeal for "the new." As the industry developed, sono-racial categories solidified into economic structures that greatly shaped artists' and consumers' encounters with the market. The music industry's foundation of sono-racial triangulation has resulted in popular conceptions of black and Asian music as separate categories or genres. World music is marketed as the sophisticated alternative for savvy, elite consumers, the model minority alternative to hip hop and R&B dominated pop. When you go to a music store—or iTunes—where do you find African American music? Under hip hop, R&B, or soul. Where do you find African music? Under the world music umbrella, because black is often conflated with African American in the U.S. racial taxonomy and Africans are seen as separate (or mistaken for African Americans). Where is Indian or East Asian music? Also in the world category. And where do you find Asian American music? You don't find it anywhere because this segment of the population has never been understood or marketed to as having a distinctive sound and audience, or they are mistaken for Asians and put in world music, as is the case for many Western artists of color who perform non-Western styles. Black and Asian (or "world") sound are thus separated both from whiteness and from each other.

Many musicians whose cultural practice does not sync up with their racial designation are challenged by body–culture determinism. And it proves detrimental to the careers of many Afro Asian artists because they straddle these divides within their work. Unable to be categorized in the industry's sono-racial system, they find themselves without contracts, gigs, or audiences. Alternately, Afro Asian and other interracial artists' work might be read as mono-racial and the specifics of its hybrid nature lost in translation. The assumption of black–Asian musical difference is similarly harmful. Forms that fall under these labels are believed to share no common ground for the musical styles are allegedly so different that they can only be understood in contrast to one another. It is presumed that there is no shared vocabulary and definitely no way one could enhance the other except in comical juxtaposition.

Sono-racial triangulation is not a reflection of inherent cultural or sonic differences, but a dynamic created through the actions of legislators, music executives, the media, the academy, and musicians themselves for monetary gain and social control.[12] The industry is structured on the notion that racialized bodies produce a limited set of cultural sounds mutually exclusive of one another. And this discourse of limitation and separation works to preserve a racial order that maintains white dominance by reproducing the hierarchical structure itself. Yet despite media representation, blacks and Asians have not been forever detached, nor have the musical cultures linked to them remained separate. Many individuals, small groups, and organizations have interacted cross-racially in spite of the dominant narrative. What is more, a number of these encounters have been hatched specifically to combat the very racist forces that attempt to keep them apart. These collaborations are the heart of Afro Asian politics and music.

Arise!

I will now turn to Paul Robeson and Liu Liangmo's *Chee Lai* as one Afro Asian engagement that countered dominant separation of black and Asian people and sound in the first half of the twentieth century. As Robeson grew increasingly aware of global anti-imperialist politics in the 1920s and 1930s, he used his musical, theatrical, and film work as space to experiment with how cultural production might support struggles for social justice. He began to perform various world folk traditions together in concert in order to demonstrate links he believed existed between "people's music" from around the world. He especially wanted to "reintroduce" African American people and culture back into a world trove of folk culture he understood as evidence of a larger and longer running shared heritage among people of color abroad. Amidst a broader anti-imperialist agenda, he posed Asians and African Americans as "spiritual fathers" and argued that by combining their unique strengths, Afro Asian artists could forge a shared path toward self-determination (Robeson 1978, 94). What led Robeson down this path and why did he think diverse cultural material should be put into dialogue? What did these musical explorations and conversations provide as an individual space of sono-racial expression? How did they help to forge a more extensive antiracist and anti-imperialist cultural project of which Afro Asian exchanges were part? And what might *Chee Lai* reveal about the limits or challenges of Afro Asian musical performance?

Robeson (b. 1898, d. 1976) forged a tremendous career as a singer, athlete, actor, and activist. An outspoken proponent of domestic civil rights and black internationalism, he exploited performance as a means toward political mobilization after turning away from a career in law (Duberman 1989, 54–55).[13] Music was central to Robeson's artistic work, in the theater, live concerts, and as a recording artist. Known for his booming baritone, he began his vocal career performing African American spirituals and extolled the virtues of the black folk tradition as a space to cultivate black national liberation through cultural reclamation and the establishment of intraracially defined aesthetic standards. He argued, however: "If the American Negro is to have a culture of his own, he will have to leave America to get it" (Robeson 1978, 81). He believed blacks should look into their own roots and place this music in conversation with other great cultures of the world. Bringing African American music into the world folk repository was meant to cultivate a black internationalism that Robeson saw as key to furthering their concerns domestically. He reasoned African Americans suffered from the same systems of oppression that other nonwhite and non-Western people did worldwide. "We know those [oppressing] hands," he said, and by seeing shared struggle and strategies for cultural survival, blacks in the United States could gain stronger political footing to work against them (Robeson 1978, 353). Robeson thus began to incorporate Russian, Welsh, Finnish, Yiddish, Yoruba, Spanish, Hebrew, Chinese, Korean, and even pre-Renaissance European songs into his repertoire.[14] Chinese revolutionary Madame Sun Yat Sen (Soong Ching-ling) called him the "voice of the people of all lands," and he indeed posed himself as an Everyman speaking for the world, to the world (Sun Yat-Sen 1941).

While only a subset of his larger repertoire, Robeson's performance of Chinese folksongs became a means to elaborate Asia and Africa as symbolic partners in anticolonial endeavors. This arm of his larger theory of cross-cultural and cross-racial connections is exemplified in the 1941 *Chee Lai: Songs of New China*, recorded in partnership with Liu Liangmo, a composer and conductor who pioneered the choral singing movement in China's mid-century resistance to Japanese colonization (Liu [1950] 2006, 204). Liu's The People's Choral Society grew to incorporate over a thousand singers, in part due to "the reemergence of the 'masses' and 'volunteers' as important religious, political, and popular cultural" symbols in anticolonial and antifascist struggles (Luo 2014, 155). But the Nationalist government shut down the organization in 1936, only a year after it had begun. Liu moved to the United States in order to escape harassment from the Kuomintang, residing there from 1940 to 1949 (Liu [1950] 2006, 204). He met Robeson through a mutual friend in 1940 and, during their meeting, taught him several Chinese songs. Robeson immediately incorporated "Chee Lai" (translated as "March of the Volunteers") into his performances, surprising Liu by singing it at a show several weeks later (Liu [1950] 2006, 205).[15] Liu recruited Robeson to record the title song and two others on *Chee Lai* and led a youth chorus of male Chinese immigrant laundry workers who also recorded three tracks.

This album and the live performances that fed it articulated a musical politics of affinity between African American and Chinese culture and anticolonial struggles. Robeson had already made statements and done fundraising to support the Chinese struggle, but Liu saw his singing as the perfect vehicle through which to make the song and its message circulate broadly through U.S. society and anti-imperialist spaces abroad. While for Liangmo, Robeson could possibly have been simply an American artist willing to support his cause, Robeson employed the Chinese songs as explicit evidence of a deeper black–Asian union.[16] *Chee Lai* thus illustrates what Afro Asian performances offer beyond the co-presence of black and Asian people and elements: the possibility for the two to mutually influence and support one another amidst a dominant Western ideology of racial division. At the same time, this sono-racial collaboration showcases multiple ways in which participants or audiences for these interracial endeavors might draw on or read these productions through dominant racial discourses.

After a relatively apolitical early career, Robeson spent much time in London in the 1930s, where he experienced a personal awakening to anti-imperialist politics.[17] He shared space with future leaders of multiple anticolonial movements, including Kwame Nkrumah, Nnamdi Azikiwe, C. L. R. James, Jomo Kenyatta, and later, Jawaharlal Nehru (Duberman 1989, 171; Monson 2007, 109). The first decades of the twentieth century were marked by an expanding global sense of solidarity between peoples of various colonial nations and saw increasing political projects that crossed cultures, races, and nations to contest the oppressive practices of the European colonial system. Early pan-African, pan-Asian, and pan-Arab organizing; the 1896 defeat of British and Italian troops in Ethiopia; the 1900 Boxer Rebellion in China; and the 1905 victory of Japan over Russia became flashpoints of a new global outlook for people of color (Prashad 2001, 28). Black activists in the United States such as W. E. B. Du Bois, Elijah Muhammad, and Marcus Garvey linked their continued struggles against slavery and Jim Crow to these international movements (Kelley and Esch 1999, Prashad 2001). Robeson was inspired by these stirrings and followed in the footsteps of these earlier black internationalists.

As his performing career grew, so did Robeson's political profile: he gave speeches, interviews, and circulated writings on geopolitical affairs and would make statements in his live performances espousing Third World unity, including African Americans in this global conversation. Alongside Robeson's fervor for these politics, he increasingly performed music he saw as an aesthetic exploration of these same concepts. Joining traditions from around the world, he developed a vocabulary for interracial music based on shared performative gestures and cultural dialogue. He detailed theories about the connections between cultures in a number of articles and interviews, and in his shows would introduce songs by laying out webs and genealogies of how the various traditions fit together.

His performance of a "musical united nations," as termed by a U.S. magazine in the 1940s, was problematic in that it generalized particularities within national cultures, such as referring to singular languages as "African" and "Chinese" (quoted in Karp 2003, 69; Steen 2010, 112). At the same time, he demonstrated more nuanced thinking by drawing connections between traditions based on their performative properties. He detailed, for example, the similar rhythm, phrasing, and technique of speak-singing shared by African American preachers and Jewish cantors: "From these songs, sung, preached or spoken by Negroes in their religious life, and in their deep trouble under slavery, it is only a step to the beautiful songs of the Jewish People which are sung or intoned [or] chanted in their synagogues" (quoted in Karp 2003, 71). He also described what he heard as the "same note of melancholy, touched with mysticism" in spirituals and songs of Russian serfs (quoted in Karp 2003, 69). It is in shared gestures (melody, tone, and form), the role of performance in sustaining a culture, and the sentiments behind the performance that Robeson found connections.

Robeson believed one of the most effective models for African American cultural enfranchisement was Asia. He claimed African Americans were an "Eastern" product and would be better served by adopting Asian rather than Western values. The West was losing an attention to "religion," he claimed, while Asian cultures maintained the central importance of spirituality in their art. In fact, he said, blacks had historically struggled to assert themselves culturally in the West because they were not of the same mind as whites: "Negro students who wrestle vainly with Plato would find a spiritual father in Confucius or Lao-tsze" [sic] (Robeson 1978, 93). For Robeson, this Afro Asian union was less about a direct dismantling of the white power structure and more about offering an alternative: "My quarrel is not with the Western culture but with the Negro imitating it," he says. "The American Negro [I believe] never thinks that he is an Eastern product: I hope to be able to show him the way" (quoted in Stuckey 1976, 107).

"Asia" is both specific and a romantic metaphor in this discourse. Robeson makes analogies between key black and Asian figures, such as calling Ho Chi Minh the Toussaint of Vietnam, comparing Jim Crow laws to Chinese feudalism, or saying Indian princes are to the Indian people as house and field slaves were to one another (Robeson 1978, 377, 273, 350). In "The Culture of the Negro" and "Negroes—Don't Ape the Whites," he argues that African languages could better convey the subtlety of Confucius versus English in translation (Robeson 1978, 87, 92). In this sense, Robeson shows there are conversations that can and should be had outside of the presence of whites or Europeans. For blacks in particular, this looking to the East as the marker of sophistication and reference could subvert the Occident–Orient formation (Karp 2003, 61). The two cannot be entirely opposed in the Afro Asian formation, especially when African *Americans* populate the "Afro" field. The dual binaries of black–white and white–Asian are crossed in Afro Asian discourse.

Shannon Steen refers to Robeson's fascination with Asia as "sino-modernity," a vision of modernity filtered through a white U.S. and European vision of the East (2010, 109-110).[18] He invests Asia with the properties he values: historically grounded, spiritual, peaceful, nonwhite, and non-European, while overlooking the realities of China that at that time was in the midst of terrible political upheaval. His notion of "Asiatic" is based on cultural rather than racial elements, but it also draws from Orientalist discourse, especially in claiming an inherent sophistication in the East. Robeson was progressive in highlighting the power of aligning distinctly oppressed people under a shared umbrella of nonwhiteness and marginalization. But while he unseats the binary scaffolding of the colonial project, he retains his own triangulated set of essentialisms. Also, while the source of racial uplift in this scenario is no longer whiteness, one might question Robeson's notion that blacks needed to prescribe to a different cultural model in order to find socioeconomic betterment. In his formulation, blacks were still positioned outside of or against the alternative modernity, perpetuating primitivist discourses.[19]

Racial/cultural questions were only part of Robeson's musical theory, for he believed that shared labor practices also stimulated similar aesthetics (Steen 2010, 111-112). Situating his racial project amidst engagement in socialist political circles shows how issues of class also became a means of drawing connections across national and cultural lines, and that music was a way in which Robeson sought to give voice to working people of any race. Aligning folk traditions with leftist political messages was a strategy embraced by numerous artists since the cultural front of the 1930s, such as Woody Guthrie, Josh White, The Almanac Singers, and The Weavers (Denning 1997). Robeson, however, received a mixed critical response to his shift from an African American to a broader folk repertoire. Biographer Martin Duberman offers examples of critics who argued Robeson should stick to singing spirituals or expressed doubts as to his ability to sing European folk styles (1989, 632). Duberman speculates that negative criticism of Robeson's expanded body of work might have been based on the ways in which it troubled the portrait of a typical black performer of the time (1989, 178).

The dynamics of the mid-twentieth-century folk scene were such that white performances of nonwhite traditions were seen, ironically, as more familiar radical gestures. Many folk artists were educated, upper-middle-class whites from the North and they were often promoted by the industry—or presented themselves—as performing forms that were old, unchanging, rural, or uncommodified. While the "original" folk was never a static culture and by the mid-twentieth century was deeply embedded in the same music industry as popular forms, the notion of "folk" music was predicated on the performance of music across time, space, culture, and/or race by people who were not "folk" themselves. Folk artists of color like Robeson and, later, Odetta, Harry Belafonte, and others, challenged these modern binaries as they were not of the dominant race clearly positioned against "folk." Due to the ascendancy of "folklore authenticity" in the music industry, as previously discussed, these artists were often seen as performing their "own"—and thus premodern—music rather than interpreting other people's. But Robeson, like the others, maintained a performative distance from the songs he sang. He was an elite, black person singing the working-class music of various races. At the same time, he was a person of color, troubling the simple conflation of race, culture, and class present in sono-racial triangulation. Amidst critical questions and continued success, it is clear he reached outside of what was racially and culturally expected of a black performer and grew increasingly fanatical about drawing cross-cultural connections regardless of his reception (Duberman 1989).

Chee Lai provided Robeson with an opportunity to perform nonnormative blackness, challenging body–culture determinism. By the 1940s, Robeson's voice had become an index for respectable, approachable, and progressive blackness. His deep baritone, forceful delivery, and minimal vibrato did not fit the aesthetic dimensions of the elite Western art tradition nor contemporary black popular forms such as blues and jazz. Robeson cultivated this vocal profile to reflect his world folk ideals. Lisa Barg says that Robeson lobbied for *Ballad for Americans* to be transposed from its original key of E-flat major to B-flat (2008, 55). While he could sing the piece in its original key, the lower tonic would allow him to "deliver the text in an assertive, informal conversational singing voice" (Barg 2008, 55). Barg notes, however, that the political significations of Robeson's voice shifted over time. In the 1920s,

> Robeson's interpretations of black folk sound stood as the benchmark of racial authenticity; by the late 1930s, however, the lines of authenticity had shifted considerably and Robeson's vocal style and concert repertoire did not fit comfortably—if at all—the criteria of authenticity based around southern rural folk stylistics that were being promoted in the urban folk song movement. (Barg, 2008, 33)

Robeson warmed the hearts of the nation's left as a "safe" and "cultured" black sound. (Although, as national fears over Communism grew, his voice again became a site of struggle over appropriate sonic blackness.)

"Chee Lai" offered further possibility for the expression of Robeson's inauthentic blackness (or an already expanded blackness) through a politics of "empathetic listening." In a separate case, Karp claims that Robeson desired his performance of "Hassidic Chant" "not to be considered as a case of Africa influencing another culture, but rather the reverse: a Jewish song exerting 'a profound impact on the *Negro* listener'" (2003, 73). While Robeson had previously wowed audiences with his mimicry of non-English language and inflection, this performance would also reveal how music of the Other impacted him. In "Chee Lai," the spectacle of a black man intoning Chinese is part of the performance. Robeson's black body was already the subject of intense fascination on the part of white U.S. society (Carby 1998).[20] A 1928 interview for *London Evening News and African World*, for example, opens with the description:

> Black as the ace of spades, immensely tall, his broad shoulders and great torso filled the chair in which he sat. But it was the broad high forehead, broader than most Negroes have, the almost gentle expression of his curiously light brown eyes, and his long, slim hands that most attracted the attention. (quoted in Robeson 1978, 76)

Even Liu was moved to comment on Robeson's physique, saying when he first met him, "I almost jumped with fright. At six feet four or five inches tall, with an imposing physique, he seemed to have come from the land of giants" ([1950] 2006, 205).[21] The performative politic of "Chee Lai" lies in how a Chinese song flows through a black body and the cultural work that makes the performance convincing. The Afro Asian project is based on interminority difference taken onto bodies as well as the naturalization of this act—the idea that Robeson could be a legitimate source of Chinese music production. The Chinese voice is broken from its source, but instead of being heard out of context, it is housed in a new Afro Asian context. And blackness, according to Robeson's theories, is returning home.

Translation is central to the interracial identity of "Chee Lai," especially as the target audience was in the United States. The recording begins with a spoken introduction in which Robeson explains the meaning of the song's words for an English-speaking listener. The piano starts and he sings the lyrics in Mandarin. A short piano interlude follows and then he sings again, this time in English.[22] The translation is not literal: the original "with flesh and blood let us build our new Great Wall" becomes "let's stand up and fight for liberty and true democracy," while "the Chinese nation faces its greatest danger" is changed to "all our world is facing the chains of the tyrants." Robeson is said to have assisted in making the translation resonate with African American concerns—something he also did with the national anthem of the Soviet Union (Luo 2014, 148)—but in the end "march on" is more of a generalized cry against tyranny that neutralizes the specific dynamics of the Chinese concerns. The most significant lyrical change is that "millions with but one heart braving the enemy's fire / march on" becomes "all of us with one heart with the torch of freedom / march on." In this instance, the violence of marching into bloodshed is replaced with a hopeful charge to carry the light of liberation ... to where? The goal is uncertain, but instead of faceless "millions," those who carry the torch are "all of us." The first-person plural includes all of the listeners in the struggle and triumph expressed.

This inclusive gesture is mirrored in the packaging of the album. Robeson's face graced the cover of many of his recordings, often almost filling the frame in a larger-than-life representation. The *Chee Lai* cover, however, has a tan background that looks like a painted stone wall. On the right side stands a soldier from the Chinese National Revolutionary Army. Just left of center, a torn-edged snapshot of four children give a thumbs-up to the camera. "Chee Lai: Songs of New China" is written in English and Chinese characters across the top. At the bottom, in a solid red strip, Robeson is listed above the Chinese chorus and Liu, in black. Chinese people are foregrounded: the soldier on the front lines of the battle and

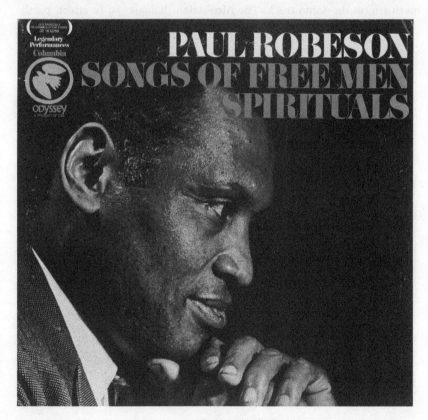

Figure 1.4. Front cover of *Songs of Free Men—Spirituals*. Photograph by Roy Pinney.

children, the future of New China. Liu needed Robeson to make the Chinese voices audible, but he is not seen anywhere in the album materials. Robeson used the sonic space of the recording to display his interracial philosophy. This was a strategic collaboration for both parties, and Robeson accepted his accompanying role for no pay, much in the manner of the "racial sidemanship" that I discuss in Chapter 2 (Liu [1950] 2006, 206). He also sent royalties to Tian Han, the lyricist of "Chee Lai," in China (Luo 2014, 167). Through *Chee Lai*, Liu and the choir's political agenda were given voice within the civic space of the United States, legitimated by a black man outspoken about racism and imperialism as an intermediary. Chinese concerns—foreign concerns—were rendered as important to the U.S. domestic space.

Yet while indicating the political possibility of black–Asian conglomeration, the *Chee Lai* project also raises questions about what does not translate in Afro Asian scenarios and reveals the tremendous work that must be done to forge a truly unified and sociopolitically informed collaboration. Robeson, for example, appears separately from the Chinese singers on the album, limiting the amount of possible Afro Asian exchanges. Robeson's songs and the choir's are interspersed on the album, but they do not ever perform on the same track. The Afro Asian dialogue is, in effect, partly studio-produced rather than something unfolding in live performance

Figure 1.5. Front cover of *Chee Lai: Songs of New China*.

(see Chapter 5). We do not hear Robeson encounter Chinese singers, only Chinese songs. And while we get a sense for how Robeson responds to Chinese songs, we do not get to hear the Chinese youth choir's reactions to Robeson's interpretations, much less African American music. This imbalance is also evidenced in the ways personnel are credited on the album. Robeson appears as an individual, while the choir members are not named, merely listed as a group under the direction of Liu. Thus, a singular black figure is the sole point of dialogue with any kind of black community, while the voices of the Chinese youth are present only in the singular rather than a variegated community of individuals.

This particular performance also did little to disrupt dominant representations of Chinese or Chinese Americans as national outsiders. The concerns presented are those of Chinese citizens—Liu in particular—and neglect domestic issues that might have been facing the laundry worker youth in the choir. The explicit distinction between Chinese and Chinese American is not made either, much in line with Robeson's other work. Very little of his theorizing or performance recognized Asian Americans as a unique population, even though he did mobilize for organizations concerned with domestic anti-Asian racism (Robinson 2006). He is said to have been interested in learning Japanese American songs, but there is no record to show he incorporated these into his performances (Robinson 2006, 272). Robeson's lack of focus on Asian America supported dominant racial constructions that conflate Asian Americans with Asians and further solidified his ideals of Asia as an exotic space.

It is also important to raise questions about how much of Robeson's translation of the Chinese material was legible to the consuming audience. Did he successfully provide a framework for U.S. audiences to understand the aesthetic and cultural resonances of the songs? A *Time* listing suggests otherwise: "Although not tuneful to Western ears, the songs are interesting and authentic examples of China's new mass music" ("Music: December Records" 1941, 54). Similarly, in a review for *The New York Times* in the same year, Howard Taubman says, "In a volume of this nature musical criticism is of no importance compared with the emotion evoked by the courage and determination of the Chinese. The songs tell us more about China's valor than about her music, and at the moment her fight is more momentous than her art" (Taubman 1941, 6X). These critics both focus on the political statements on the album, but see the music as foreign and unimportant. By contrast, Taubman follows his review with one for an album by Robeson, Richard Wright, and Count Basie, in which he thoroughly dissects the music. On *Chee Lai*, Robeson explains the lyrical sentiments of the songs, important given the fact that the record was produced in order to raise funds for the China Aid Council and American Committee for Chinese War Orphans, organizations helping provide medical supplies and care for Chinese who were wounded, orphaned, or refugees. But the project was not pedagogical in the sense of interpreting Chinese music for a U.S. American audience. Robeson's voice gave the Chinese songs an air of familiarity, but perhaps not enough to make it past the melodic and lingual differences from Anglo-American culture.[23]

Questions of translation must also be asked of the actual lyrics Robeson performed in "Chee Lai." In a 1950 newspaper column, Liu praised Robeson's "perfect Mandarin" and the clarity of his diction ([1950] 2006, 206). But it is possible that this was the reflection of an Afro Asian ideal rather than reality. Knowing there was poetic license taken with the recorded English version of "Chee Lai"—and unable to translate it myself—I asked a colleague to provide me with a literal translation of the Mandarin text. Listening to Robeson's performance, she found herself unable to make out what he was singing, even with the lyrics in front of her.[24] I do not raise this critique to condemn the project or suggest that fruitful racial and cultural exchange did not happen. But it does prompt questions about what is lost in these kinds of interracial formations. With an emphasis on interaction and dialogue, there can be a loss of mono-cultural fidelity and the strength of cultural resource available in a more insular environment. In Afro Asian performance, we see the growing of cross-cultural knowledge, not always the end result. In fact, the notion of an end result is in some ways moot. Value is placed on sincere attempts to gain new perspective and speak across difference, rather than how authentically someone sits within it.

Throughout the 1940s and subsequent decades, Robeson continued to denounce domestic racial injustice and its links to U.S. foreign policy. For example, he released a statement against the 1950 Korean invasion and in the years following argued that African Americans should not serve in African or Asian wars for a nation that would not respect their own rights, predating Muhammad Ali's refusal by a decade (Robeson 1978, 252, 367, 378). Between his outspoken politics and the growing Red Scare of McCarthyism, the U.S. State Department rescinded his status as an ex officio cultural ambassador by revoking his passport in 1950.[25] A State Department brief explicitly stated Robeson was not allowed to travel because of his aid to African anticolonial struggles and his "recognized status as a spokesman for large sections of Negro Americans" (State Department brief quoted in Robeson and Lloyd [1958] 1988, 64). While the official government word is couched in terms of Robeson's blackness and work on behalf of African people, his broader socialist and anti-imperialist agenda—in part inspired by connections to China and Asia—was certainly an even greater threat to U.S. foreign policy.

Amidst a U.S. cultural space marked by racial triangulation, *Chee Lai* negotiated what an Afro Asian musical exchange might be. In particular, the album shows how Afro Asian expressions can sit within a larger leftist framework, stretching beyond black–Asian and even racial concerns on a whole. Aesthetics are an important part of the project: the performance of Chinese music by a black person was an important way in which the creators sonically modeled the anti-imperialist political dialogues that were fomenting in the early twentieth century. But the shared motivation to articulate these politics and forge a new future in coalition was also tantamount. This recording, the collaboration that fueled it, and Robeson's other relationships were all spaces in which he tried out the possibility of crafting a unified tradition not labeled by a singular racial or cultural marker. Robeson's interracial musical gestures forged an aesthetic and political vocabulary that proposed a new relationship between sound and identity. Rather than simply expressing African American concerns through Asian forms—or vice versa—Robeson suggested the possibility that people of color might draw on multiple traditions to express a collective identity and joint concerns.

Bandung and Beyond

The latter half of Robeson's prolific career coincided with the growth and solidification of the Afro Asian movement (and broader Third World movement) in the second half of the twentieth century. There was no "start" to Afro Asian engagements; encounters between African and Asian people date back to at least the fifteenth century (Prashad 2001). The concept of Afro Asia as a modern political union, however, was born out of the anticolonial struggles of the early and mid-twentieth century, what David Kimche deems "a new awakening among coloured peoples, the gathering of momentum of ideas and emotions which were to develop into national movements and finally into sovereign nation-states" (1973, 1). By the second half of the twentieth century, what had been more local or nation-based engagements grew into multiple global conglomerations forged to jointly work toward liberation of and self-determination for nonwhite and non-Western people.

One apotheosis of these stirrings was the Bandung Afro-Asian Solidarity Conference held in Indonesia in 1955.[26] This meeting of twenty-nine African and Asian nations was a forum for the newly or soon-to-be independent countries to discuss forging paths free from the shackles of imperialism.[27] These conversations formed the groundwork for the Non-Aligned Movement (NAM) and an Afro Asian taskforce within the United Nations (Prashad 2007). In the heyday of the Cold War, the United States and Soviet Union jockeyed for global domination by inducing other countries to become their allies. Conference delegates advocated that participating nations remain unaligned to either super-power and create a separate "Third World" (Prashad 2007).[28] While this term now has a pejorative connotation, its original meaning was as a hopeful alternative to Western-led global conflict. Unfortunately, Bandung attendees put in place no specific political policy and most of their countries held little economic power; therefore, this early Afro Asian solidarity had minimal tangible sway over geopolitics (Kimche 1973). Kimche notes that in the two years after the conference, India's total volume of trade with other Asian countries actually dropped 28 percent, suggesting the neglect—or impossibility—of forging political-economic coalitions (1973, 81). The global super-powers soon established neocolonial control over many of the recently sovereign African and Asian nations, exercised through economic dependence and martial presence.

Bandung was more important as a symbolic union. The conference attendees asserted a joint identity based on shared experiences of colonization. This union was decidedly racialized: no white-identified countries from the two continents—Israel, South Africa, and the USSR—were invited. Yet this merger was not homogenizing. The final conference communiqué states the importance of each nation cultivating its local culture alongside cross-cultural pursuits (Romulo 1956, 95). There were also significant political disagreements amongst the delegates, particularly related to whether the People's Republic of China and the Communist doctrine were a new imperial force. Black delegates from the United States stood by their country's anti-Communist stance and walked out of the talks because China was represented (Prashad 2001, 145). Still, the conference was a watershed moment of Afro Asian pride. "Beginning with the 1955 meeting of decolonizing African and Asian nations in Bandung, Indonesia, until at least the early 1970s," Bill V. Mullen rhapsodizes, "African American and Asian radicals imagined themselves as antipodal partners in cultural revolution, pen pals for world liberation" (2004, 76).

The Afro Asian partnership reached fruition in the United States with the social movements of the mid-twentieth century (Young 2006). Black and white cadres of organizers combated segregation in the Southern states beginning in the 1950s and 1960s, resulting in the passing of the 1964 Civil Rights Act, the 1965 Voting Rights Act, and open housing legislation in 1968 (Burns 1990). Martin Luther King Jr. was, in part, inspired to advocate for nonviolent conflict by Mahatma Gandhi's *satyagraha* practice, developed in the struggle for Indian independence, and King traveled to India in 1959 to meet proponents of this tactic (Horne 2008, 212). In 1967, King nominated Vietnamese monk Thich Nhat Hanh for the Nobel Peace Prize, further exemplifying the mutual support among leaders in global antiracist and anti-imperialist efforts. In the same decades, black nationalist politics fomented in many U.S. communities and figures like Malcolm X argued against integration as the path toward racial justice. The image of Japanese American radical Yuri Kochiyama holding her friend X's head moments after he was assassinated in 1965 is one potent example of the cross-racial reach of X's messages and alliances (Prashad 2001, 104).

Black Power gained fervor in the late 1960s and 1970s and a new generation of activists took a more militant revolutionary stance. Organizations like the Black Panther Party—founded in 1967—worked to build black nationhood through social, cultural, and political mobilization, rejecting nonviolence as a guiding philosophy and engaging in armed conflict with law enforcement. Despite how they were depicted in popular media, a major pillar of the group's work were welfare programs aimed at strengthening black children and families and the self-determination of black communities (Pulido 2006, 96–97). Holding a large influence over these movements were Mao Tse Tung and Chinese Communism as a whole, which black radicals looked to as Third World models for Marxist class struggle (Kelley and Esch 1999).

Other U.S.-based organizations such as the Brown Berets, I Wor Kuen, and the Red Guard Party modeled themselves on the Black Power movement and the Panthers, in particular, in their fight for Latino and Asian American liberation.[29] Because of these dialogues, Asian ethnic minorities began to assert themselves through racial labels. "Asian American," for example, was embraced during this period as a politicized coalition "that united under a single banner people from many different nations (including former historical rivals, antagonists, and colonizer/colonized), who were marked by different immigration histories and positioned differently with regard to class, gender, and sexuality" (Kondo 1997, 9). This term was an alternative to the state-defined "Oriental" label used to lump them all together. The impulse to signify and organize around new racial meaning, dis-identifying from its previous connotations, is at the heart of Afro Asian practice.

Music was an important medium in this mobilization, providing a marker of nonwhite and non-Western heritage, rousing emotional support, and serving as a tool for professing political sentiments. Many specifically Afro Asian endeavors grew out of the interracial and international consciousness of this historical moment. A review of these projects reflects multiple impetuses, including the desire to unearth forgotten connections across racial and cultural barriers or to explore possibilities for dialogue across differences. Other projects explicitly grounded their politics in Marxist struggle, seeing music as a space to talk about shared experiences of oppression or strategize through culture toward joint political struggle. Some projects are also evidence of unintended Afro Asian politics, brought about through personal interests but certainly aided by geopolitical shifts resulting from Third World movements. Still, I argue, even the most apolitically motivated collaborations have political implications in their crossing of colonial and neocolonial boundaries. Afro Asian formations have promoted various forms of social, political, and aesthetic solidarity but have also explicitly or implicitly worked toward reconstructing the modern racial system.

Afro Asian music is a theoretical framework through which I examine specifically how some black–Asian collaborations counter racial segregation through unearthing cultural connections or finding new ones. Numerous scholars have engaged Afro Asian and other Third World movements as acts of solidarity between disparate populations, but they are also early manifestations of a unified people of color, even though this term would not appear in heavy usage until later in the twentieth century. "People of color" is an alternative to "nonwhite" or "minority." The term was used to refer to free blacks in French colonial settings (*gens de couleur libre*) and was picked up by racial justice activists in the United States from radical theorists such as Franz Fanon in the 1970s (Sen 2007). It allows for the recognition of racial difference that is not solely framed as the lack of whiteness and, thus, more accurately reflects the demographic proportions of the globe. The formation also allows for racial difference alongside a unity that defies colonial racial logic. People of color (POC) discourse illuminates the continuity between European colonial and U.S. racist formations and identifies a shared experience of racialized oppression. Rather than being defined by singular racial, cultural, or national unity, a POC community is based on this joint experience and the performative naming of itself as a unified body. The resulting politics of affinity are based on similar concerns and desires for a postcolonial future.[30]

I would like to propose *music of color* as an aesthetic counterpart to this political formation, which recognizes a connection between nonwhite or non-Western practices based on their coming out of and being connected to people of color's experiences. I use this term to indicate traditions from within and outside of the United States that are subdominantly positioned in U.S. racial and cultural discourses, that is, forms that share a similar set of sociopolitical problematics. Music of color, like its progenitor, draws connections between cultures of minority populations in the United States and nonwhite populations abroad based on notions of marginalized identity, similar experiences of oppression, and cultural similarities shared across national lines. This concept suggests that cultural forms associated with nonwhite or non-Western people should be understood not only in relationship to white or Western forms but also as part of a larger swirl of cultural forms that can interact freely. Music of color is also a purposefully political merger that pushes against colonial compartmentalization by proposing an affinity between these various forms of music despite racial and cultural difference.

Music of color provides a different set of criteria for defining a body of listeners, one based on experience as the basis for cultural similarity rather than race or nation. In particular, music of color suggests that audiences (and artists) of various backgrounds can draw on music not related to their heritage as a symbol or tool toward their liberation. Rather than simply expressing African American concerns through Asian forms—or vice versa—Afro Asian music offers the possibility that people of color might use multiple traditions to express a joint identity and communal concerns.[31] But this formation does not require the erasure of independent roots or significances of traditions. The beauty of individual styles, the sum of them together, and the relationship between them are all equally relevant in this line of thinking. This multifarious culture is not exclusive to the modern West, but it has been furthered by the convergence of many nonwhite populations due to European colonization, in a sense providing a singular adversary to well-being and self-determination.

The Afro Asian and Third World political projects had a tremendous impact on cultural production, resulting in numerous expressions of music of color that continued to generate further explorations. There were a number of experiments at the nexus of jazz and Indian classical traditions in the 1950s and 1960s, drawing on the improvisational element in both as a medium for cross-musical experimentation. The earliest of these projects did not express explicit coalitional politics; however, the meetings of blacks and Asian in postcolonial environments were a key necessity for their emergence. In the United Kingdom, for example, black British saxophonist Joe Harriott (originally from Jamaica) worked with Indian violinist and composer John Mayer on several projects and they formed their own ensemble of Indian classical and jazz musicians (Shipton 2007, 691-692). The pair toured extensively in Europe and released albums such as *Indo-Jazz Fusions* (1967) and *The Indo-Jazz Suite* (1966). The expansion of jazz to incorporate South Asian styles and rock continued in subsequent decades in the United Kingdom and United States with bands such as Mahavishnu Orchestra, Shakti, Garaj Mahal, the Brown Indian Band, and Indofunk.

In the United States, the dialogues between social movements of the 1960s and 1970s formed artistic networks that fostered interracial and intercultural musical interaction. For example, pan-Asian activism on the West Coast inspired the rise of the Bay Area Asian American jazz scene of the 1970s and 1980s. There had been a thriving Asian American jazz scene in the United States that started in the 1930s (and numerous Asian American players), but it, much like the larger black and white scene, was more about entertainment than politics (Dong 1989, Yoshida 1997). In the 1970s, inspired by the black Association for the Advancement of Creative Musicians, Asian American artists such as Jon Jang, Francis Wong, Glen Horiuchi, Mark Izu, and Fred Ho (see Chapter 4) began to explore how to represent a more politicized Asian American musical identity. Their work often incorporated Asian and Asian American musical styles, instruments, and subject matter in a free jazz context as a means to express cultural pride and pan-Asian political unity.

In addition to these symbolic links, a number of Asian American artists collaborated with black artists, producing work that denounced racism and reflected the intersection of African and Asian diasporic identities. In fact, artists in the West Coast Asian American jazz scene were quite keen on collaborating with black artists, never fully operating with a narrow singular racial perspective (Dessen 2006). Groups like Marron and United Front brought together some of the same Asian American players with black artists including Lewis Jordan and George Sams. Asian American jazz continued to develop into the 1980s and beyond, with artists such as Hiroshima, Miya Masaoka, Asian Crisis, Vijay Iyer, and Rudresh Mahanthappa further growing the conversation. Important among this next wave was an increased participation of female musicians (Masaoka and Meena Makhijani of Asian Crisis), expansion of cross-racial explorations to include South Asian traditions (Iyer and Mahanthappa), and continued collaboration with black, white, Latino, and Native American musicians.

Black artists have also initiated cross-racial explorations with Asian/ American artists and traditions. Some blacks historically used Asian material to symbolize an escape from Western cultural hegemony, romanticizing or exoticizing it much like in dominant discourse. Examples of these gestures include pieces like Sun Ra's "India" (recorded in 1956) and Duke Ellington's *The Afro Eurasian Eclipse* (recorded in 1971). In their own idiosyncratic ways, each of these pieces demonstrates the composers looking to the East as a spiritual foundation and increasing global cultural and political force. These recordings resonate with Bill Mullen's notion of Afro-Orientalism, the black use of sometimes stereotyped representations of Asian entities in order to draw connections rather than separation, "a counterdiscourse that at times shares with its dominant namesake certain features" (Mullen 2004, xv). But black musicians also engaged more closely with actual Asian cultures as a means toward cross-racial identification and symbolic solidarity. In the 1950s and 1960s, John Coltrane turned increasingly to a number of non-Western musical forms, incorporating Indian, African, and Middle Eastern musics, and Hindu and Chinese symbolism into his work.[32] He had ongoing conversations with Ravi Shankar and studied with him briefly before his death in 1967 (Monson 1998, 158).[33] Alice Coltrane, who began to perform with her husband's quartet in the final years of his life, took these explorations further in her own compositions, drawing on black church forms, Indian music, and Hindu themes (Berkman 2010).[34]

In more recent years, hip hop has provided fertile ground for both what Nitasha Sharma calls "appropriation as othering" and "appropriation as identification" in the employment of Asian images (2010, 234–282).[35] As I discuss in Chapter 5, various hip hop and R&B artists have employed stereotypical representations of East and South Asian people and cultures, often in an Orientalist hodgepodge. In contrast, the Wu Tang Clan, formed in 1992, based their entire output on an ethos overlaying Staten Island, New York, with elements of Shaolin Kung Fu history and mythology. While employing some stereotypical imagery, their project also reflected their personal knowledge of and training in martial arts, a key site for Afro Asian youth solidarities.[36] In solo projects such as the soundtracks for the animated television series *Afro Samurai* and film *Ghost Dog: The Way of the Samurai*, Wu Tang's RZA has continued to blend East Coast beats with his interpretations of martial arts film scores. While these projects do not actively include Asian participants in the foreground, they express a desire to forge community built on shared Otherness and the revolutionary potential of self-defense. Other hip hop artists who have explicitly connected their work to radical Asian/American politics or feature mixed black and Asian membership include The Coup, Zion I, and Dilated Peoples.

This brief sample reveals some of the major contours of musical projects in which black and Asian sonic signifiers, traditions, or people share space: Asian/American performances of black music, black Orientalist productions, and fusions of style or membership. And there are others that do not fit into these categories, such as mixed-raced artists like Anthony Brown or Sugar Pie DeSanto, the *gamelan*-based compositions of black composer Anthony Davis, or even Sidi Goma, an ensemble of African-Indian Sufis from Gujarat.[37] My purpose here is not to detail every black–Asian exchange but rather to raise questions about what some of them reveal. The Afro Asian impulse has been variously explored in close and distant relationship to similarly named political ideologies. How then do we demarcate the racial politics of "The Wedding of the Chinee and the Coon" from Alice Coltrane's "Journey in Satchidananda"? Or black musician Bill Cole's performance of Asian double reed instruments from Carl Douglas's "Everybody Was Kung Fu Fighting"?[38] The following chapters in this book provide a set of tools with which to discuss the myriad confrontations of musical blackness and Asianness, those that explicitly serve projects of Afro Asian solidarity, others that implicitly intervene in racially triangulating discourses, and everything in between.

March On

Just as Afro Asian sociopolitical engagements are not a recent phenomenon, neither are sono-racial collaborations between black and Asian people and musics. "The Wedding of the Chinee and the Coon," *Chee Lai*, and other Afro Asian musical endeavors following showcase multiple roots of contemporary Afro Asian music making and how they link to broader interminority politics. Post–Civil War racial discourses and policies have historically separated blacks and Asians from whites and from each other. In many eras, Asians have been elevated above blacks in racial discourse, posed as a model minority to a decidedly "un-model" black underclass. This dynamic has been carried into popular culture figurations of blackness and Asianness, resulting in industry structures in which black musics are integrated into domestic culture—and circulated globally as an emblem of the nation—while Asian musics are categorized as of the "world" rather than homegrown phenomena. The veneration of African American culture in the United States (and world) complicates a tidy portrait of (sono-)racial triangulation, however, as music and other practices are elevated within the sono-racial taxonomy while black people continue to be subjugated.

Artists of color have operated within these sono-racial structures in ways that promote and defy dominant formulations of sound and race. Bob Cole and Billy Johnson offered a "take" on the minstrel show that argued for blacks' ability to perform cross-racially, although their use of stereotyped images of blackness, whiteness, and Asianness continued to promote static and problematic representations of these populations. Paul Robeson sought to unite African Americans with their spiritual and political kinfolk around the world, but romanticized this union in ways that exoticized non-Western (especially Asian) people and forms. Post-Bandung sono-racial collaborations showcased a range of approaches to bringing together different people and sounds, although they varied in participants' commitment to long-term relationship building. Rather than a linear unfolding of a unified Afro Asian project, the cases in this chapter show the many separate streams that feed into a larger pool, reflecting the ways in which artists of color have struggled to operate within a culture industry that fetishizes them.

These artists' and their surrounding industry's use of race as a form of currency—monetary, social, or political—is a precursor to the sono-racial dynamics of multiculturalism I explore in the remainder of this book. In each of these projects, sounds were not just sounds; they instead were used as surrogates for racialized bodies, to varying ends. "Wedding" and *Coontown* presented racialized sound as shorthand for forms of racial difference and comic fodder as artists collaborated with sounds that were not seen to "match" the race of the person performing them. *Chee Lai* capitalized on the unique blackness of Robeson's voice, funneling a Chinese song through his black body to argue for larger connections between people around the globe. And in the final examples, sounds became the vocabulary for artists seeking to hold lesser-heard conversations with others across race and to more fully express themselves as individuals, aesthetically and politically. Ultimately, I showed how people of color use dominantly managed terms and racial figurations as a means to engage with one another. At the same time, I queried how these gestures signify differently when executed by nonwhites, questions I will continue to return to in the following chapters.

Rather than viewing the politics of "The Wedding of the Chinee and the Coon," *Chee Lai*, and the various post-Bandung projects as disparate, I argue that they all demonstrate ways in which body–culture determinism manifested in historic popular culture formations, as well as how artists disrupted this simple equation. In the remainder of the book, I aim to connect the dots between these historical moments and later Afro Asian performances, those that explicitly cite this history and those that do not. Each of the cases I explored here was important in showing that people of color are not only able to perform their "own" difference, they can perform the Other just like white interpreters. In the following chapters, I will show how artists have continued to push on this white-non-white divide by drawing attention to whiteness, ignoring it, or posing different relationships between racial categories in which white is merely one other actor. We will also see, even in the acknowledgment of whiteness, the variegated dialogues that are developed when projects are not created simply to respond to it. Longstanding interracial conversations have developed among artists that refigure racial relationships and stretch well beyond the expression of purely oppositional identities.

2

Becoming Afro Asian
Yoko Noge's Jazz Me Blues and Japanesque

Katerina's stands on a busy block at the meeting point of Chicago's Lincoln Square, Uptown, and Lakeview neighborhoods. A combination restaurant, bar, and performance venue, its unassuming façade is marked by a thinly lettered blue neon sign. I have come tonight to hear local artist Yoko Noge and her mixed-race ensemble, Japanesque, perform their monthly gig featuring a blend of blues and Japanese *minyo* or folksongs.¹ Entering the long, narrow room, I notice the club's red walls with gold trim, about twenty weathered wooden tables of various sizes, and kitschy accoutrements such as retro lamps fitted with feather-trimmed shades. While I usually sit at the bar that stretches along the wall to my left, tonight I sit at a small round table right in front of the small stage tucked into the back corner. The drum kit rests less than a foot from me and drummer Avreeayl Ra greets me, joking, "Up close and personal, right?"² The music begins and the room is filled with the sounds of Noge's gruff singing, accompanied by piano, guitar, bass, *shamisen, taiko*, and the drum kit.³ As the group alternates between blues standards, *minyo*, and Noge's original compositions, the sheer kinetic force of the music strikes me. The kick drum rattles my legs, accented by a pound in my chest from the interlocking *taiko* parts. The steady pulse of a walking bassline blankets my body in vibration, while my ears tingle from the sharp plink of the *shamisen*. At the most basic, physical level, I experience Japanesque as an intimate engagement with sounds and the people who produce them.

Japanesque (and Noge's Jazz Me Blues Band) is an example of sono-racial collaboration between black and Asian people, African and Japanese diasporic cultures, and racial discourses of blackness and Asianness in Chicago. Racialized sounds, their histories, and the people who play them all come into contact in the moment of performance. But they are also evidence of much longer and larger social and political currents articulated in the previous chapter. While the sounds are "real"—evidenced by their effect on my body—in Afro Asian performance they also become symbols of interracial and intercultural engagement. Japanesque creates spaces in which artists of multiple racial and cultural identifications participate in making music sono-racially construed as belonging to "each other." In concerts, musical, cultural, national, and racial boundaries are performatively constructed and simultaneously blurred or traversed.

As in other interracial endeavors, however, Noge's ensembles raise questions about how and why one lays claim to material not deemed their "own." Typical models of cross-racial performance fall into several categories: minstrelsy, passing, and identification. Motivated by curiosity, desire, and revulsion, minstrelsy is about defining the self while performing the Other (Rogin 1998, Lott 1995). The temporary crossing of racial lines serves to distance the performer from the performed—presumed to be of a different racial category—and keeps the performer's identity intact. Passing, however, involves a provisional disavowal of the self and capitalizes on the paradoxical rigidity and permeability of racial categories in order to forge a new social identity (Lipsitz 2007). While minstrelsy gains power from its transparency, passing requires the obfuscation of racial transgression. And rather than temporary racial transformation in minstrelsy, passing narratives often unfold over much longer stretches of time, even an entire lifetime. Finally, cross-racial "appropriation as identification" (Sharma 2010) posits retention of the self while drawing performative connections to the Other. The Other provides gestures, sounds, or techniques that allow the performer to express an alternate or more complete version of themselves than previously available. In each of these approaches, self-definition is paramount and the Other serves as a model or point of contrast.

Noge's work mixes all three of these approaches, although, since these appropriations occur in interracial settings, they can work against notions of racial cohesion at either end of the exchange. Michael Rogin argues that "blackface made new identities for white men by fixing the identities of women and African Americans" (1995, 52). But performing the self alongside the Other—rather than just music sono-racially associated with them—allows for the possibility of shifting one's conception of self and the Other through interaction. Others are "selves," too, and they grow and change in response to one another. Noge's groups provide example of how Asian/American performance of black music has historically been about self-definition, but also frequently about understanding blacks by using music to forge relationships with them. This process also shapes African American identity and blacks' understanding of Asian/Americans people and cultural practices. We hear in these projects a process of negotiation on multiple axes and from various subject positions.

Lisa Lowe suggests that "rather than considering 'Asian American identity' as a fixed, established 'given,' perhaps we can consider instead 'Asian American cultural practices' that produce identity; the processes that produce such identity are never complete and are always constituted in relation to historical and material differences" (1996, 64). In the work I explore here, I argue that instead of racial endpoints, Noge and collaborators are constantly changing selves who collectively produce Asian/American and African American identities and cultures through their Afro Asian engagements. In the previous chapter, I proposed the possibility for "music of color" to allow for cross-racial nonwhite access to a shared body of mixed cultural material. In this chapter, I explore how this aesthetic tome is interracially built.

Noge's case also reveals how the immigrant experience in the United States—Asian or otherwise—is rooted in the negotiation of a racial system based on the polarities of black and white. Or, to put it a different way, the Asian immigrant experience *is* an Afro Asian performance through which interminority difference is brokered. As has been shown in several studies, jazz (and to a lesser extent blues) has been an important tool through which Asian musicians have negotiated their relationship to modernity and the West.[4] Performing black music provides a space in which Noge and her Japanese bandmates become U.S. American by moving toward blackness rather than whiteness. By doing so in Afro Asian spaces, their music becomes a means through which they practice how to sit within African American history and community as a nonblack person.

To get at these points, I will first discuss the musical backgrounds of Noge and her band members to show how they reflect what I call the "Afro-Asianization" of Asian/American and African American cultures. Examining a few of their stories in detail, I suggest they jointly reflect one of the pillars of Afro Asian performance: the de-linking of nation and race from culture. Next, I will analyze several of Noge's pieces to illustrate how she locates herself within African American practices, not as simply another practitioner but as a cultural "sidewoman." This discussion opens up to consider the ways in which gender impacts the processes of Afro Asian identity formation, as well as the possibilities for remaining between masculine and feminine, black and Asian, rather than either one. Finally, I illustrate the ways in which Chicago civic arts programs have had difficulty in representing the dynamic racial and cultural processes in Noge's groups, especially the ways in which they showcase identities that shift through time. Their work troubles clear dichotomies of black/Asian, American/Japanese, and native/foreign, yet their performances often reinscribe these very demarcations due to the authenticating hand of the culture industry.

As you will see in other case studies in this book, some Afro Asian artists infuse their work with fervent antiracist or anti-imperialist politics. Noge's work is not overtly political. Born out of her life, career, and idiosyncratic interests, she claims no goals for her performances other than to play interesting music and engage audiences through active listening and participatory dance. But we should not overlook the quotidian as a politically productive site of Afro Asian community formation, and this chapter is an attempt to understand the very intimate spaces in which sono-racial collaboration might unfold. Through discourse on romance, sexuality, and "home," Noge's music impacts broader racial and cultural conversations as civic and corporate bodies encounter it. She does not do politics "in" her work; her work "does" politics by endorsing and opposing racially triangulating discourses and institutions.

Afro-Asianization

In the 1989 film *Forbidden City, U.S.A.*, several elderly Chinese American singers and dancers recount their first encounters with segregation while touring in the Jim Crow South. The binary conception of race embedded in the national psyche was more tangibly present there than in San Francisco where the artists lived, and they were confounded by segregated public facilities that seemed to only allow for white and black use. Which bathrooms should they choose? In the end, some performers went in restrooms for whites, others for blacks, not necessarily feeling like either was a space for them. Getting on a bus, singer Toy Yat Mar faced a similar dilemma, although the vehicle's layout allowed her to choose to sit in the racially ambiguous middle. The performers knew they were not white even though some could pass enough to not draw attention in a brief encounter. The more pressing question was whether they were black, since they felt little similarity or rapport with blacks despite their mutual marginalization. Forced to query their relationship to blackness, some of the artists elected to define this relationship as one of kinship, while others one of negation.[5]

For many, the Asian American experience is an Afro Asian negotiation rather than a singular, linear assimilation toward whiteness. Whether recent immigrants or fourth-generation, Asians in the United States cannot help but encounter African American culture and people. For artists, this exposure is often more pronounced, as they respond to stimuli around them and find their voice amidst a culture heavily marked by the production of blacks. Nitasha Sharma has shown that South Asian American hip hop artists use African American music to assert racialized identities unique to their experience in the United States (2010). Black music, she argues, is a vehicle that allows for the construction of a racial discourse previously unavailable to desis. Sharma claims this phenomenon is fueled by both the ubiquity of African American culture and artists' seeking out hip hop as an inherently political tool. As I discussed in Chapter 1, the culture industry has long proffered triangulating constructions of black–Asian racial separation. But artists like Toy Yat Mar, Sharma's subjects, and Yoko Noge—albeit from different ethnic groups—indicate that this is not the cultural reality for many Asian Americans. Looking closely at Noge and her bandmates, we see an example of the ways in which Asian/American identity is Afro Asian because of the "African-Americanization" of U.S. culture (Rollefson 2014).

Noge is a stalwart of the Chicago blues scene. She formed the Jazz Me Blues Band with her husband Clark Dean in the mid-1980s and it has featured a shifting roster of some of the city's best-known musicians, including guitarist Floyd McDaniel, drummer Darlene Payne Wells, saxophonist Sonny Seals, drummer Phil Thomas, and trombonist/singer/actor John Watson. Dean was friends with HotHouse club founder Marguerite Horberg and pitched her the idea of having a regular Monday evening gig at the space—a night many musicians had no work—and Horberg agreed.[6] The event began as "Blue Monday" and became the primary venue for the band's repertoire of classic Chicago blues standards, old-style New Orleans tunes, and Noge's original compositions. The Jazz Me Blues Band has recorded four albums, including several recorded live at the HotHouse, and the *Chicago Tribune* named Noge Chicagoan of the year in 2006.

During the period of my research, the Jazz Me Blues Band consisted of: Noge on vocals and piano, Clark Dean (white) on soprano saxophone, Tatsu Aoki (Japanese/American) on bass and *shamisen*, Jimmy Ellis (African American) on alto saxophone, Jeff Chan (Chinese American) on tenor saxophone, Kaz Terashima (Japanese) on trumpet, and Avreeayl Ra (African American) on drum set. Noge launched Japanesque in 2006, a separate project devoted to experimenting with blending *minyo* with blues. Japanesque performances often featured guest musicians who were regulars from the Chicago blues scene including guitarists John Primer, Lurie Bell, and George Freeman, and bassist Bob Stroger (all African American) and drummers Hide Yoshihashi, Amy Homma, and Jason Matsumoto (all Japanese American) from the Tsukasa Taiko ensemble. A shifting roster of core Jazz Me Blues members (Aoki, Ellis, Terashima, and Ra) also participated. As evidenced from the list, the bands embody a mix of players from different racial, ethnic, cultural, and national backgrounds, as well as musical traditions.

Jazz Me Blues and Japanesque also bring together musicians from different segments of the Chicago music industry: jazz/creative music, blues, and Asian American community performance (music and other arts). The members additionally encompass multiple generations and reflect a range of secondary employment. Several of the members are full-time, working-class musicians who make their living performing and teaching. Noge, however, also works as a journalist for the Japanese financial paper *Nikkei*, writing articles on finance and social trends. Terashima moved to the United States from Japan in 2006 to pursue a master's degree in music at DePaul University. And Aoki is, among other things, an adjunct professor at the School of the Art Institute of Chicago and Northwestern University.

Noge's ensembles are the pinnacle of her long engagement with U.S. American and specifically African American music. She was born in Osaka, Japan, and began singing U.S. American folk music in high school. A friend had her listen to a recording by black American blues singer and guitarist Elmore James. Noge says the music "just gave me a chill and somehow I knew everything kind of connected together, what I was trying to find out in the music, singing-wise. This is it. And so I started to sing the blues music. And I met several other people who shared the love of the blues." While in college, she formed a band with some of these people, entered a competition for money, and won. Soon after, she became a recording artist for the Japan Victor label and began to tour while still in school. Thus, Noge started her professional music career as a blues performer. Yet, despite her success in Japan, she says, "My dream was always coming to Chicago, because I knew there was real blues music going on and I had to check it out one day." So in 1984, at age 26, she and her then husband—a Japanese blues guitarist from her group—moved to Chicago.

Noge and her husband purposefully began to frequent blues clubs on the West Side of the city, choosing black neighborhoods "because we knew the blues was supposed to be the music born from the community and the black voices." Shortly after arriving, they met Willy Kent, a celebrated black blues singer, bassist, and songwriter. Her husband was soon hired as a side player and Noge went with them when they performed around town, often joining the group as a guest vocalist. Two years later, Noge's husband returned to Japan, but she decided to stay in Chicago and they divorced. At age 30, she began to study piano with white boogie-woogie impresario Erwin Helfer, so she could accompany herself and have another tool with which to experiment in finding her own musical voice. She has since formed a winning partnership with Dean and performs with an ever-increasing roster of musicians from the city's blues and jazz communities.

The fact that Noge was first a blues performer in Japan illustrates that, for many Asian immigrants, the Afro-Asianization process starts before their arrival in the United States. Blues and jazz have circulated internationally since the 1920s and held a significant presence in many Asian countries. As E. Taylor Atkins argues, "In the interwar period America gradually displaced Europe as the principal cultural influence in Asia, securing its hold through the spectacle of motion pictures and the rhythmic power of American dance music" (2001, 85). Jazz, the first black style disseminated on a wide scale in Japan, took hold in the 1920s and soon cities such as Osaka and Tokyo harbored cafés, dance halls, and movie theaters offering performances by Japanese and foreign bands. Amidst this popularity, the music carried multiple and conflicting significations. Jazz "allowed Japanese to experience an authentic 'modernity' that placed them squarely in the politically and culturally prestigious company of elite Western nations," a new tool furthering the adoption of various Western cultural forms begun during the Meiji restoration (Atkins 2001, 47). At the same time, the music was often—and continues to be—viewed in conjunction with blackness: its perceived authenticity and potential sexual danger (Atkins 2001, 102). Much as in the United States, these beliefs have also been rendered onto other black musical forms such as the blues.

Japanese audiences first grew interested in the blues in the late 1930s (Atkins 2001, 132). Noge describes the 1970s and 1980s as that country's "first blues boom," a moment of wide-scale discovery of the blues that inspired the formation of hundreds of bands.[7] This history demonstrates that it is quite common for Japanese musicians to have encountered or even grown up with this music. We have seen an example of this already in Noge's case, but it holds true for some of her bandmates as well. Trumpeter Terashima, who is from Tokyo, began to play the trumpet in the seventh grade and performed in his school's ensemble. But he found that while classical music offered much activity for string players, trumpeters would often wait a long time to play just a few notes. So he turned to jazz at age 20 as a way to play more actively. Terashima describes his jazz skills as self-taught and says he felt a connection to the style because he grew up with a father who listened to it. As Andre Millard suggests, "Recorded sound was the great educator, attracting generations of performers into musical careers and schooling them in styles of music which were often not written down" (2005, 12). Like many U.S. American players, Japanese jazz musicians often learned their licks by listening to recordings and studying improvised solos.[8]

Yet while hearing and playing the blues was an everyday experience for Noge in Japan, the performance of *minyo* was not. The Jazz Me Blues Band has performed Noge's compositions since their inception, the songs often containing Japanese lyrics or references to events, topics, or images from Japan. But Noge's turn to performing *minyo* is a relatively new move, one that occurred only once she had moved to the United States. She first incorporated these songs into her repertoire at the request of a Japanese producer who wanted her to sing "Tankobushi," a regional coal miners' work song, when she played in Kyushu. The audience loved it, she says; some of them even came on stage and began to perform the accompanying dance. Noge started to incorporate more *minyo* into her sets and now performs songs including "Shide Mai" and "Sanosa." Her continued interest in the genre has also been supported through her work as a vocalist with Aoki and his Miyumi Project, a group blending Japanese classical and folk music with experimental jazz.

Noge's performance of *minyo* is not based in an innate racial connection to the material. Many of the songs she now performs she knew from childhood but has had to go through, she says, "sort of a re-learning process, making sure the words are right." For many immigrants, interest in the traditions of home grows in diasporic spaces, offering opportunities for them to combine with cultural material from their new surroundings. Recognizing Noge's "return" to Japanese music complicates a simplistic immigrant narrative of increasing acculturation. It also means her becoming "more" Japanese occurs through hybrid musical experimentation. The exploration of intersections between Western classical and popular music with Japanese traditions has been a hallmark of contemporary Japanese musical practice since the post-Meiji 1930s.[9] Composers have long sought to reconcile decades of government-forced Western classical training with local cultural forms neglected in the push for modernization-cum-Westernization and have often relearned forgotten folk traditions in the process (Herd 2004). Noge did not uncover a pristine Japanese musical identity in the *minyo*. Like other Japanese composers, she is actively engaged in a search for musical identity through *minyo*. In the United States, this pursuit takes place within the dominant white landscape and in relation to the nation's trove of African American culture.

Noge's case offers a nuanced portrait of an individual negotiating her cultural and aesthetic ties to both the United States and Japan and negates essentialist links between nationality, race, culture, and musical practice. Expanding my frame to her band members confirms this same function. Aoki's musical background is in both Japanese traditional music and jazz: his mother was a geisha and he thus grew up amidst intensive arts practice. Aoki began to learn *shamisen* and *taiko* at age 3 and started playing rock and jazz bass as a young adult. He is the founder and artistic director of the Chicago Asian American Jazz Festival (Noge is a cofounder) as well as the executive director of Asian Improv aRts Midwest, an offshoot of the West Coast–based Asian Improv aRts organization. In Terashima's case, he grew up with jazz as part of his daily culture thanks to his father's listening habits. And Jeff Chan underscores the Afro Asianness of the Asian American experience given that the bulk of his musical background is situated within an African American cultural form.

Black musicians also engage in the Afro-Asianization process but with some key differences. Drummer Avreeayl Ra, for example, has performed in Aoki's Miyumi Project for years. And from his experience playing with a host of other musicians—including Sun Ra—and performing instruments such as Native American flute, he says he feels adept at working in a variety of world music environments. Yet while cross-racial musical knowledge can move both ways in Afro Asian performance, performers of black music—both blacks and others—tend to have less knowledge of Asian musical traditions. In talking with several of the black blues musicians who play in Japanesque (not Jazz Me Blues members), they often did not know the names of the Japanese instruments in the ensemble or, at times, the names of the Japanese/American musicians. In addition, fewer of the black jazz and blues artists had previously played with Asian instruments or traditions. This fact testifies to the power of sono-racial triangulation as an organizing logic in the States. Asian/American musicians generally have more exposure to black music because of its prominent role in U.S. and global popular culture. But because of predominant assumptions of Asian practices as foreign, there are fewer opportunities for blacks to experience these traditions on a practical level. In Japanesque, the black blues artists are generally guests joining Noge's usual crew, so there is not as much time or space to befriend fellow band members or learn the particulars of the Japanese instruments. Still, as many of the regular band members have said to me, these guests have tended to be quite open to collaborating with Asian/American artists and Asian traditions, allowing for the Asian–Americanization of African American culture as well.

The Jazz Me Blues Band and Japanesque feature musicians whose individual musical histories reveal non-essential identities, but also provide fertile ground for their various histories to intersect with one another in rehearsal and performance. Noge, for example, made a point to learn the blues by connecting with black players. This roots seeking started as a romanticized journey to learn from racial "insiders" but resulted in the formation and fostering of long-term relationships. Evidence of one such partnership can be found in the album *Yoko Meets John*, a 1999 release that showcases Noge and the late John Watson. The album title is a reference to the long-term collaborative process between the two as well as another interracial music duo—John Lennon and Yoko Ono. Watson was an actor, singer, and trombone player who performed with the Jazz

Me Blues until he passed away in 2006. He was integral to the formation of the group and helped recruit several of its other members. For years, Noge and Watson met each other weekly to talk about music, eat at the South Side soul food restaurant Ms. Biscuit, and play. Justin O'Brien's liner notes suggest that the album chronicles "the blossoming of a musical friendship" and "the discovery of the common spiritual ground in cultures from two far-flung continents and its expression through Chicago blues, swing, bop and straight-ahead and free jazz" (1999). This friendship unfolds musically through witty and sometimes sexually suggestive sung and spoken exchanges.

Despite an album cover displaying the two in smiles and intimate engagement, Noge claims there were difficulties in forging this relationship. Watson was reluctant to open up and trust her, a response she attributes to the fact of their racial difference. At times, she says, he would "just look at me" or even say things that she found offensive, in one sense giving Noge an experience of racial marginalization likely felt by the black artists with whom she tried to connect.[10] Still, she says, she enjoyed their

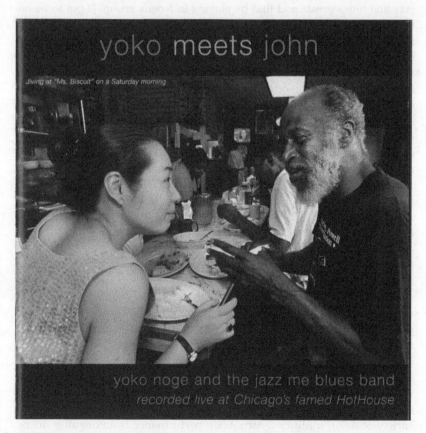

Figure 2.1. Front cover of *Yoko Meets John*. Photograph by Clark Dean. Album design by Justin O'Brien. Courtesy of Yoko Noge.

"rehearsals"—sometimes just breakfast with only ten minutes of music played—and they connected through their music. The personal relationship took longer to establish, but over a period of five or six years they grew closer. She suggests that Watson went through a difficult time and she was there to support him. O'Brien's notes state that the album is "mostly about serious musicians rediscovering and exploring the humor and creative tension in relationships as well as in some wonderful, rhapsodic and meaningful music" (1999). This forging of bonds amidst interpersonal tensions and the ability of music to support them are critical to their Afro Asian enterprise. Noge claims that fostering feelings of trust and reliance with fellow band members is rarely seen as important by solely business-minded bandleaders. But, for her, this extended investment in personal relationships is crucial to the kind of music she and her collaborators produce.

The Jazz Me Blues Band has also inspired and fostered interracial collaborations between other band members. Jeff Chan and Jimmy Ellis have worked together on numerous other performances with Chan's trio and Ellis's ensemble. Moving from the Bay Area to Chicago in 2002, Chan says he was struck by the access to and approachability of many of the city's jazz and blues greats and that by playing in Noge's group, "I got to be on the stage with these guys every week." He smiles broadly, saying, "One of my most important musical relationships right now is my relationship with Jimmy Ellis" and that it "wouldn't have happened" without working with him in the Jazz Me Blues Band. As another example, Aoki has forged his career collaborating with black members of the Association for the Advancement of Creative Musicians, including Von Freeman, Mwata Bowden, and Fred Anderson. And, at their Monday night HotHouse gigs, the Jazz Me Blues Band often features younger guest artists of various races who sit in for a song or two, cultivating the next generation of players. Further evidence of the group's interest in fostering communication and building bonds are the recordings several members generously gifted to me. On one HotHouse Monday, Aoki presented me with a stack of around ten CDs and DVDs of his work. When I asked what I should pay him, he said he wanted only for me to "write a good paper."

In all, the backgrounds of Noge and collaborators present a more nuanced image of black–Asian encounter. First, "black" and "Asian" are not monolithic entities artists move between, but instead overlapping spaces that have in various ways flowed into one another. Rather than vessels for unadulterated traditions from the homeland, Asian immigrants Noge, Terashima, and Aoki's histories suggest a more complicated relationship to black and Japanese music. The triangulation of the Asian immigrant experience is key to the formation of new lateral engagements among musicians of color. And black members' encounters with Japanese music have stretched on, in some cases, for decades, and by working with Asian/American artists, they have had space in which to learn about a variety of Asian traditions. Afro Asian performance is an ongoing sitting beside other people of color, spawning collaborations and racial understanding through prolonged engagement. But interracial community is not a given and requires long-term efforts and understanding of the larger racial taxonomy. These dialogues begin in personal associations and are worked out through the musical texts they inspire.

Accompanying Diaspora

Noge's songs demonstrate a desire to reside between Japanese and African American cultures, raising questions about the racial makeup of her sound. In the Jazz Me Blues Band, she writes original songs dealing with Japanese topics and incorporates Japanese language or themes into existing ones. In Japanesque, she extends this dialogue between forms to incorporate intensive instrumental interplay between *minyo* and blues players. Thus, she performatively places herself within African American history and culture through her lyrics and gestures. Instead of fully laying claim to this heritage as her own, however, she presents herself as a supporter, a "sidewoman." The sideman is an important jazz figure: this player is not the star but supports the entire musical endeavor, bearing tradition out of the spotlight. In Noge's case, this position is not simply a musical one; it reflects the ways in which she situates herself amidst the U.S. racial terrain and in relation to blackness, in ways that both resist and reinforce stereotypes of black and Japanese musicality. She has chosen to surround herself with black, white, and Asian American artists—all relative national insiders compared to her—and provided space for them to speak to her participation in the form. The notion of a "side*woman*" also indicates the gendered contours of the spaces Noge fosters, in which she is frequently the only female.[11] While she sometimes operates from a position of racial superiority in relation to black artists, her femininity can place her in a subordinate gender position. We will see that in both of Noge's groups, the field of power differentials is complicated, multilayered, and ever-shifting.

Several of Noge's songs illuminate the performative ways in which she displays racial sidewomanship within African diasporic histories and traditions. Performance is central to the ways in which racial and cultural diaspora are lived.[12] As James Clifford notes: "The language of diaspora is increasingly invoked by displaced peoples who feel (maintain, revive, invent) a connection with a prior home" (1994, 310). Emigrants are concerned with the creation and maintenance of the culture of the homeland within diasporic spaces and often join together to perpetuate it despite differences in class, generation, or other social fissures. It is the actions of living in the diaspora that bind these communities—not extant links formed in the place of origin. When a tangible connection to home is not available, the symbol of the homeland is central to the experience of diaspora. Social and political organizations, clothing, and music serve as ways to continually imagine a connection to one's native land. So, since diaspora often operates in the realm of metaphor, can one's attachment to it be based solely on an intangible allegiance versus "blood"? If diasporas can overlap and people can be mixed-race, can one individual be a part of more than one diaspora?[13] And what does it take to appropriately claim a diaspora not your own? I believe new racial and cultural models—and realms of political efficacy—open if we understand diaspora as a process of affiliation, rather than as a given based on heritage alone.

On a cool evening in June 2007, I head into the HotHouse to see the Jazz Me Blues Band after being away for a few months. The venue (a now defunct performance space/art gallery in Chicago's South Loop neighborhood) boasts an international reputation for presenting jazz, blues, world music, hip hop, spoken word, film, and theater artists. I strong-armed a friend into attending with me, desiring the presence of someone else as I reacquainted myself with the band and space. Much like Katerina's, the walls are painted deep red and eclectically decorated with murals and paintings of musicians, retro lounge lamps, and "imports" such as small statues of Hindu gods and intricately carved wooden benches. Except for the free entrance price (formerly $5–$7), the space remains the same, down to the paper plates of Doritos and potato chips on the tables. The presence of snacks alerts me that there will be a birthday celebration tonight. Thinking back to the prior year, I realize it is yet another for Clark Dean who is turning 81. We take a seat in the booth in the center back of the small house, snagging a plate of chips from another table on our way.

Partway into the second set, Noge begins a slow piece and dedicates it to a visiting professor who has brought along his class. She starts on the piano with several descending, multi-octave cascades on a blues scale, like rain trickling down the keys. Laying on the pedal, Noge blends the notes into a resonant hum that lingers once the opening figure concludes. Then, over the decaying sound, she sings:

> Sometimes I feel like a motherless child
> Sometimes I feel like a motherless child
> Sometimes I feel like a motherless child
> A long way from home
> Sometimes I feel like an eagle in the air
> Sometimes I feel like an eagle in the air
> Sometimes I feel like an eagle in the air
> A long way from home

Noge accompanies herself sparsely with occasional chords. By the second verse, the piano grows into a steady four-beat pulse with small embellishments on the fourth beat, her voice always trailing slightly behind the piano. Drummer Avreeayl Ra plays accents with mallets on toms—subtle, gentle, anticipatory, and never fully carrying the pulse.

Near the end of the second verse, saxophonist Jimmy Ellis hobbles to a microphone downstage center to begin a long solo. He plays the melody twice in a meditative manner, full of longing but not sad. On the third time through, Ellis opens up, playing higher and diverging more from the melody in his improvisations. Noge matches this shift by punctuating his phrases with clipped, syncopated chords. After this most plaintive verse,

Ellis drops down for a final time through the progression, playing a lower, more economical improvisation. He extends this verse, repeating the melodic section "a long way from home" several times, ultimately resolving to the tonic while the piano lingers on the subdominant. Eventually, this harmonic tug gives way and the piano resolves.

Vamping, Noge acknowledges Ellis's solo and sings again, this time in Japanese:

Atashi ga konoyoni umareta karanya
Moichido anata ni aitai atashi
Tooku no osora ni yobikake te mita
Anata no ohiza ni dakarete atashi
Yumemite nemutte waratte mitai
Wakatte irunoyo moo nido to anata
Sugata o misenai atashi no kokoro ni
Soredemo yappari kono omoi no take
Ituska ha anata ni kotaete hoshii
Mou korekiri de aenai nante atashi gaman dekinai
Mou korekiri de aenai nante atashi gaman dekinai
(It's because I was born to this world
I long to see you one more time
I called for you toward far away sky
Wish to be held on your lap
Dreaming, sleeping, smiling, I wish
I know that you would never show yourself in my heart
But still I can't stop longing for you to return
I just can't bear that I can't see you ever again
I just can't bear that I can't see you ever again)[14]

At first, Ellis echoes each of Noge's short phrases on saxophone in a call-and-response that reinforces the simple beauty of the melody. As the song progresses, Noge remains on the melody and Ellis's answers diverge into an antiphonal dialogue with the main theme. Ra ramps up the percussion, adding the clang of the cowbell to the toms. Soon, Aoki—who had previously been sitting to the side eating a piece of birthday cake—comes onto the stage and in one swoop picks up his bass and launches into a line that transforms the proceedings from reserved to full-out pathos. The pulse shifts to a groove in which Ra and Aoki emphasize the backbeat. The stark texture grows more full and vibrant as everyone builds to a full frenzy, over which Noge repeatedly growls "sometimes I feel" in an improvised coda. The band comes to a shimmering rest as Noge holds a final "feeeeeel." The audience breaks their rapt silence, overlapping the end of the song with applause.

"Sometimes I Feel Like a Motherless Child" is a spiritual that deals with the destruction of black families as children and parents were sold away during the Trans-Atlantic slave trade. The song is a staple in the repertoires of many blues, jazz, and gospel performers, including the Blind Boys of

Alabama, Louis Armstrong, Eric Clapton, Mahalia Jackson, Ike and Tina Turner, and Odetta. Noge's arrangement of the song is one of the Jazz Me Blues Band's signature pieces and is a musical interpolation of her persona into a symbolic African American lineage. Bearing witness to the diasporic history of Africans in the Americas, Noge's version is unique in her insertion of additional text referring to the death of her own mother. The loss of family and longing for home present in the original resonate with Noge's own inability to return home, metaphorically, to Japan and the family she knew. The new lyrics stretch beyond personal expression; Noge draws a thematic link to broader feelings of homelessness and displacement for foreign nationals. Her attempt to establish a dialogue between these two experiences is met by Ellis's saxophone responses, literally in conversation with the Japanese lyrics. But the additional narrative is not equated with the black experience—it takes up but one verse amidst the rest. The song remains true to the original, preserving its recognizable contours and molding the Japanese sentiments to its shape.

In a similar fashion, Noge inserts herself into a narrative of African American history in her original composition "I Confess." The song is told from the point of view of a woman falling in love with Dr. Martin Luther King:

> I confess I fell for you
> I confess I fell for you
> I confess I fell for you
> I confess I fell for you
> The way you talk, the way you walk
> The way you think with your arms crossed
> The way you smile, the way you dress
> The way you feel when I touch your arm
> . . .
> You can talk your talk and walk your walk
> Dream your dreams to change this world
> Think your thoughts and write a book
> Teach your people to trust and love

"I Confess" features a sensual groove and is popular among the dancers in Noge's audiences. Its quirky text is framed with a romantic device and traces a well-worn path of blues sexuality. Noge avoids turning King into the stereotypical hypersexual black male, however, for the lyrics suggest the speaker's love is a response to King's mind and ideals in addition to his physical features. At the same time, the song remains somewhat risqué, especially when one considers the rumors of King's alleged infidelities. But perhaps this also serves to present him as a man rather than a demagogue on a pedestal, capable of indiscretions and of being loved as something other than a leader. Inserting her voice into the story, Noge attempts to relate to black civil rights history by meeting it on its own turf and bearing witness to it.

Noge's work also poses the possibility that history can be both ances-
tral and metaphysical, exemplified in her performance of the Ray Charles
classic "Georgia on My Mind," a yearning paean to the Southern United
States, geographically distant but in the narrator's mind and heart. Noge
covers this song in a tribute to both her hereditary and symbolic homelands. As with "Motherless Child," she inserts lyrics that place the original song in conversation with her Japanese identity, singing first about
Georgia and then Osaka, like Chicago, a "second city" to Tokyo. She even
names several districts to specifically locate this home, much in the *minyo*
tradition of marking place. Noge longs for Osaka from a nonnormative position within the U.S. Japanese diaspora. The first major wave of
Japanese migration to the United States occurred in the late nineteenth
and early twentieth centuries, called the "issei" or first generation. The
children and grandchildren of this group are subsequently referred to
as "nissei" and "sansei," second and third generations (Asai 1995, 429).
Noge—like several of her Japanese bandmates—is "shin-issei," a diverse
category of "new" immigrants who arrived after 1945 and are not part of
the dominant tripartite formulation (Wong 2006, 8). Unbound by the standard narratives of assimilation or rebellion marking the major migrations,
she diasporically longs from an idiosyncratic point of view.

Yet she also longs for Georgia. Like many black and other musicians
who sing this song, she has no ties to the South via her ancestry. But with
a musical lineage that stretches back to Southern roots cultures—through
her teachers and collaborators—she lays claim to the symbolic capital
of the song. Jointly pining for these two homelands creates a dialogue
in which multiple locations of home are linked and interrogated cross-
racially. By lending their support, the rest of the band acknowledges this
dual yearning and confirms that, at least for Noge, both locations can be
considered home: Osaka, her place of birth, and Georgia, a symbolic evocation of the Southern roots of black popular music she performs.

The presence of the rest of the band—an interracial band—is important
to reading Noge's performances as acts of solidarity. Instead of removing
"Motherless Child" or the figure of Dr. King from their cultural context,
she performs them in a venue important to the culture and alongside individuals from within the blues community. The other players are allowed
space to offer their own insights into the pieces. Ellis, for example, told
me that in his long solo in "Motherless Child," he inserts melodies from
other spirituals to highlight the roots of the song in that particular tradition. Those of a given race or culture also hold a certain amount of power
to accept or reject an outsider. John Watson's initial resistance to Noge's
overtures is one instance of this kind of agency. Thus, the band's performances become multivocal dialogues on the search for home and history
amidst global movement and varied experiences within these currents.

"Accompanying diaspora" stretches beyond the symbolic embrace
of cultural material. Clifford suggests that diaspora operates as "a signifier, not simply of transnationality and movement but of political
struggles to define the local, as distinctive community, in historical

contexts of displacement" (1994, 308). The sharing of cultural material and politics allows for the building of interracial coalitions based on witnessing mutual experience of displacement and supporting its remedies. Yet these are not simple tasks and there are many possible pitfalls. Differently raced bodies carry distinct histories, and labels cannot freely be traded in all directions. Further, while the African diaspora is understood as primarily symbolic, I believe there has been an injustice in distinguishing it from more tangible diasporic histories. We should question the motivations behind the longstanding narrative of the "missing link" palpably connecting African Americans to Africa.[15] And even if "intangible," African American heritage is part of a world economy with very tangible ramifications. So how does one effectively build interdiasporic affiliations that resist dominant tendencies for cultural fetishization?

In short, to be in a performed diaspora, one must do the material work to sustain the diaspora. By inserting her voice into the African American blues tradition, Noge creates a unique means to relate to it as an admirer and supporter, a sidewoman to African American history rather than a lead soloist. Noge's performatics, stage persona, and backstage operations function as a feminine practice of collectivity rather than Western and masculine models of single authorship and stardom. Noge leads her group and decides on its repertoire, but she generally gives the other members more foreground stage time than herself. She rarely solos on the piano, instead providing a base for the individual voices of her collaborators. She also turns moments that could be used for promoting just her projects to advocate more broadly for the cultural value of the blues in U.S. American life. I have heard her speak at several celebrations and fundraising events about the blues as the nation's unique, classical music and lament the lack of financial support given to the music and musicians. She testifies to a rich blues legacy and does her small part to perpetuate it by supporting other musicians, especially providing gigs for aging black musicians and offering guest spots in her HotHouse gigs as training ground for up-and-coming artists. At one point, in 2010, Noge and Dean learned that their pay for a weekly Thursday night gig would be reduced, to which Dean told me he would just play for free, so they could keep more of the other players employed. Ellis confirms this giving spirit, saying Noge is good to her band members and puts herself "right out there with you."

As another example, Aoki shares in this supportive role: although a key jazz innovator in Chicago, he claims that he is not seeking to be regarded as a central voice within African American forms. Instead, he desires to support black musicians and the larger tradition. The bass is the perfect instrument for his approach, providing a rhythmic and harmonic foundation for other players who will then solo and command primary focus from an audience. Noge and Aoki work to sustain the blues and jazz legacies rather than simply make a name for themselves.

These Afro Asian performances are not, however, immune from essentialism, ignorance, or stereotype, and Noge does not sit within the

African American diaspora unproblematically. For example, she couches her move to the United States in terms of the inauthenticity of her blues voice, based on her self-described "comical" mimicking of blues vocalists and English. Alongside the extensive jazz and blues industry in Japan, Atkins describes an accompanying discourse that expresses "a consistent ambivalence about the authenticity of its own jazz expressions (an ambivalence similar in nature to that with which several generations of white American and European jazz musicians have grappled)" (2001, 11–12). Noge describes her initial performances in Japan as "sort of blues music" or "copying," hence her decision to move to Chicago. Similarly, Terashima describes liking Chicago's music and architecture because it is individual and unique, in contrast to work by Japanese artists he feels often imitate Western creators. Atkins confirms this sentiment: "Throughout its history Japan's jazz community has had to locate itself in an aesthetic hierarchy that explicitly reflects and reinforces asymmetries of power and cultural prestige in the Japan-U.S. relationship by placing American jazz artists at the apex as 'innovators' and non-Americans at the bottom as 'imitators'" (Atkins 2001, 11). In the case of Noge and her associates, this innovation is specifically linked to blackness.

Once in Chicago, Noge found her move did not bring her closer to becoming what she had considered to be an authentic blues performer:

> I realized that there are a lot of people who can sing better than I do. And what I have to do over the years. . . . I would never be black woman even how hard I try, how hard I mimic their accent or their lifestyle. I can't be black. I wasn't raised as a black person, so musically I can learn from them, and as a human being I can learn from them, but I have to crush my idea of totally becoming a black woman. It's out. And then, why do I have to sing the blues, and why do I have to listen to the blues, and why do I, what do I learn from the blues? And those questions arise. So I decided that, you know, I have to create my own voice. And it's me who was attracted by the blues music. Well I'll admit that. It's me that came to Chicago because of the attraction of the blues music. I'll admit that. And it's me who fought with men and sometimes physically, and all those things. I admit myself . . . and find my voice. Somewhere. So that was the start of the finding my own voice trip.

Noge's realization of her place within the racial image of the blues in a sense freed her to develop her own style. But getting to this point took her through moments in which she desired and even made efforts to try to be black—or what she perceived as black—as if doing so would unlock the secret to blues authenticity. She then turned her focus to establishing dialogues with black artists as a means to learn from them but, especially in her earlier days, this was also based on cultural knowledge assumed to come with blackness. It is interesting, then, that one of her most influential teachers ended up being white—pianist Erwin Helfer.

Figure 2.2. Yoko Noge performs with Japanesque at the Chicago Cultural Center. Photograph by Tomoko Sawairi Nagle. Courtesy of Yoko Noge.

Noge slowly morphed from a position of racial expectation to one in which she sought to find her own voice and learn to interpret African American music through it. But she frames this realization as a series of questions that reveal how she grappled with understanding why a person who did not grow up with a black experience could have such a strong connection to music supposedly born from it. Even though she related this story years later, it is clear that she has hardly come to an "end"; her decisions launched an open-ended journey that may never reach an easy conclusion. Noge retains her ambivalence, framing her unique voice within blues tradition as something else because of her racial and national difference. This is particularly indicative of her Japaneseness. Nonblack players from the United States might claim a certain understanding or proprietary right to blues or jazz because they are part of the nation's cultural milieu. But nonblack and non-U.S.-American artists like Noge do not have this domestic relationship to argue for inclusion. Asian outsider narratives, while replicating stereotypes of Asian rigidity, show that nationality plays a significant role alongside race in notions of authenticity in blues and jazz, regardless of the influence of this music in Asian countries.

Critics also fall into their own authenticating narratives when trying to locate Noge within the blues form. Several features and reviews question her vocal skills or refer to her singing as "broken English" (Kopp 2000, Hunger 2005). I, however, hear her singing as quite consistent, regardless of language. In a performance with the Miyumi Project, Noge sang a song that began in Japanese and, at a climactic moment, started to repeat a phrase that I only slowly came to realize was in English. This seamless flow was aided by the fact that, in either language, her style is quite consistent: guttural, angular, and with a tendency to bend and protract words. Still, one anonymous reviewer asserts, "She's not much of a blues singer," while Ed Kopp claims, "Noge sings in an affected blues style" and has a "limited voice" ("Yoko Noge" 2006, Kopp 2000). These statements specifically question her performance as a blues singer, possibly revealing assumptions about what an authentic female blues persona must be: the voluptuous sapphire, a little bit raw, and a whole lot sassy.

A short, thin Japanese woman, Noge will never physically match the blues shouter image visually, but she does performatively invoke the feminist counterhistory of the form through her vocals and instrumental arrangements. She, in fact, embodies multiple streams of women's participation in blues history. The first commercially successful style of blues was the "classic blues" of the 1920s, and featured female vocalists such as Ma Rainey, Bessie Smith, and Mamie Smith. Historically, the classic blues tradition provided a space that allowed for the public performance of alternative black, female, and sometimes queer sexualities, forging a feminist counterpublic through coded lyrics and artists' publicly known "private" lifestyles (Davis 1998). This form, based on vaudeville and Tin Pan Alley aesthetics, stood in contrast to the later "downhome blues" style of a male singer with guitar, which mainly offered heteronormative or misogynistic representations of women. Yet there were also women who wielded instruments and performed in the downhome tradition—such as Memphis Minnie—as well as musicians of multiple genders who did not fit the mold of either form. Noge performs at the recent edge of both of these feminist histories, presenting the blues as a living space of reinterpretation and change while bringing to light the diversity of participants in the past.

As Noge channels these multiple blues through an Asian body, she signifies on this diversity by placing herself within it, forging a space for a more aggressive portrayal of Asian femininity than readily available in the public sphere. This is best evidenced in her cover of blues classic "I Want a Little Girl" from *Yoko Meets John*. The song was written by Bill Moll and Murray Mencher in 1930 and has been performed by artists such as Ray Charles, Nat King Cole, Eric Clapton, and Louis Armstrong. The original lyrics are sung, assumedly, by a male narrator who discusses his desire for a "little girl" to call his own: one who doesn't have to "fry" her hair, wear fancy pantyhose, or look like a *Playboy* pin-up as long as she falls in love with him and can cook. While allowing for a slightly-less-than-normative femininity, the female subject remains a silent object of male desire, a passive entity to be longed for and only materialized through her interactions with the narrator. And she is "little," implying subservience either due to age, size, or both.

Noge's version is a feminist spin on the original. Her version opens with John Watson playing a muted trombone solo and then singing the original lyrics with ad-libbed additions. Saxophonist Sonny Seals then performs a solo, riffing off of the melody Watson introduced. Over seven minutes into the piece, Noge remains silent except for comping on the piano. But after the sax solo, she begins to sing an altered version of the lyrics: "I want a little boy to love a lot / I'll give anything I've got / for a little boy to fall in love with me, with me / I want a little boy, he may not look / like the kind in my *Playgirl* book / but if he can cook, mmmm, he will suit me to a T." She goes on to say that her "little boy" doesn't have to have a lot of money or hair but, again, should be able to "cook," turning the expectation of what it means to be taken care of on its head. The song ends with a back-and-forth between Noge and Watson in which he again asks for a "little girl" who can cook and she replies in a very sultry manner, "I can cook." Noge then begins to play an aggressive piano lick, suggesting she can do so in the bedroom and in the masculine realm of instrumental performance.

Even though maintaining the frame of romance, Noge's verse diverges from the common blues presentation of female sexuality. First, it is active—she becomes the desiring party, not merely the subject of male desire as in patriarchal blues texts or Orientalist portrayals of Asian femininity. This is even more pronounced in that Noge inserted her verse into a song performed widely in its original form, in effect opening a new space within the blues tradition unexplored by the male interpreters of the song. Second, in retaining the pejorative "little boy" in her verse, Noge rejects the power dynamics discursively indicated in the pairing of girl/man and baby/Daddy, typical lyrical couples. Finally, the "little boy" she desires is given the same liberties in appearance but still must cook with her musically and sexually, placing both on an even keel. While Noge remains unusually silent as the piece unfolds, she does so to let the heteronormative male fantasy play out, so she can insert herself into it and twist it to her liking.

Noge draws on the power of the classic shouters' in-your-face sexual strength and a lineage of female instrumentalists, disavowing notions of passive Asian and black femininity. She shows that she does not have to choose between being a "blues woman" and a Japanese woman, pushing on the limited representations of both black and Asian women in dominant media. And by interpreting the song in her own voice, she honors the tradition by not limiting what a blues voice "should" be to a profile that even black singers might not be able to match.

Of course, Noge's use of "boy" is a moment of feminine strength and possible racial dominance. And flipping the script on sexual expectations asks Watson to jump into a stereotypical lusty black male role. When one piece of the race and gender puzzle is moved, they all shift. But this movement is productive in that tropes and roles are shaken from long frozen positions—where and how they settle are part of the Afro Asian process.

Despite the challenges of locating home—musically, culturally, nationally— Noge and her collaborators have committed a great deal to continuing to forge one together. In their reinterpretations of classic texts, and voicings of Noge's originals, we see the ways in which they musically construct a joint identity with the performative power to shape new possibilities for Japanese and African American culture. Listening closely to their "Motherless Child," for example, we hear how they move the piece from a tone of sorrow and despair to one of potential hope, in the end all supporting Noge singing "sometimes I feel." No longer a speaker without a home, Noge repeats this phrase, reflecting an awakening, a sense of release, and the ability to feel connected again to one or multiple homes.

Most important to this reinterpreted spiritual—and the band's other repertoire—is its continued unfolding and changing as guests join the ensemble or band members have new experiences. In a show the Jazz Me Blues played at Cuatro, an upscale Latin American and Caribbean restaurant, Noge played the piano introduction to "Motherless Child," but then began to sing words and a melody I had never heard before. After this excursion, she eventually brought the piece back around to its usual format. Later that evening, I asked her about the additional material and she said it was a Japanese fisherman's song. She had recently returned from a trip to Alaska and had a number of meaningful interactions with Native Alaskans. She said she could not fully explain why she ended up singing the fisherman song, but she had been thinking about the importance of fish to those communities and it just came out. I do not raise this last interpolation to glorify polyglot performance as inherently valuable by virtue of its multivalence. Rather, I suggest Afro Asian performance is at its best when its practitioners treat it as a living negotiation rendered through diverse personal experiences and approach it with the desire to experiment and remain open to new voices.

Silk Road Blues

Despite the longstanding Afro Asian relationships present in Noge's ensembles, their music has continuously been presented as a new fad within the Chicago culture industry. Noge and her collaborators are deeply imbedded in this economy, as city arts programming and grants form a significant portion of the opportunities for working musicians. Cities also use the arts as a means to increase tourism and revenue. Sharon Zukin contends, "With the disappearance of local manufacturing industries and periodic crises in government and finance, culture is more and more the business of cities—the basis of their tourist attractions and their unique, competitive edge" (1995, 1–2). Often, performance sites sponsored by city arts programmers promote representations that simplify or reinterpret artists' texts or encourage artists to do so themselves. Because Noge's music and ensembles are places where multiple racial and cultural discourses come together, examining how her work functions in the civic arts scene of Chicago can indicate broader ways in which blackness and Asianness figure into projects of civic representation. In particular, Noge's reception in city arts spaces reveals how cultural officials have tried to mold an image of the city that uses "Asia" as a symbol of progress and globality, while discarding older representations based on the blues and blackness. This new municipal branding reflects dynamics of racial triangulation I discussed in Chapter 1, but with local differences and even contradictions in order to suit the specific needs of early-twenty-first-century Chicago.

Starting in June 2006, the Chicago Office of Tourism, Department of Cultural Affairs, Chicago Symphony Orchestra, Art Institute of Chicago, and Yo-Yo Ma's Silk Road Project launched a venture called Silk Road Chicago. This series of performances and exhibits was an umbrella under which much of the city's cultural programming was herded as municipal officials made use of an Orientalist vision of the old trade route as a symbol of the contemporary global nexus and vitality of the city. The Silk Road as symbolic economy was not employed to investigate the roots of contemporary practice, but rather to explicitly proclaim Chicago as a forward-looking, cosmopolitan city. Most of the performers on the mammoth event calendar, however, were the same local artists who regularly performed in Chicago, with a few big stars like members of Ma's Silk Road Ensemble or *sitar* master Ravi Shankar thrown in as highlights. Not much new programming was actually produced, and while the project showcased a diverse array of performers and traditions, most of it was not featured within the same performance. Rather, individual cultural or ethnic performances were connected to the others only by residing on the same calendar. Japanesque performed several concerts in conjunction with this project, and these gigs were some of the few that explicitly spotlighted interracial and intercultural musical interactions. In all, Silk Road Chicago was not really a new initiative bringing the wonders of the world to Chicago, but a reframing of what was already there. In fact, some of the included material had nothing to do with the Silk Road. The Silk Road Cabaret series, for example, spotlighted primarily white lounge acts, although Japanesque was also presented on this bill.[16]

Despite the attempt to identify Chicago as an intense amalgam of cultural fusion, the global rhetoric replicated triangulated racial dynamics that simplified and stereotyped traditions. Much publicity evoked the Silk Road as ancient and foreign. Asian and Middle Eastern arts were represented as a homogenized stronghold of old-world tradition, not living practices performed by people in Asia, the Middle East, and the rest of the world. This neglect of lived experience was also reflected in the representation of the economic route as a set of cultural practices and artifacts rather than humans. Many of the promotional images of the campaign were close-up shots of instruments, maps, ceramics, and tapestries. The Silk Road Chicago website even contained a page with a glossary of instrument names and descriptions, each one labeled with a specific country of origin. The attachment of these instruments to fixed locations negates the new Silk Road Chicago discourse of travel and intercultural interaction as well as the cultural mixing and evolution that formed the original Silk Road and is present in Ma's project. The passive nature of the objects also reveals a feminizing aspect to this "historical" Orientalism. The East and Middle East are depicted as fragile, empty vessels existing solely to be filled by a consuming audience's desires.

When it came to people, the Silk Road and Asia were employed as symbols of newness, futurity, and "the world." Chicago inarguably functions as a global city that is greatly marked by the circulation of people, goods, and media from outside of the United States, while also having significant influence on global political-economic affairs (Abu-Lughod 1999). At the turn of the twenty-first century, images of the international diversity of the city were increasingly employed as symbols for civic promotion—versus historic depiction as a black–white city—and Asians were used as evidence of the city's interpenetration with the globe. This discourse is consistent with the racially triangulating equation of all things Asian with "out there." However, Asia-as-global has also become a symbol for demographic changes within the nation and a possible threat to national cultural homogeneity, as exemplified in films such as *Blade Runner* (Lowe 1996, 84–85). This inevitable "new world" to come is often personified as a masculine subject: whether a corporate drone or robotic techno-citizen, this version of Asianness pierces the membrane of the U.S. national fabric and penetrates institutions with model minority prowess.

The focus on Asian arts in Silk Road Chicago provided a momentary opportunity for Asian/American artists in the city. Because of the figuration of Asian people and cultures as forever foreign, Asian/American musicians have long faced the cultural equivalent of Asian exclusion laws. In Chicago specifically, Asian/American jazz and creative musicians have been virtually ignored in broader civic discourses. Aoki tells me there is only one critic who actively follows his and Noge's work: Howard Reich, who writes for the *Chicago Tribune*. And it is rare for Asian/American musicians to be featured in major, city-sponsored jazz/blues events like the Chicago Jazz Festival.[17] Aoki was fortunate to book a high-profile performance of his Miyumi Project at the festival in Millennium Park in the summer of 2006, but says this only happened because he had a friend on the planning committee who advocated for him. In Silk Road Chicago programs, Asian/American artists had greater temporary access to arts spaces, but in many cases were selected for—or required to perform—the role of "exotic" in order to gain entry. For instance, my former *erhu* teacher, Betti Xiang—a prominent musician in Chicago and China—received her Chicago Symphony Orchestra debut via a Silk Road–related concert. Playing "The Butterfly Lovers Concerto" by He Zhanhao and Chen Gang, Xiang graced a stage that is a bedrock of elite music in the city, but only as a temporary visitor with (sono-)racial difference clearly marked. (In previous appearances with prominent orchestras, she similarly played "Butterfly Lovers" or Tan Dun's *erhu* concerto based on the score from the film *Crouching Tiger, Hidden Dragon*.)

While the global Silk Road rhetoric temporarily embraced Asianness, it left out blackness despite the presence of black performers on the roster (not to mention blacks who were part of the original Silk Road). This is particularly interesting given that for decades, the Chicago Board of Tourism marketed the city as the "Home of the Blues," the genre representing the city's gritty industrial past and role as a Great Migration destination (Grazian 2003, 27). But as Chicago, like many cities, de-industrialized and tipped toward the financial services sector, the black working-class image fails to symbolize an upscale, sophisticated, vacation destination. The blues, one might say, are so twentieth century. Further, as Zukin states, "Culture is also a powerful means of controlling cities ... it symbolizes 'who belongs' in specific places" (1995, 1). The majority of the Silk Road Chicago events took place at venues within the Loop (the city center) or on the North Side of the city, stopping short of the more heavily black South and West Sides of town. The Silk Road Chicago project aestheticized diversity and ignored "the material inequalities of city life," maintaining extant racial segregation in the city by inviting locals and tourists into nonblack locations and discouraging black audiences (Zukin 1995, 2).

These two contrasting images of Chicago's musical identity—global, Asian Silk Road and local, black blues—came face-to-face in a series of Japanesque performances in May and June 2006. The concerts unfolded over several weeks in venues such as the Chicago Sister Cities celebration in downtown Daley Plaza, the Old Town School of Folk Music, and the Jazz Me Blues Band's regular Monday evening HotHouse gig. The performances were sponsored by Silk Road Chicago and culminated in an appearance at the Chicago Blues Festival. The primary venues for these events operate with typical multicultural dynamics that celebrate cultural difference, but offer little in the way of interracial and intercultural engagement. The Sister Cities celebration, for example, showcased booths and performances from countries including South Africa, Australia, and Japan. But the represented food, crafts, and music were presented in separate tents or never shared the stage with one another.[18] Another venue, the Old Town School of Folk music, is an institution that offers classes and concerts representing many world roots traditions that rarely cross paths as each class is sealed into its own classroom and time slot. A simple evocation of this dynamic was that the preshow and intermission music played for the Japanesque performance at Old Town was Appalachian folk music. While this recording was probably just a favorite of the sound engineer's, it illuminates the type of cultural tourism that venues like these can promote. Dropping into the performances, audiences are confronted with a hodgepodge of cultural material with little context, differentiation, or grounding in material histories. Cultural difference is celebrated—while racial difference is ignored—and audiences have scant room to query their makeup or intersections.

The expression of diversity within these venues ultimately made for limited views of the dialogue between traditions and people in Japanesque. In performances, both promoters and the musicians framed their work in ways that reflected simplified and reified renderings of African American and Japanese music. First, the latter elements were represented as foreign practices reinvigorating the blues with "an international tinge," as Blues Festival organizer Barry Dolins would say in his introductions for the group. The *minyo* tradition was rhetorically linked to the static, spatially distant, and titillating Silk Road. Further, at the Daley Plaza performance, Dolins introduced Noge as "from Osaka" even though she had lived in Chicago for more than twenty years. Several of the performances were billed as "Jazz, Blues, and Beyond," suggesting the Japanese elements were from somewhere "out there," rather than something that resided within Chicago. By contrast, the ensemble's black guitarist, John Primer, was often introduced to authenticate his blues roots. He was repeatedly billed as Muddy Waters's "last great guitar player" and said to play original Delta blues from Mississippi. Dolins also stressed that Primer lived on the South Side of Chicago, suggesting an inherent authenticity based solely on the heavy black presence in that portion of the city. The images of both musical traditions reified them into static roots as opposed to living, changing practices, and the same spatial separation between cultures in Daley Plaza or Old Town was made manifest between the members of Japanesque.

Dolins told audiences that they would go "from the far East to the far South Side" during Japanesque performances, suggesting a great geographic and cultural distance between the musical traditions and performers. And the structure of shows served to illustrate the *minyo* and blues as entirely separate genres by showcasing them distinctly before they were joined. In the Old Town performance, for example, Primer first played a solo set and was then joined by the other players for several fusion pieces. After the intermission, Aoki, Hide Yoshihashi, and Amy Homma performed a *taiko* trio and were then joined by Primer and Noge to play versions of several blues standards. Similarly, at the Daley Plaza performance, Primer began playing solo, added Dan Beaver—a white blues harmonica player—for a few songs, and was then joined by Noge and the rest. Each tradition was thus spotlighted in its supposed "original" form before it was merged with the other. This framing did serve a pedagogical function for listeners less knowledgeable about either tradition. But by making these dynamics more intelligible, it also promoted a simplified "East meets (black) West" dynamic.

The participants also referred to their musical merging as new and unusual. A number of times Noge introduced the *minyo*-blues by stating it was a crazy new thing they were trying and "we'll see how it works out!" Statements made by presenters reflected a similar skepticism or amazement at how the two traditions might join. Also, on several occasions, Dolins introduced the concert by saying "blues is Chicago's global muse." He explained that Chicago had inspired many worldwide to come and play with its great blues musicians, while also claiming that a "global muse" is what makes Chicago music so special. The muddled reasoning of this sentiment suggests it was just a colorful catchphrase to denote intercultural interaction.

John Hutnyk argues that "fusion"—or one of its code names such as "hybridity" or "East meets West"—is a buzzword in the multicultural culture industry (2000). As much a marketing category as an aesthetic trend, it is used to describe everything from food and fashion to leisure activities and music. Hutnyk claims further that the increasing buzz around the "global" has spawned popular interest in the supposed results of this phenomenon—the mix of West and non-West, North and South, First and Third World, modern and primitive. The popular discourse celebrating fusion in music, for example, maintains these very dichotomies, often praising minority musicians for melding "the best of both worlds," but requiring a partial or full assimilation to supposedly mainstream Western pop values, a lack of explicit politics, and token sonic exoticism. "Fusion" thus falls into a long history of Westerners selling and consuming difference, a "multicultural trick that sells exotica as race relations and visibility as redress" (Hutnyk 2000, 3). What is more, in minority–minority blends, the whole engagement is often clouded over with racial connotations in which the entire exchange is figured as unusual and outlandish. This discourse lacks historicized grounding, ultimately making fusion itself the object of focus and what is mixing irrelevant. Appropriately, on the Chicago Blues Fest program, the culminating performance of the Japanesque ensemble was not even billed by the artists' names—like other acts—but merely as "Blues: Chicago's World Music."

But looking at the Japanesque performances through an Afro Asian lens reveals ruptures to the Silk Road Chicago logic. First, Japanese instruments and music were used in the performances in ways that countered notions of reified tradition. For example, when used in festivals and community events, *taiko* are usually played alone, as the primary instrument, and loudly. In Japanesque's pieces, *taiko* players Yoshihashi and Homma provide accompaniment to the ensemble, generally accentuating the

Figure 2.3. Japanesque at Andy's Jazz Club, Chicago. Courtesy of Yoko Noge.

backbeat.[19] Primer and several subsequent Japanesque blues guests have commented to me on the strong blues feeling the two have in their *taiko* playing, Primer going further to suggest that the *taiko* actually carry the bassline in a lot of Japanesque pieces. Aoki's *shamisen* playing also differs from traditional iterations. When playing the instrument on pieces he usually performs on bass with the Jazz Me Blues Band, he will sometimes play the existing basslines and then use these as the basis for melodic improvisation.

The blues and jazz elements are also not presented traditionally in the ensemble. While Primer was billed as an authentic voice of the Delta blues, he tells me he does not know why people call it that: "All I know is, it's the blues"—his style. When improvising with Japanesque, Primer does not hold onto static technique or licks, but uses the *minyo* material as a basis to create new solos that reflect what he is hearing in the larger musical context. In the Blues Festival performance, the ensemble included Ra on drum set alongside Yoshihashi and Homma, as opposed to the drum kit being the sole percussive voice as in typical jazz or blues groups. Ra claims this shift was not difficult, however, due to his experience playing with *taiko* in Aoki's Miyumi Project and with Sun Ra, who often included multiple percussionists in his ensembles.

Japanesque performances also revealed similarities between the supposedly vastly different blues and *minyo*. A promotional postcard for one concert proclaims:

> Both musical forms are deeply rooted in people's souls and grew from their everyday life experience. Some songs are about hard labor, some are about crying for lost love, some are about paying the rent. You will be surprised to hear music from these two very different cultures meld together to create a new cross-border root music.

In the same vein, Noge routinely gave the audience English translations of some of the songs she sings in Japanese. For example, she translates lyrics from "Sanosa" as "Well, you're gonna leave me honey / Well, go right ahead, see if I care / If you're gonna leave me / I'll put some money in an envelope / And shove it in your face." After explaining this at one show, Noge asked the audience, "Doesn't it sound familiar?," suggesting the thematic and formal similarities to blues songs including the signature punch line at the end. The female strength revealed in these lyrics highlights the alternative ways in which the feminine functions in Noge's performances versus the feminizing Orientalism in some of the other Silk Road Chicago events. Noge's expressions are also distinct from the assumed male citizen of the global-futurist "Asia." As in "I Want a Little Girl," Noge presents a subject that is assertive and in control, matched in her top-name billing within the Silk Road Chicago events.

Beyond lyrics, Noge draws connections between the vocal styles of the two traditions, suggesting that in both, precision or delicacy is not appropriate. Rather, "soul" is more important than pitch accuracy or flawless execution. Even more, she claims the two traditions are similar because "the main voice is the vocal. And the accompaniment is very simple. And chord structure is very simple. Because it's not supposed to be a, you know, performance piece on the big Carnegie Hall. It's the people's music in the field, in the temples or shrines or churches or whatever." Similarly, Primer calls *minyo* "Japanese blues" and says it uses scales and forms similar to the blues.[20] He thinks the Japanese instruments fit perfectly into a blues setting even though they have different timbres than standard blues instruments. He also suggests the *taiko* sound much like his understanding of early blues drumming, which he says contained only the low-end kick drum and toms. The possibility of this aesthetic common ground was realized in the Old Town School performance when, during a solo in the *minyo* "Shide Mai," Primer morphed the song into "Sweet Home Chicago." The others picked up this interpolation, seamlessly moving into the Chicago blues standard.

Japanesque performances also presented a different notion of fusion than that of other Silk Road Chicago fare, revealing instances in which the traditions did not merely sit side-by-side. In one moment near the end of the Old Town show, Primer and Aoki launched into an improvised exchange between guitar and *shamisen*. For several minutes, they traded fours back and forth, trying to one-up each other in a playful version of a jazz cutting session. The audience grew very attentive during this exchange, recognizing the uniqueness of this dialogue. At one point, Primer played a curly line, elaborating on a descending scale that, to the delight of the audience, Aoki replicated on the *shamisen*. This conversation between the two instruments and musicians placed them on equal footing, negating the notion that one was merely providing color to the other tradition. Noge and ensemble signified on the multicultural exploration of global "fusion" culture and turned it into interracial and intercultural interaction.

Dolins suggested that the Japanesque performances depicted "what the Silk Road brought to the world, a new, modern culture," and, certainly, interracial and intercultural musical performance is not new to Chicago. In fact, the city possesses a long history of improvisatory music that has encompassed black, white, Asian, Middle Eastern, Latino, and many other musicians. And this local scene is merely one node of a long genealogy of experimentation across cultural lines that runs through African American jazz, blues, and hip hop. Noge's groups are emblematic of this history, with players representing the 1950s "golden era" of Chicago blues performance, the West Coast Asian American jazz scene, the Association for the Advancement of Creative Musicians, and younger artists working between genres and scenes. The members of the Jazz Me Blues Band have engaged in these exchanges for decades: Aoki, for example, has been doing Japanese and creative music fusion work for twenty years. When I asked what the reasons were behind the popular focus on his work during the Silk Road Chicago era, he replied simply, "Asian is in right now."

Diversity with a Difference

There is no such thing as "Asian blues" or "Asian/American jazz"—they are both Afro Asian. Asian/American musical artists are influenced by the black–white (sono-)racial binary even as they are placed outside of this continuum. Yoko Noge first felt this influence when she discovered blues in Japan and later as she forged relationships with black blues artists in Chicago. And the black, Asian, and white artists she has worked with over the past three decades have been similarly influenced in their own cultural productions, resulting in continually changing expressions of Asian/American and African American musical identities. The process of finding, holding, and losing the self is an ongoing negotiation. Self (and Other) may solidify in moments of performance, but who we are shifts through time and space. And while performing blackness or Asianness does not make one into either, someone of any background has the potential to shape their configuration. Through a process of growing racial understanding, Noge does not remain Japanese/Asian: she becomes Asian American and Afro Asian. And while she does not become racially black, she does in some sense become culturally African American through her performative contributions to the culture.

The Jazz Me Blues Band and Japanesque reflect features at the heart of Afro Asian musical history: the desire to look, play, and sing across sono-racial boundaries in order to form bonds, create new sounds, and contest limiting categories. In particular, Noge and crew have developed aesthetic and cultural strategies that reveal the ways in which: (1) diasporas vary and intersect, often in more than one location; (2) cultural knowledge is not a natural consequence of nationality or race; and (3) the symbolic longing for home can be a shared space between diasporic people. They do not let go of notions of black and Japanese authenticity, but they do offer spaces to inhabit that are not simply "inside" or "outside" of either one as all members jointly produce both Japanese and African American music regardless of heritage. Their work asks us to rethink what authenticity is and how it might not be rooted in a fixed relationship between body and sound. Afro Asian performance suggests authenticity should not be based solely on *who* you are, but rather *what* you do. As saxophonist Jimmy Ellis says, "You know, I don't want to achieve *this*, 'cause that's the end. I'd like to keep on being something tomorrow. Better than say, 'okay I made it.' Now, made what? You know, you don't ever want to make it. Because that's the end. You want to keep on *making* it. You know what I mean?"

As multiply raced artists produce culture that is sono-racially "theirs" and "not theirs," they raise questions about how cultural ownership should be determined. Afro Asian and other interracial settings provide space for artists to inform, sanction, or police their co-creators' cross-racial performances. But whether one is an authority based on who they are, knowledge they have, or work they have done is very much in dispute. Amidst inevitable questions of racial and cultural legitimacy, Noge and collaborators propose new criteria for determining cultural owner-ship based in experience, participation, and advocacy. Examining these dynamics between two nonwhite racial positions complicates how we understand the politics of cross-racial exchange, especially since "up/down" and "out/in" are often the only options in relation to whiteness. Especially as black and Asian artists and musical practices do not sit in typical dominant–subdominant relation to one another, these settings can complicate how power differentials are managed. Noge's work indicates that racial appropriation and solidarity, while often conceived of as politi-cal opposites, often actually reside together in interracial entanglements. Good intentions and desires for true communication can and usually do occur alongside racial assumptions and misperceptions.

The lines blurred by Noge's collective are sharpened in their engage-ments with people and spaces in the multicultural Chicago culture indus-try. Presenting the coming together of black and Japanese as a novelty, presenters, critics, and artists continue to propose East meets West narra-tives.[21] Dynamic Afro Asian negotiations are frozen in presentations that frame these processes as a perpetual meeting. But Noge's life and work prove the two musical cultures she performs met long ago as opposed to in the moment of performance. The circulation of black music to Japan, Japanese and other Asian/American artists' influences on the creative music scene, and flexibility of improvisatory black music to incorporate diverse material all allow for something more complex and ongoing. The industry struggles to effectively portray evolving interracial identities, and artists like Noge are in a sense made more Japanese by being continually pushed out of what is considered U.S. American.

It is important to remember, though, that the inevitability of Afro Asian interaction is not a given, especially for black artists. The imbalance of the triangulated system means that blacks have a larger chasm to traverse in order to connect with Asian/American artists and experiences. But black artists have clearly been served in this respect by the exploratory projects of Asian/Americans. What began as Noge's personal interest in the blues has blossomed into a multi-ensemble project redefining the intersection of Japan and the blues and has brought musicians, industries, communities, and audiences into shared spaces with the potential for interracial and intercultural dialogue. Yet proximity does not ensure conversation. In the next chapter, I will examine the potential for these dialogues to unfold in physical space and the circumstances that foster this possibility.

3

Articulating Interracial Space
Funkadesi's "One Family"

$\mathcal{S}$cholars herald New York, Los Angeles, and Chicago as global cities that simultaneously portend a more diverse U.S. future and a reduction of the nation as an economic entity and primary identity marker.[1] These cities have been held as exemplars of "the browning of America," a popular phrase used to signal demographic changes in the United States due to the influx of people from South and Central America, the Caribbean, South Asia, and Southeast Asia since the 1965 Immigration and Nationality Act.[2] In combination with an economy that thrives on the labor of undocumented workers from Mexico and Central America, and the compounding growth of existing racial and ethnic "minority" communities, a multifarious brown population has increased markedly within the nation's bounds and forms ever-expanding networks that stretch beyond it.

Yet unlike what the phrase implies, this browning has not been steady or even in its unfolding. Chicago, for example, is a city notorious for its racial and cultural diversity as well as segregation. Fondly called the "city of neighborhoods" for its many ethnic enclaves, Chicago has long been a haven for new immigrants and their families (Peterson 2002, 258–259). The 2010 U.S. Census breaks down the city's racial population as, roughly, 32.9 percent black, 31.7 percent non-Hispanic white, 28.9 percent Hispanic of any race, 5.5 percent Asian, and 0.5 percent American Indian or Alaska native (United States Census Bureau [accessed] 2012).[3] But despite the presence of a variety of races and ethnicities within the city and surrounding areas, there may be little interaction between them. Blacks reside heavily on the South and West Sides of the city, in upwards of 90 percent. In contrast, many communities on the North and Southwest Sides have 10 percent or fewer black residents. Some Latinos live in segregated pockets—although less dramatically—and others in neighborhoods with blacks, whites, or both (Bogira 2011).

Racial and ethnic groups coincide in Chicago, but often only at the macro level. While the city harbors the nation's third largest black and South Asian populations, for instance, South Asians live primarily in the north and west suburbs or far North Side, essentially on the other side of the city from the heaviest concentration of blacks.[4] There are economic differences as well: higher percentages of lower-income residents live on the South and West Sides of the city, while the north and greater suburbs have populations with higher incomes (Rankin 2009). Chicago's desi population only grew to a notable size after the 1965 Act, rapidly increasing from 713 in 1970 to 30,000 in 1981, the majority of whom were from middle- and upper-middle Indian classes and well educated (Diethrich 1999/ 2000). African Americans are a more diverse population in these respects and an older presence in the city, the black parts of town having grown exponentially in the first half of the twentieth century (Wilkerson 2010).

Afro Asian band Funkadesi emerged against this backdrop. The group was founded by Rahul Sharma in 1996, the culmination of personal experimentation with mixing North Indian classical music with African American and Caribbean popular forms. He began his musical life playing bass in funk, reggae, and blues bands, and later studied *tabla* and *sitar* in India. As an undergraduate at the University of Michigan, he decided to do a little "showing off with some slap bass mixed in with Indian elements" at a student Diwali event and delighted the audience by joining styles he had been learning separately.[5] The following year, 1993, Sharma moved to Chicago to work toward a doctorate in clinical psychology with a specialization in intercultural psychology. While in school, he found it challenging to find the right musicians to continue his explorations. But in 1996, shortly after applying for internships around the country, he says, "The band fell in my lap." Luckily, he was offered an internship in Chicago and started to build the band in earnest. To motivate his collaborators—perhaps more than just bringing them together to jam—he booked a gig at the Heartland Café before having fully assembled a group; in fact, the two lead singers did not even meet until the moment of their first performance.[6]

My initial assumptions led me to suppose that Chicago is a city that helped foster this sono-racial collaboration. I saw Funkadesi's membership and sound as a microcosm of the city's diversity and what I assumed (hoped?) was evidence of a local black–brown alliance that countered problematic representations of this relationship in mainstream popular culture. Sharma suggested instead that Chicago *needs* the band in order to spur interaction that counters its segregated demographics. Afro Asian spaces do not simply appear; people desiring their materiality bring them about. In the right circumstances, this desire can tangibly congeal, creating an environment unlike that which exists in the urban expanse beyond the performance venue. At the same time, as prototype utopias, Afro Asian performances become sites in which the complications and tensions of interracial life flare up and participants actively engage in the difficult processes of "browning" at the micro level.

In the last chapter, I explored the ways in which the symbolic overlapping of Japanese and African American musics and histories manifests in the work of Yoko Noge, forming sono-racial collaborations expressing an interdiasproc longing for home. Scholars have argued for the theorization of diaspora beyond the singular.[7] But while acknowledging "overlapping diasporas," there has been less detailed attention paid to how this unfolds beyond simply laying one on top of one another, as well as the specific racial implications when populations intersect in the United States.[8]

In this chapter, I investigate in more concrete detail aesthetic and social processes through which people of varied racial and musical communities rub against one another and begin to mesh their lives together in sonic and physical space. In particular, I examine how these sono-racial collaborations offer alternatives to multicultural spaces in which diversity exists in broad strokes, but people and practices are often segmented from one another. I argue that Funkadesi engenders spaces that promote the formation of interracial communities in segregated Chicago through their music, audiences, and a performative discourse espousing unity-through-diversity. For the brief moment of a concert, audiences have the opportunity to experience a form of interracial and intercultural interaction that is unsupported in the city at large. These communities are imagined for, as Benedict Anderson theorizes, they are intentionally constructed out of people who would not otherwise feel a kinship (1983). The difference between Funkadesi and Anderson's nation-state, however, is that a small-scale collective offers the possibility for face-to-face contact among all members. The Afro Asian spaces produced are akin to what Josh Kun calls "audiotopias"; that is, "sonic spaces of effective utopian longings where several sites normally deemed incompatible are brought together, not only in the space of a particular piece of music itself, but in the production of social space and the mapping of geographical space that music makes possible as well" (2005, 23). I do not contend that the desire for Afro Asian audiotopias is a given, although Funkadesi's success certainly indicates there are many people hungry for it.

To illustrate my claims, I demonstrate how Funkadesi draws from multiple racialized traditions and weaves them together in ways that extend beyond simple juxtaposition. Their music has been an important laboratory for experimenting with ways to incorporate difference into a whole that does not require uniformity. I go on to consider the ways in which Funkadesi's performances generate provisional physical spaces that reflect a blend of people similar to their musical output. I show how sono-racial triangulation is revealed by where venues are located in the city and how human interactions unfold within them. I then indicate how Afro Asian sites contrast these trends, while raising questions about how we define audiences in relation to sono-racial categories and identifying possible fissures between musical and sociopolitical coalitions. Finally, I suggest some of the complications that the culture industry poses to the realization of new Afro Asian environments due to sono-racial/spatial practices that specifically promote black–brown (or black music–world music) separation.

Articulating Race and Sound

Funkadesi's membership is an apt illustration of the result of national "browning" in Chicago. Sharma was born to ethnic-Indian parents shortly after they immigrated to the United States from Kenya—thus he is the product of both the Indian diaspora in Africa and African/South Asian diasporas in the United States. During my field research, the group also featured desi artists Navraaz Basati (Punjabi), Pavithra (Tamil), Inder Paul Singh (Punjabi), and Maninderpal Singh (Punjabi); black members Valroy Dawkins (Jamaican), Kwame Steve Cobb (African American), and Abdul Hakeem (African American); and Carlos Cornier (Nuyorican), Rich Conti (white), and Lloyd King (mixed black and white).[9] The players collectively reflect movement to the United States from Europe, Asia, Africa, the Caribbean, and Latin America and range from new immigrants to those whose families have been in the United States for generations. Beyond racial and ethnic diversity, the band also encompasses a range of ages (thirties to sixties) and class backgrounds. Several members are working musicians who make a living performing and teaching, while others hold day jobs and do artistic work on the side. One member held a fundraiser in order to pay for his cancer treatment, while another is a doctor. Current and former members hold Ph.D.s, while another has worked full-time in a big box bookstore. The result is an atypically racially and culturally diverse ensemble of artists leading contrasting lives spread across the Chicago area. What they share is a conscious desire to create music across this difference.

Funkadesi's music blends numerous African diasporic and South Asian traditions. Sharma plays funk bass and Hindustani *sitar*; Basati and Pavithra sing multiple classical and popular Indian styles (including folk, classical, and Bollywood); Cobb plays jazz, R&B, and funk drum kit as well as West African *djembe*; Cornier plays Latin percussion; Conti plays Brazilian percussion and the vibraphone; Dawkins provides reggae-inflected vocals; Hakeem plays rock, reggae, and funk guitar; King plays jazz flute and saxophone; Inder Paul Singh plays keyboard and sings; and Maninderpal Singh plays *tabla* and *dhol*.[10] The group's songs incorporate lyrics in languages including Hindi, Punjabi, "Punjindi" (a combination of the two), English, Telugu, Tamil, Jamaican patois, and occasionally Spanish. On a general level, the sounds produced by the ensemble match the diversity of membership. Yet their aural profile is not a strict representation of who is there, as members' musical competencies may or may not "match" their race or ethnicity, a point I will return to later. Almost all of the current and former members play in other ensembles, participating in the city's jazz, West African, reggae, R&B, Latin, rock, and South Asian popular and classical scenes.

What this list of identities and traditions does not indicate is how exactly they imbricate within the space of the group, a process modeled in the concept of "articulation." In his seminal "Race, Articulation, and

Societies Structured in Dominance" ([1980] 1996), Stuart Hall proposes a discourse through which race and racism can be understood in both social and economic terms. "Articulation" is the way in which dissimilar elements—in Hall's case capitalism and racial categories—form a greater system that functions as a unified whole. While the separate entities work together, "they are the product of an articulation of contradictions, not directly reduced to one another" (Hall [1980] 1996, 39). Articulation can only occur if unlike entities come together, drawing attention to the affective and sociopolitical potential of sono-racial difference. Afro Asian sonic and physical spaces consist of elements that unify not by becoming alike, but through fitting together in their difference; in fact, it is their dissimilarity that allows them to bind. Articulation helps me to theorize how Afro Asian sonic-racial negotiations unfold through time rather than exist as static entities. These spaces are constantly in a state of articulating and disarticulating as interracial propositions are made, taken up, or discarded.

The articulation of sono-racial categories is much like interlocking rhythms. West African drumming, Afro-Cuban *son* and *rumba*, Balinese and Javanese *gamelan*, and many other genres are built on the concept of separate rhythmic patterns interlacing with one another in order to create a unified voice. Depending on the tradition, interlocking rhythms might be voiced through one instrument or one instrument family (West African drumming or *rumba*), or split between various instrumental sources (*son* and *gamelan*). For a player, this musical texture requires a different mindset than if one were playing on their own. A *rumba*, for example, might split its percussive melody between different drums, which multiple musicians execute in a hocket style. A player must know the entire context and how their specific hits fit into it, sometimes at odd intervals. In this sense, playing interlocking rhythms can be more challenging than simply playing a pattern on one's own. But dividing the duty among players can also allow for the production of structures more complex than one could render alone. In either case, interlocking rhythms are a performative expression of ensemble that differs from what is standard in most Western popular or classical forms.

Funkadesi focuses tremendous energy on the articulation process. But they also throw into relief the less intense everyday processes undertaken by diverse people who share space in neighborhoods or workplaces, cohabitations only bound to increase as the United States becomes a "majority minority" nation. Thus, the band's more marked articulations exemplify techniques that can be instructive for future interracial community building. Their music demonstrates ways in which people weave together practices and beliefs through trial and error, over time, and within space. In contrast to "overlapping," which accounts for demographic overlay on a large scale, my focus on articulation is more attuned to the nuanced ways in which people fit together their lives, while accounting for the maintenance of racial and cultural differences in the course of their melding. In Hall's theorization, dominant and subdominant entities are imbedded in the same articulating system and the negotiation of power differentials is an integral part of the process. Consequently, Afro Asian endeavors are not romantic, egalitarian havens; rather, they are places in which deeply entrenched hierarchies are repeatedly interrogated.

Performing original compositions, arrangements of traditional pieces, and covers of popular songs, Funkadesi employs several articulating mechanisms. First and most simply, they interweave songs from various traditions. For example, they insert quotes from well-known popular songs into their original pieces, such as the Temptations' "Just My Imagination (Running Away with Me)" or Lynyrd Skynyrd's "Sweet Home Alabama," a device that typically produces much excitement in audiences. In "Time So Serious/Mustt Kalandar" (blending Admiral Tibet's reggae classic "Serious Time" and a traditional *qawwali* song), this gesture extends into a full cover of both songs in which the singers alternate verses and choruses over the same chord progression and accompaniment. Beyond a reflection of two cultural currents in the group—Jamaican and South Asian—the pieces reflect a connection based on thematic material. The Tibet song considers the rush of the modern world and the inability of people to see one another as their true selves amidst it. Amidst this confusion, only in Jah does the singer put his trust. "Mustt Kalandar" describes a Sufi devotee dancing passionately, "intoxicated with the spirit of God" (*It's About Time* 2003). Similar to "Time," this song asks God to keep the singer safe on their path through the world. In this method of articulation, Funkadesi demonstrates a simple, outer layer to the onion of interracial and intercultural conversation.

The group also blends traditions within a single song, allowing listeners to engage multiple musical cultures simultaneously. "T-shirt," for example, opens with a brief flourish on *timbales* that leads into a bouncy saxophone–trumpet duet over a reggae backbeat played on keyboard.[11] The *tabla* begins to keep time as vocalist Radhika Chimata sings a legato *alaap* before launching into Hindi lyrics: "Khushi khusi zindagi jeena hai / Sharaafat ki zindagi jeena hai" ("Live a joy-filled life / Live a righteous life").[12] The straight rhythm of the vocals against the syncopated accompaniment creates a subtle lilt that unfolds into a more intense pulse as the bass enters and another *timbales* fill ushers in the main body of the song. Dawkins (who brought this song to the band) takes over from Chimata, singing: "Hear dis! / When I was a boy me never have any toys / Say when I was a boy me never have any toys." The accompaniment becomes more funk-resonant, fleshed out by drum kit, electric guitar, *congas*, and keyboard-produced steelpan drums. While the singers alternate, the instrumental voices play simultaneously, creating timbral combinations unlike those found in any of their respective styles.

The band highlights these cross-genre conversations by extending instrumental roles and techniques. Once, late into the band's set at a street festival, Sharma on bass and percussionist Meshach Silas on *djembe* moved center stage for a duet. What emerged was a dialogue in which the drum made calls that the bass realized in melodic pitches as responses.

This exchange recalled the standard improvisatory give-and-take of a *sitar* (or other melodic instrument) and *tabla* player in North Indian classical music as well as the antiphonic drumming and singing found in many West African traditions. The shared formal relationship of the two instruments provided a link and context for each to extend toward one another, expanding the sounds listeners would expect to hear from both of them in a traditional setting.

These types of musical dialogues are successful due to sono-racial articulation at the level of individual group members. Many members are the product of multitradition training and have spent years finding their unique voice through this mixture. In live shows, for example, Sharma often delivers a solo bass introduction to the group's arrangement of the Punjabi traditional "Laung Gawacha." He begins with a slow, meditative section in which he treats his bass like a *sitar*, playing a melody while simultaneously striking the other strings as a drone. He then transforms the texture into a funk riff in which he hits heavily accented single notes. Finally, the solo turns into a smoother, continuous groove that introduces the song proper. Sharma says, "Playing the [bass] guitar and the *sitar* satisfies the ABCD (American Born Confused Desi) predicament in me. I can play the *sitar* in a very Western way and the [bass] guitar in a very Indian way" (quoted in Shankarkumar 2000). His hybrid technique indicates an ability to flow between styles and a long-running negotiation between them. But instead of a double consciousness in which two cultures stand in tension with one another, Sharma's playing reveals their ability to coexist. In fact, the solo is actually a tri-cultural moment for he simultaneously inhabits two unrelated South Asian traditions in addition to the African American one.

This musical multivocality is present in other members of the group. Carlos Cornier honed his percussion skills in New York's Latin music communities, but diverged from the singular path of a *salsero* by playing in folk and rock groups and even studying Middle Eastern drumming. Maninderpal Singh grew up performing Western classical music and jazz in school, while simultaneously playing Sikh devotional music at home and *gurdwara* (temple). As artists in a multicultural society, Funkadesi members have encountered traditions outside of their personal heritages in schools, community spaces, and arts venues. Their musical vocabulary is marked by this experience of multiple forms, even if not in their primary training. In a rehearsal I witnessed, members used references to styles such as reggae, merengue, or blues as shorthand for the feel or form of a song. These terms provide a vocabulary that cuts across their gathered styles and gives context to guide how each individual fits themself into a piece.

Cross-cultural musical training works to contest body–culture determinism, as members perform genres not associated with their racial identities. This gesture occurs most strongly in the South Asian members: Sharma playing funk bass, Basati providing vocals on R&B covers, and Maninderpal Singh playing *cajon* in live performance. But in some instances, Dawkins will sing in Hindi to accentuate the female singers' vocals. Or black R&B artist Jasper Stone will fill in for Inder Singh on keyboard and vocals. Stone successfully improvises solos on the group's covers of Indian songs and has even accompanied traditional Hindustani *sitar* and Punjabi vocal numbers, treating the keyboard as a harmonium. Within the band, the sounds a musician makes are not always those that the racialized industry would dictate for them. Further, while world music discourses feature many narratives of white artists participating in music of color, cross-cultural/racial musical knowledge among people of color is less frequently spotlighted, mirroring body–culture determinism in the music industry as I detailed in Chapter 1.

Funkadesi members also work to build their cross-cultural fluency in order to better create amidst multiple styles. Several players describe being taught patterns and techniques by their bandmates, or listening to each other's parts and transcribing them onto their own instrument. One player, for example, says he listened to Singh's *bhangra*-based keyboard lines in order to determine how to compose his own solos in a similar style. And former saxophonist Kristin McGee—coming from a jazz and Western classical background—solicited recordings from other members so that she could learn the Indian modes in which she was to improvise.

This ongoing pedagogical process is best seen in the interactions of the four percussionists. Before he passed away, drummer Meshach Silas educated the others on how rhythms from various traditions could fit with one another, as well as the commonalities between instrument functions so that they could stand in for one another. Maninderpal Singh told me, "The *dun-dun* drum and the *dhol* have very similar roles within the cultures of Africa and India, respectively. I was able to learn African rhythms that I could play on the *dhol* to represent a *dun-dun* in traditional African songs that we would perform."[13] The merging of rhythmic traditions is facilitated by improvisation sessions in which the drummers experiment with fitting together patterns. They also define signals they can use to communicate when playing multiple patterns simultaneously, such as a break built on *rumba* clave.

The common vocabulary born from these experiments provides all of the percussionists with a sense of what patterns from their traditions might fit well together and with the overall groove of the piece. As Singh says:

When you have a specific "feel" like a Caribbean calypso, the rhythm that translates the best is the Punjabi *bhangra* played on the *dhol*. The slow reggae songs have a nice amount of space where more intricate *taals* of classical Indian *tabla* fill in the space and enhance the song. The African "six-eight" vibes sound more complete with a *tabla taal* that represents a double-time rhythm of a six-beat *taal* called *Dadra*.

As Singh describes, the array of rhythms from the represented traditions becomes fodder for a joint percussive web, irrespective of the song's primary style.

The fitting of rhythms to a song is not unlike what a percussionist would do in a monocultural ensemble. But in Funkadesi, this negotiation requires more intercultural knowledge and a new musical vocabulary that can translate between traditions. In Singh's case, he describes shifting his technique when playing in the group versus a traditional ensemble: "I play rhythms with a style that emphasizes the beauty and sound of *tabla* and *dhol* without 'losing' the sound that would happen if I were to limit myself to strict adherence to 'classical *tabla* repertoire.' I play a little louder, and a little more sparse than regular *tabla* performances." He also plays *tabla* standing up to give him more flexibility to move to the *dhol* and sing. Singh seeks to present the idiosyncratic acoustic elements of the drums he plays—and to support non-Indian songs—without adhering strictly to the ways tradition might dictate he play. Whether this choice is culturally "correct" may very well be argued; however, Singh and his bandmates bend their respective styles toward the Funkadesi sound in ways that retain their ability to be recognized as part of a root tradition. The ways in which players morph these genres demonstrate a strong grasp of the forms while making a statement that the new musical scenario of the group is just as valuable as a monocultural one.[14]

It is specifically in the realm of rhythm that Sharma early on envisioned the Funkadesi sound. He says, "I kept thinking about things that would serve as a bridge. The reggae beat, for example, is so in synch with Indian beats and *soca* sounds to me just like Indian folk rhythms speeded up. The combination of reggae and Indian folk music was easy because there is such a marriage of rhythm" (quoted in Shankarkumar 2000). Sharma also notes that he was "enthralled with the concept of the 'pocket' in funk and reggae grooves playing the role of a drone or *tanpura* in Indian classical music." Similarly, Singh says: "The correlations between the rhythms, the drums, and the music that we're playing are almost self-evident and sometimes it's just a little 'jam session' with a 'cultural learning session' that allows us to map out the rhythms from our own traditions to any particular genre that we play." There is a flexibility that exists within rhythm, such as varying speed, which can allow for musical articulation in a manner unlike pitch and mode. Yet changing the tempo of a rhythm can alter its feel and traditions will likely shed some of their qualitative traits—which are, of course, not static either—as they move toward one another. Sharma says that the band's percussionists are "expert accompanists who are particularly flexible in 'bending' the swing or feel in order to match the ensemble" and this ability has been a boon to the group's rhythmic play.

The Funkadesi percussionists describe their creations as a new unified whole rather than a merging of separate elements. They generally perform as a team, even when playing for monocultural events. Thus, band members are accustomed to performing in settings in which they have to translate between their own and other musical traditions. And, while they have strong ties to various communities and industries, they simultaneously venture from them to interact with members of others. This process is best served by listening; remaining open to new sounds is as much of a technique in interracial and intercultural performance as any physical manipulation of an instrument. This is also somewhat of a requirement for musicians trying to make a living in the Chicago arts economy. A bassist who guests with the band told me that an intercultural sensibility is necessary in order to work in the ethnic music scenes in Chicago. An artist cannot make a living from *salsa*, *bhangra*, or reggae alone: they must be able to float among bands and styles to get enough paying gigs. Sharma confirms this idea, highlighting in particular the versatility of the city's African American musicians:

> A signature quality of Chicago gigging musicians is their proficiency and adaptability across a wide range of genres (jazz, blues, funk, reggae, R&B, gospel, etc.). Perhaps because of the diversity of talent passing through Chicago, this multi-proficiency has been seen by some as a necessity. It is worthy to note that this versatility phenomenon may have increased the likelihood that a project like Funkadesi took off in Chicago.

Despite self-reflexivity in creation—and the scholarly pedigrees of band members like Sharma—Funkadesi is not an intellectual project. The weaving together of traditions with which they experiment is grounded in the tactile: long-term experimentation in the co-presence of other musicians. The result is an unfolding performative vocabulary that pushes on the boundaries erected in multicultural frameworks. This is best illuminated in a performance the band gave at the 2005 Dance Chicago festival. In the show, troupes presented examples of tango, tap, *kathak*, modern,

Figure 3.1. Funkadesi percussionists Kwame Steve Cobb, Rich Conti, Carlos Cornier, and Maninderpal Singh with flutist/saxophonist Lloyd King. Photograph by Mark Ness. Courtesy of the photographer.

bharatnatyam, West African, and other styles. While drawn from around the city, the troupes only came together because they were featured on the bill and each performed on the program separately—a typical multicultural presentation. In contrast, after each piece, Funkadesi played an improvised number expanding from a musical tradition associated with the previous dance form. After the tango company, for example, Cornier began to play the *cajon*—traditionally used to accompany the dance—and the rest of the group filled in parts that drew from their full palette of styles. In a space in which an assortment of forms was presented without interaction, Funkadesi broke through the racial and cultural barriers erected by the Dance Chicago frame.

The close negotiations required for musical interlocking have resulted in some instances of the same in band members' lives. Much like Singh's depiction of the percussion jams as "cultural learning sessions," being in the group has facilitated broader relationship building among its members. One player describes going to an engagement ceremony for singer Basati, and how interesting it was to eat new foods, hear different prayers, and wholly engage with a different culture. In another instance, Cornier was honored by a Punjabi organization for his contributions to the Chicago Punjabi community, having performed for numerous events as part of the "percussion team." The community's affection for Cornier was so strong, they fêted him without even knowing his last name and simply addressed his award "to Carlos." Unlike many other musical communities that have garnered scholarly attention, Funkadesi members do not live together, share a workplace, or sit in the same racial or ethnic communities. And yet the intimate process of making music together has opened them up to experience each other's lives in extra-musical ways, forming the basis for interracial bonds.

Funkadesi's mixing of musical traditions also blurs boundaries between high and low and sacred and secular. A *sitar*-like bass opening to a *bhangra* piece—as in "Laung Gawacha"—places side-by-side an elite classical tradition with a folk one. This merger of so-called high and low culture indicates the possibility for different class-based "worlds" to articulate and speak to each other just as cultures or races. The incorporation of classical elements into a popular setting is also a key indication of the ways in which the, primarily, Indian elements are bent to meet the African diasporic traditions. This gesture argues for the equal importance of folk and classical forms or, perhaps, calls into question these designations and normative cultural hierarchies.

Thus, Funkadesi's music pushes on traditional cultural formulations in multiple ways. Watching the group perform in a club one night, however, I was reminded of Ravi Shankar's admonition against patrons drinking alcohol or being high at his shows, something he tolerated at times and, at others, refused to play to. Shankar's feelings were due, in part, to his sense of the proper etiquette required of those who engaged his treasured music, a formal decorum Funkadesi eschews in its subtle party vibe. At the same time, Shankar hoped to inspire experiences of spiritual transcendence in listeners, something he saw being thwarted when they were intoxicated ("Ravi Shankar" 2012). Funkadesi proposes that this transcendence can come in a popular environment even though it may mean not necessarily honoring the traditional parameters of some of the styles they perform. Just before the group's first full-length CD release, writer Achy Obejas mused: "In a world with a precious balance of rhythm and melody, of black and white and Latino and Asian, of just-for-fun banalities and clever word play, of sexuality and propriety, the house band would have to be Funkadesi" (2000). Funkadesi presents a portrait of interracial negotiation that is unique to their historical moment as well as part of a perpetual cycle of younger generations questioning the parameters and meanings of "tradition." While there are ways in which industry pressures can push musicians to compromise their ideals, it is clear that Funkadesi members also do so because they are themselves working through how they fit into a world that is sacred, secular, high, and low.

Interracial Space

Successful sono-racial articulation requires particular spaces in which to unfold, spaces where different types of people can gather and be inspired to push beyond their usual routines. Jacques Attali suggests:

> Music is prophecy. Its styles and economic organization are ahead of the rest of society because it explores, much faster than material reality can, the entire range of possibilities in a given code. It makes audible the new world that will gradually become visible, that will impose itself and regulate the order of things; it is not only the image of things, but the transcending of the everyday, the herald of the future. (1985, 11)

Funkadesi's musical mélange portends a new kind of interracial conversation in the city of Chicago. But this phenomenon stretches beyond their texts to the physical spaces their music engenders. Because they pull from multiple musical traditions and are connected to many racial/cultural communities and industries, their shows often attract a range of listeners, forming audiences that reflect the mix of the band. Embodied within a Funkadesi performance is a dialogue between people who share the diverse, urban landscape of Chicago, but rarely converse with one another in the segregated world beyond the concert.

Culture and race are manifested through space; you can read these sociopolitical phenomena in landscapes and cityscapes, as well as produce them through the engineering of the physical environment (de Certeau 1984). While Attali is accurate in his notion that music provides a space within which to experiment in the realm of the ephemeral, it is not cordoned off from the tangible world. Groups like Funkadesi can only produce their sounds through the conjunction of bodies in concrete places. This occurs in their membership and production process, but they also construct settings that offer the potential for such interactions to extend into a broader community.

The mechanism that allows for this transition from sound to space, ephemeral to physical, is what Jill Dolan calls the "utopian performative": moments in performance when audiences or performers experience a flash of the "what if" rather than the "as is" (2002, 515). Drawing from Thomas More's literary "no-place," this concept suggests that representation can at times have a palpable effect on the corporeal realm by allowing for the physical realization of things that do not yet exist. The imaginative becomes a place of political import, for it provides a vision of what might be and breaks possibility from the strictures of contemporary reality. Afro Asian performances like those of Funkadesi translate aural spaces of dialogue into tangible realities by allowing the music to shape the space in which it unfolds. But the translation from sound to body is not foolproof, nor does their music produce an exact replica in physical form. Rather, the music engenders spaces that allow for similar dialogues to emerge with the potential for very different outcomes. Funkadesi concerts are spaces in which audiences work out how to be in interracial community to varying ends. The "no-places" of these performances are refracting mirrors to the music, illuminating its sociopolitical potential and highlighting its shortcomings.

The segregated diversity of Chicago is reproduced in its culture industry. The city's music scenes feature an impressive offering of styles, but they generally interact little and draw racially differentiated audiences. This dynamic can be seen in the ways in which racialized venues are spaced throughout the city. As events push beyond the downtown area and central music venues, they tend to attract more racially/culturally homogenous audiences. Conversely, as they move closer to the city center, audiences grow more heterogeneous, whiter, or both (meaning, an increase in white participants even if a mix of other races is present). For example, Funkadesi drummer Cobb and his wife and performance partner Chavunduka put on a Kwanzaa/Tanzania Water Project benefit on the South Side that drew approximately 150 attendees, all black except for one middle-aged white couple. Alternately, a Bhangratheque party held on the western edge of downtown attracted a majority desi crowd, but also a sizable presence of whites and blacks. Bhangratheque events also indicate how racial spatialization occurs within a single venue. At a 2009 party celebrating the Hindu festival of Holi, *bhangra* played in the first room populated almost exclusively by desis, while a different DJ spun hip hop in a second room with a majority black, minority white, and sparse desi and Latino crowd.

This dynamic works against interracial engagement, as a 2008 study on cross-ethnic attendance conducted at the Dance Center of Columbia College Chicago makes clear. The study "data confirms the anecdotal assumption that culturally-specific performances attract larger percentages of audiences reflective of the tradition or heritage represented in the work performed" and whites (Slover Linett Strategies Inc. 2008, 6). While the Dance Center's whole season attracts 45 percent nonwhite attendance—one of the highest in the city—the patrons are segregated within performances, what study authors describe as "macro-level diversity but micro-level clustering" (Slover Linett Strategies Inc. 2008, 4). Although not the focus of the Dance Center study, I would add that white and European ethnic performances draw majority white audiences. This trend is echoed in the city's music scene. There are several venues that feature a broad mix of traditions, styles, and people, such as the Chicago Cultural Center, Old Town School of Folk Music, Daley Plaza, the former HotHouse, and various summer festivals. In general, these spaces are like the Dance Chicago performance I mentioned before: they present a variety of genres but on different nights, programs, or in otherwise separate ways so that audiences do not mix. An overall diverse roster can still mean that audience demographics shift dramatically day-to-day or within the spatial arrangement of a multivenue festival.

The Old Town School of Folk Music's Folk and Roots Festival is a good example of how these dynamics play out. When I attended the second day of the festival in July 2010, there was a wealth of music performed, including *bhangra, son jarocho*, Egyptian, Irish, and U.S. folk and rock. The festival was divided into multiple stages that were spread throughout North Side Welles Park: the mainstage, *Nuestra Musica* tent, faculty performance tent, gazebo, dance tent, and children's area. Depending on the artist featured, the mainstage audiences tended to be majority white with a minority of members who mirrored the group's racial or cultural makeup, most notably when the headliner for the day, Red Baraat, appeared and the previously non-existent desi contingent grew to about 30 percent of the audience. Separately, there was much representation of Latino and Latin American artists on the festival program due to the *Nuestra Musica* tent, but they were physically set apart from the mainstage. Venezuelan harpist Leonard Jacome performed a set with his band on the mainstage to an audience that was 80 percent white. When they were featured in the *Nuestra Musica* tent later that day, the audience was almost entirely Latino. The second performance was much more participatory and many at the festival missed out on this communal experience because of the lack of interracial audiences. At the same time, it was a more homogenous audience familiar with the conventions of this type of presentation that made this engagement possible.[15]

Old Town School is one of several venues in which Funkadesi has played, in addition to other performance halls, local street festivals, national music festivals, nightclubs, and universities. They are also hired for private gigs such as weddings, school carnivals, and corporate meetings, and volunteer their time to support benefits for various political causes. Each of these spaces has a particular framework for presenting culture. There are single ethnic community spaces in which audiences share the same background as the performers. There are corporate exhibitions that cater to an elite, often whiter crowd that might contrast with the band's racial or cultural makeup. Multicultural stand-alone venues or festivals make up a third category, in which there is the possibility of mixed audiences and an emphasis placed on the consumption of diversity in a bohemian spirit. Finally, universities and civic festivals attempt to present diverse performers for diverse audiences, but often with greater formal limitations and emphasis on family-friendly material versus a club or bar. These venue categories are distinguished by different relationships of audience and performers as well as an assumed shared cultural knowledge. They are also marked by contrasting intentions on the part of listeners, some who seek out the familiar and others who desire difference.

Depending on the venue type and theme of their shows, Funkadesi audiences can be more homogenous than the band's makeup. A mall opening they played on the city's Northwest Side drew a mostly Latino crowd, while the "Desi Crossroads" concert they were featured in at Old Town School was heavily South Asian. Because their sound is so chameleonic, the group has the ability to be hired to play in various racialized venues. Members appear comfortable in a range of spaces and even make small adaptations—such as Sharma giving introductions in Spanish—depending on who is in the crowd. Varied audiences find resonance in their work because the mix of musical styles provides multiple points of identification for diverse listeners.

Of course, as I have shown, mono-racial crowds are not unique in Chicagoland and playing to separate audiences contributes to segregating dynamics. Funkadesi also ends up having a body of listeners who are not part of a single scene, which can mean greater difficulty in cultivating a following and building a continuing conversation. Still, the fact that a single ensemble is drawing such a range of people is unique. In U.S. popular music since at least the 1920s, target audience (or "market") has been an important determinant of a genre's racial profile (Miller 2010). With such varied intended and unintended audiences, a group like Funkadesi calls into question the utility of race as the default means to define a body of listeners because so many differently raced people consume their fare. In essence, they illuminate what has been true since the beginnings of the pop industry—consumers have always exceeded the bounds of marketing categories. People listen across racial lines even as their person-to-person interactions may be more conservative.

Funkadesi is able to move through multiple racialized spaces but, at times, they also defy the segregated logic of the Chicago music scene by attracting racially diverse audiences in a single show. Because the band members are aligned with various cultural and musical communities through teaching, studying, performing, family, and friends, they draw in listeners from these circles. At the shows they headline in centrally located venues in which multiple populations have physical and cultural access, they often attract a crowd that reflects their sound: black, white, and South Asian—split relatively evenly among the three—with a smaller presence of East Asians and Latinos. There is also a more notable presence of interracial couples at their shows. The fact that these audiences are black and white, or white and South Asian, is less important than that they are black and South Asian. As the Dance Center study shows, white patrons roam the city center freely and white-nonwhite racial pairings are typical. Funkadesi creates space for interminority engagement and makes possible a more integrated audience of people of color. This is an increasing phenomenon in major metropolitan areas such as Chicago, New York, and the San Francisco Bay Area, and Funkadesi and other interracial bands stood at the front edge of this trend. When mixed groups of people are brought together through interracial sound, the concert becomes a space for the articulation of racial/cultural groups and offers the possibility of building community that complicates typical racial binaries and hierarchies.

The idiosyncratic Funkadesi audience is less diverse in terms of other identity markers. They tend to attract an older adult audience—thirties to sixties—rather than a younger pop or rock crowd. Their fans have also aged with the band, so were decidedly younger when the group first started in the mid-1990s. Listeners are also middle- or upper-middle-class for the most part, many who came to know the band as friends of members or artistic collaborators. It is interesting to note that concerts with lower ticket prices are not necessarily their most diverse. Free shows tend to be part of private events that attract more homogenous listeners or public events in mono-racial neighborhoods. However, shows the group would do at the downtown HotHouse with midrange ticket prices of $10–$20 were consistently the most mixed.[16] This suggests that the Funkadesi audience has more expendable income and a certain amount of social capital to more freely explore the city. Further, despite their individual incomes, the group performs middle classness in their presentation—wearing dressy casual attire and speaking and behaving with a sense of informal decorum. Audience members typically display a comfort in engaging in this type of scene. Class-wise, this is not unlike a typical world music audience; however, Funkadesi shows are markedly less white.

The HotHouse is worth considering in greater detail, especially as Funkadesi frequently performed there. This club highlights both the racial geographies I am discussing, as well as architectural features that allow for certain types of audience interactions and aid the articulation process. The HotHouse/Center for International Performance Exhibition (CIPEX) was founded by Marguerite Horberg in 1987 as a space dedicated to featuring performance artists and supporting community activism. It became renowned for presenting international guests, including serving as a key venue in the annual Chicago World Music Festival. The HotHouse was also a critical node of the local creative music scene, presenting many of Chicago's greats. It additionally provided gallery space and rentals for community events and performances, mainly for progressive organizations. The venue was originally located in the Wicker Park neighborhood, where it thrived until pushed out in a wave of gentrification in the mid-1990s. In 1995 it moved to a new location in the downtown South Loop area, where it remained until 2007.

The South Loop iteration of the club (the one in which I conducted the bulk of my research) sat in a neighborhood in the midst of urban renewal: loft conversions, chains such as Dunkin Donuts, Kinkos, and Quiznos, and the campus of Columbia College intermixed with bleak parking lots, the Pacific Garden Mission—a large store-front ministry—and the divey South Loop Club bar and grill. Black panhandlers, white businessmen, and multiraced students and concertgoers often walked past each other on dimly lit sidewalks, directly underneath the elevated train tracks of the Chicago Transit Authority's Orange line. The venue had the potential to bring in people from various communities because of its location just on the edge of the city center. At the same time, as arts institutions are typically part of the "first wave" of gentrification, the club held a tenuous position between a community hub and a space of "revitalization" that could ultimately serve as an agent to forcing out lower-income neighbors (Cameron and Coaffee 2005, 39).[17]

Of other venues in Chicago, the HotHouse, in particular, fostered diverse audiences and supported artists in presenting their work in their chosen manner. Still, while it attracted audiences that reflected the racial, ethnic, and national range of its acts, micro-level clustering was the norm: Polish/white audiences for the electro-folk Warsaw Village Band; desi for a fundraiser for a South Asian organization; Asian/American and white for the experimental Japanese Miyumi Project; Asian/American, black, and white for Yoko Noge's blues/Japanese *minyo* explorations, discussed in Chapter 2. As the last two examples suggest, however, this mirror between the house and the stage made for racially, ethnically, or nationally mixed audiences for interracial music performances. Audiences did not always reflect quite the degree of boundary crossing interaction as the music, but the shows did promote an environment where patrons of all kinds were comfortable talking or dancing with one another, and also attracted mixed couples and groups.

The HotHouse's closing had a less visible effect on Funkadesi than Yoko Noge and her groups, for they did not singularly rely on the space like Noge did. Funkadesi also performs quite a bit at the Old Town School of Folk Music, Martyr's, Fitzgerald's, the Double Door, and Park West, and they have continued to produce shows with large turnouts at these locations. The HotHouse did, however, foster a milieu well-suited to Funkadesi's style. Horberg proposes that the eclectic decor of the venue presented a visual counterpart to the group's multicultural makeup, along with its track record for attracting audiences of color. Beyond surface representation of difference, the conjunction of Chicago creative music and world music in the HotHouse's programming reflects the dual forces that have marked the band. This connection is supported by the fact that Funkadesi members perform in other ensembles that also found a home at HotHouse, reinforcing the venue as a space of their own.

On a more concrete level, the main performance room encouraged the rubbing of elbows between participants, providing the opportunity for interracial encounter. It featured a bar in one corner, just inside the entrance from the neighboring gallery space. Surrounding the edges of the room was an elevated bank of red-upholstered booths with a small walkway connecting them. Another row of wood tables often formed an inner ring of seating at floor level, sometimes absent in shows when a large number of dancing audience members were anticipated. Most importantly, the stage was only slightly elevated from the surrounding dance floor and thrust into the space, rather than being recessed behind a proscenium. Replete with soft lighting and large windows that showed off the Chicago skyline, the HotHouse was cozy and beautiful. The close quarters sometimes meant strangers shared space at a table or were pressed against one another on the dance floor. And the lack of performer–audience separation gave a sense that everyone was jointly taking part in the show. Thus, venue, performers, audience, and music worked together to craft a space conducive to sono-racial articulation. The geographic placement of the HotHouse, its interior spatial arrangement, and its promotion of cultural difference provided a flexible environment that could be filled in by an interracial band such as Funkadesi. The band, in turn, pushed on the limitations of the space by cross-pollinating audiences and using the room's features to engineer atypical audience behavior.

Audiences, Dolan claims, are temporary communities, and at times Funkadesi helps to build ones that do not readily exist outside the venue (2005, 10). What does it mean, then, for Funkadesi's listeners to be so multifarious? Can they be considered a unified community and what might this entail? The way an audience acts inside of a space is consequential for generating the utopian performative. Funkadesi concerts at times promote a space in which people who would not normally interact on a daily basis might do so. The band is notorious for their danceability, and a typical performance features a large number of audience members on their feet and moving together to the music. In key moments, the audience is also invited to do the same gestures together: when Inder Singh will call out "do the *bhangra!*" and demonstrates the signature shoulder and arm movements, most of the crowd's hands will start to pump up and down in the air along with him. As spectators join in, sonic fusions are transcribed onto bodies that perform movements aligned with the various musical genres.

Audience members also share intimate moments with the performers, as evidenced in Funkadesi's live performance of "Laung Gawacha." Partway through the piece, the instrumentation drops down to a sparser texture, foregrounding percussionists Conti, Cornier, and Maninderpal Singh playing the *dhol, chekere,* and *surdo.*[18] The three players leave the stage and go into the crowd, moving through the audience as a miniature drumline. This moment generally produces an enthusiastic response from patrons as they are able to dance right alongside the musicians. These drumbreaks sometimes inspire individual audience members to approach the drummers and begin highlighted solo movements and exchanges with the players. What is most interesting in this moment is the skin-to-skin contact between audience and performers as they crowd around the drummers. The breach of the "fourth wall" transitions the performance into a carnivalesque mode in which usual inhibitions are temporarily suspended (Bhaktin [1965] 1984).

In these moments of cross-racial and cross-cultural encounter, there is the potential for recognition and appreciation. In the spring of 2007, Funkadesi opened for neo-soul singer Jill Scott at a benefit for the Chicago Foundation for Women. Held at the downtown Auditorium Theater, the concert drew a primarily middle- and upper-middle-class black crowd. The opening act—a local white, Jewish, lesbian comic—received a lukewarm response from the audience. Despite the fundraising goal, it was clear the audience was there for Scott and, when Funkadesi went on next, I wondered whether the audience would have the patience to hear another opener. In one moment, to confirm my suspicion, an exasperated man yelled out "Jill Scott!," while singer Basati introduced a song about violence against women. Overall, though, the audience embraced the group and the "funk" elements formed the bridge. When Sharma launched into his bass solo before "Laung Gawacha," the audience was enraptured, clapping or cheering at its virtuosic "sitar" moments. When he transitioned to the funkier section, the audience grew even more animated and called out appreciations. Listeners there to hear Scott were familiar with percussive basslines that drip with attitude and were hailed by this sound, even as it emerged from an ensemble that did not fit a standard funk profile, sonically or racially. The novelty of these lines being played by an Indian man wearing a *kurta* must have contributed to the audience's interest. But the sonic blackness of Sharma's playing helped push past only the recognition of difference.

The embodiment of Funkadesi's aural message, in fact, allows for this confrontation with racial and cultural variance. The utopian performative does not create a magical space of ready-made harmony, but rather one in which the real coming together of human beings presents the potential for sociopolitical triumphs and failures. In part, this is because, as Michael Warner argues: "All public addresses have some social basis.... They fail if they have no reception in the world, but the exact composition of their addressed publics cannot entirely be known in advance. A public is always in excess of its known social basis. It must be more than a list of one's friends. It must include strangers" (2002, 55). In order to exceed the bounds of the "as is," the space of a Funkadesi performance must incorporate and translate difference. The chance to interact on some level with people who are different is actually part of the draw of a group like Funkadesi. And the performative technology of the live concert provides the physical dynamics that foster the coming together of strangers more so than, for instance, a play or gallery show.

But there are limits to the amount concertgoers laterally engage with their neighbors. As at other shows, listeners frequently sit, stand, and dance with their companions without breaking out to engage people they do not know. In a small survey I administered via a Funkadesi e-blast, a third of the respondents said they are compelled to strike up conversation with audience members they do not know.[19] The majority, however, tend to keep to themselves or their group of friends. The loud concert space is not necessarily the most conducive to new social engagements or extensive conversation. Venues with fixed seating, that seem more formal, or that discourage dancing also thwart the potential for cross-audience interaction. Thus, while it is indeed important that people of various backgrounds share space at Funkadesi shows, their contact does not automatically lend itself to deeper interaction. The band opens up space that can allow for extraordinary audience behavior, but participants decide how to inhabit it.

And there is no guarantee that attendees, regardless of background, will possess a desire for interracial or intercultural socialization. Some audience members may only be interested in hearing a sonic melding of traditions. At Midsommarfest, a quiet middle-aged black woman beside me grew increasingly animated during a piece in which the band inserts several verses of Carlos Santana's "Black Magic Woman." Moving her hand up and down and compelled to speak to me, she progressed from saying: "It's an interesting mix," to "This is a MIX," to "nice, niice, niiiiiice," and finally to "I love it!" The woman then described what elements she was hearing in the blend and how she found it pleasurable to hear them combined. Sifting through the layers of a piece while hearing them coherently function within the same context is part of the group's appeal. Some listeners also crave the familiar. Audiences often express delight when the band performs a popular song from the U.S. mainstream, such as "Sweet Home Alabama" or Alicia Keys's "No One." Listeners are tolerant of lesser-known songs, but tunes well known by a majority of the audience allow them to relax into a shared reference, know the words to sing along, and have something to latch onto amidst the mélange.

Further, Dolan reminds us that strong feelings of connection engendered through performance do not exist "outside of ideology," and it is true that audience members may not know how to properly understand or show respect for individuals unlike themselves (2005, 62). A concert-goer might, for example, enjoy Funkadesi because they have an "exotic" female singer, regardless of how other elements of their praxis work to dissuade Orientalism. At a show at the Kinetic Playground in Uptown, two young white women danced near the front of the stage and interacted a lot with the performers. One of the women was celebrating her birthday and the band sang "Happy Birthday" to celebrate. Having been invited into the performance space as more active participants, the women proceeded to do faux *mudras*, swirling their hands above their heads to the music. While certainly not meaning any harm, the women resorted to a stereotype of how to engage kinetically with the scene rather than looking around to see how their fellows were dancing (in this case, not doing *mudras*). This gesture speaks less of cultural ill will and more so of miscommunication. The dancing women were attempting to connect to the scene of the performance, but did not possess the proper tools through which to respectfully do so.

At a different show—a fundraiser barbecue for a Catholic school in Lincoln Square—the primarily white audience was appreciative but less engaged, especially as parents attempted to entertain their small children. After singer Dawkins wished the crowd goodnight, an intoxicated white man near me started imitating his Jamaican accent and shouting at him to go smoke some *ganja*, invoking stereotypes of Jamaican and Rastafarian culture. For this man, the performance generated a knee-jerk resort to stereotypes rather than cross-racial interest or union. Funkadesi shows can open a space for interracial and intercultural contact, but the dynamic cultural learning sessions that occur backstage are not necessarily continued onstage because of the necessities of keeping the show moving, the audience engaged, and spirits high. And because of the ephemeral nature of a concert, many audience members may come and go without developing deeper relationships with the band, the setting, or the rest of the audience, minimizing Funkadesi's pedagogical potential.

Both of these examples have gendered contours. In the *mudras* incident, the exotic feminine was performed as a broader symbol of Indianness, despite the lack of women within Funkadesi. In the *ganja* episode, the patron's invocation of a stereotype of Jamaincanness was through the specifically masculine rastaman, a racially marked figure without feminine counterpart. Gender is an important framework through which listeners' deeply held racial and cultural assumptions are amplified.

These occurrences are not ruptures in an a priori harmonious fabric; they are a necessary and productive part of sono-racial articulation. Utopian performatives are about process rather than end results, and Funkadesi intentionally creates space for the city's segregated populations to come together and develop better ways to be with each other (Dolan 2005, 13, 23). In the right circumstances, these spaces become temporary Afro Asian communities unlike those that exist in the world beyond the performance venue. For the brief moment of the performance, audiences have the opportunity to experience in the flesh what a more racially or culturally integrated world might be like, even if it is only inside their own minds. This feeling can be inspiring, but also a double-edged sword that can lead a participant to assume everything is "alright" despite lingered social disparities in and outside of the performance space. When a listener says that at a concert, "Everyone around me was saying that Funkadesi can bring world peace!," how might that lead audiences to assume the work has been done and they need only bathe in the luxurious new world (quoted in Funkadesi [accessed] 2004b)?

Dolan emphasizes the moments of ideal "what ifs," but Funkadesi performances indicate the messiness of lesser-held interactions that may never resolve in the dissolution of social hierarchies. What does it take for participants to move in new patterns and how can new social structures be built inside lingering hierarchies? Perhaps by giving them space to develop without predetermining the outcomes in the language and vision of the existing world. Sharma hatched the Funkadesi project from his own interests, but it has grown to incorporate styles, personalities, and songs that were brought by his collaborators and allowed to develop without being forced into a static formula. So, too, interracial communities must muddle along with creativity and imagination, fashioning perpetual utopias we will perhaps only recognize when we look back on them.

Theater of Diversity

Funkadesi's production of interracial space is complicated by the spatial dynamics of the culture industry that presents black and South Asian identities and expressions as geographically and culturally exclusive. Industry channels operate using a multicultural framework that, even in its promotion of hybridity, promotes simplified representations of Otherness by forcing cultural material into distinct racial boxes. Funkadesi's Afro Asian music has the power to disrupt binary constructions of difference, but is often represented within racially triangulating industry structures that stereotype and marginalize artists of color. In particular, as I discussed in Chapter 2, while hybridity discourse portends a fusion of first/third, North/South, and West/non-West, it often does so through a vocabulary of exoticism and essentialism that highlights the distance between the two poles rather than their merger (Hutnyk 2000). Funkadesi's music is thus (mis)represented by extra-musical elements that tend to highlight difference over unity, end product over process, and certain types of difference over others. "Moreover," Sharma says, "as a 'world music' band, [Funkadesi seems] to lose appeal to some arts presenters who wish to see exotic or 'ethnic' music coming from other countries."

The band wants to make it big—actively courting major festivals, radio play, and recording labels. Beyond self-produced gigs in Chicago, they have been featured in the Chicago World Music Festival, the Lotus World Music Festival, and venues throughout the Midwest, the San Francisco Bay area, and New York. Their version of "Real Situation" was included on a Putumayo compilation of Bob Marley covers in 2010. Most impressive is their winning of the Chicago Music Award five times (Award of Honor for Contribution to World Music and Most Outstanding Band) and the *Chicago Reader*'s Readers' Choice Award for Best World Music Group in 2013 and 2014. As they attempt to gain stature in the world music industry, the discursive and visual rendering of "unity-through-diversity" has been key to how the group markets their musical project and politics.

Their promotion and staging, however, illuminate the challenges of accurately representing interracial music in the culture industry. As Hall suggests, the revelation of the "complex structure" of an articulated entity "requires that the mechanisms which connect dissimilar features must be shown" for there is no "necessary correspondence" between the constitutive elements ([1980] 1996, 38). Likewise, Funkadesi pointedly performs race and ethnicity in order to make their unification legible. The group's lyrics, for example, showcase the panoply of roots traditions they perform.

In "Wayo," Dawkins sings: "If you want funk or reggae / *bhangra* ragga say we're rough 'n ready / calypso, *kaiso*, classical roots rock / if it's the blues we got the good news."[20] In a later moment, he sings a call and response with the instrumentalists who demonstrate the traditions he names. When he sings, "Give a little *bhangra* 'pon on the left-hand side," the ensemble responds with several measures of *dhol*, a playful flute melody, and male voices rhythmically chanting vocables common in the genre. He next sings, "Give a little *bomba* 'pon on the right-hand side" and is met by the *bomba sicá* rhythm played on congas accompanied by a keyboard drone. The lyrics describe *what* styles are present, but not *how* these traditions relate to one another.

In promotional materials and live performance, the group employs a whirlwind of images that showcase diverse instruments, colorful patterns, and brown faces to present visible diversity. The cover of their third album, *Yo Baba*, is a grid of ten boxes, each holding a picture of hands of various shades—presumably those of each band member.[21] Nine of the pairs of hands hold instruments, such as a *sitar*, flute, drumsticks, mallets, and various rattles. In the center, a larger photo shows two female hands with palms open; one wears a silver bracelet, the other is decorated with henna, and both show a glimpse of red nail polish on the thumbs. The range of skin hues, visible clothing and accessories, and instruments clearly indicate racial and cultural heterogeneity. But each box is self-contained and separated by a black border, so we do not see the ways in which this diversity fits together. Further, except for the center photo, the other boxes present the hands in the same set-up, presenting difference within a common gestural package. The images lack context such as full bodies, how the instruments are played, or how the ensemble moves together. What remains to a viewer—unless already knowledgeable about a featured element—is a display of multicultural fragments.

The cover of the group's first album, *Uncut Roots* (2000), does a stronger job of bringing visual cultural references into a unified whole. The painted album art features an outline of the African continent in red with an inlay of India in brown. In the center of India is a hand drawn in black with the palm facing out. All of these elements are contained within a green globe that sits on the branches of a tree with roots that descend to the edge of the image. Alongside this component are two female faces, one dark brown with curly black hair and the other lighter brown with straight black hair and a *bindi*. The geographic entities and people conjured by these images highlight African and Indian people and traditions, although they do not speak to the range, intricacies, or melding of the two. While Africa and India are layered on top of one another, they remain discrete, bounded entities. Further, the important role the United States plays in their interdiasporic conjunction is visually absent with only the "world" roots represented.

Both album covers are interesting in their emphasis on brown women, despite the majority of band members being male. We can read this feminine presence in multiple ways. On *Yo Baba* (2008), the female hands are

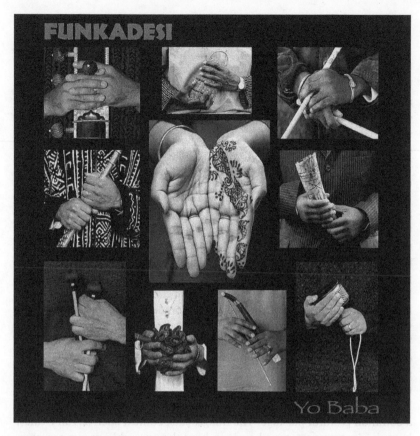

Figure 3.2. Front cover of *Yo Baba*. Photographs and design by Rich Conti. Courtesy of Rahul Sharma.

the focal point of the cover and their size and placement highlight the feminine. Their appearance serves to accent the "exotic" of the band through a gendered image of South Asianness. On *Uncut Roots*, the use of the female faces again draws on gendered depictions of race to indicate the coming together of difference. Women also serve as the embodiment of rootedness and "Motherland," especially as the visages correlate with Africa and India. This cover also recalls the many tributes to women offered up in various Third World and Afro Asian movements of the mid-twentieth century. The love of brown femininity and representation of women as the heart of a culture—even if they were marginalized from organizing—symbolically link Funkadesi to this political past (Pulido 2006, 182–183; Ward 2006, 124–125).

In the case of both covers, let me be clear, I am not condemning the band's choices. Rather than suggest Funkadesi do anything differently, I am providing these critical reflections to highlight the many traps artists will inevitably fall into within the established representational system.

Figure 3.3. Front cover of *Uncut Roots*. Artwork by Christina Cornier. Courtesy of Rahul Sharma.

The possible racist interpretations made about hennaed hands, exotic instruments, and ethnic fabrics would certainly be a symptom of a listener's or viewer's ignorance, not the band's. But I am trying to draw out a possible reading through a dominant lens to highlight the difficulties for artists and artists of color, in particular, to have their work read in their intended ways. I will pick up this issue in relation to sound in Chapter 4.

For Funkadesi, good interracial and intercultural vibes are what sell and they use diversity as a marketing point. On their website and in other press materials, they proclaim:

> Funkadesi proudly hails from Chicago, representing the diverse multiethnic communities within the city. What distinguishes Funkadesi as a group is each band member's unique and uncompromised cultural/musical contribution merging to create one unifying sound and vision. With their not-to-be-missed live shows and *visible racial and*

musical diversity, the band is ideally suited for festivals, nightclubs, world music concerts, weddings and commitment ceremonies, corporate events, as well children's programs. Funkadesi's one-world sound, roots-watering vision, and positive vibe make the band a unique and compelling musical force. (Funkadesi [accessed] 2004a, my emphasis)

The group uses visual elements to explicitly communicate what is occurring in their music, providing extra-musical clues through which to help their audiences hear their work more acutely.

Their discursive representation of unity is summed up in their motto "One Family, Many Children," a tagline displayed on promotional materials, merchandise such as t-shirts, and on their website. Family has been a longstanding trope used to discuss the U.S. national body and the incorporation of people of color into it (Kun 2005, 11). In Funkadesi's case, being a part of the family does not mean assimilating into a space of one race or culture, but rather being part of a unified agenda while retaining your distinctiveness. This is a "chosen family," as there is a wide range of people in the group with little to connect them other than the group. There is power in the notion of forming tight-knit bonds with others that are considered on par with blood and history, but do not require shared genetics or physiognomy. The Funkadesi version of family also differs from a heteronormative nuclear arrangement, offering many different ways to belong amidst a loose assortment of extended kin with nontraditional relationships. At the same time, this portrait of family exudes a sense of wholesomeness, respectability, and stability. Funkadesi presents itself as a group that will nurture and enrich you rather than one bent on confrontation or angry politics. Several of the band's press photos form a visual counterpart, depicting them in family portraitlike formations: neat rows, big smiles, basking in the glow of their kin.

Even though the band uses family as a marketing image, this spirit is a reality for many members, and they and their relatives have grown to share intimate relationships. One member's son calls the other men in the group his fathers and even bears a tattoo with the late drummer Silas's name on his upper arm. Sharma beams as he notes that his two children have "a Tio Carlos, a Baba Kwame, Baba Valroy, and Baba Abdul, a Lloyd Uncle and Rich Uncle, a Pavi Auntie, and a Maninder Chacha and Inder Chacha." Family members are also integral to the band's marketing and performance: photos of them are used to decorate their album covers and liner notes, and they join in concerts as guest artists. The group has also cultivated a circle of loyal friends who repeatedly attend shows, help sell merchandise, and are invited onstage to play with the band or dance. Fellow performers describe the amiable atmosphere the band cultivates. Comedian Jessica Halem, who shared a bill with the group, told me they were genuinely warm to her backstage and invited her into their preshow prayer circle (an act they will occasionally perform in full view of the audience, further showcasing togetherness). On a more practical note, Cornier

Figure 3.4. Funkadesi. Photograph by Mark Ness. Courtesy of the photographer.

commented to me that Sharma looks out for members who make their living solely as musicians, trying to get them gigs even when the whole band is not performing. In both symbolic and tangible ways, Funkadesi exudes a communal spirit.

The promotional images do not always reflect the multiplicity of voices in the band, however. One member tells me he chooses not to participate in group prayers in a religious way, instead looking up at his colleague's faces while they pray. And some members have claimed they have less of a voice in band decisions, while others hold more sway over their project. Current and former members have mentioned their lack of interest in playing the same songs show after show, not expanding their repertoire fast enough, or that they want the group to be consistently more polished. The players also articulate a range of investment in the outwardly unified aesthetic and political mission of the group. While some actively promote an explicit solidarity-building politics, others are more interested in building community through playing fun music and having a good time. Family, like other interracial units, does not always mean agreement or lack of conflict. However, through articulation, varying values and desires can complement one another and build a stronger ensemble. Even more, the open negotiation of these differences illustrates the particular social and political faculties needed for productive interracial engagement. "Funkadesi" is not a monolithic product of different people merging together, but the space in which this process continually unfolds, a complexity missed when glossed simply as "unity."

Accurate—or more complicated—representations of Funkadesi's unity-through-diversity are further challenged by the ways in which various types of Otherness carry disparate currencies with the culture industry. Industry forces tend to racialize cultural material, focusing on visible and often phenotypic images as evidence of ethnicity. One way in which Funkadesi members engage in this symbolic economy is through their clothing choices. Many members of the group wear colorful ethnic attire that reflects their respective heritages. Typically, the male Indian members of the group wear a *kurta* and pants, and female members a *salwar kameez* or *kurta* with pants such as jeans. Inder Singh and Maninderpal Singh also wear a turban or *dastar* as part of their ensembles. All of these outfits are clear visual indicators of the players' ethnic identifications and signal general "Indianness" even to viewers with less cultural knowledge. Black group members often wear West African *dashiki* and *sokoto*, sometimes with *kufi*, items that bear a long history of identification with blackness in the United States. Like the band logo, these garments highlight the African and Indian roots of the group, but they are tied specifically to bodies of those backgrounds and do not intermix.

Players who do not fit into one of these categories tend not to wear distinctively "ethnic" clothing. Cornier often wears track pants (black with colored stripes down the side) and a sleeveless white undershirt. King generally wears jeans and t-shirts, sometimes with a blazer. Conti generally appears in similar attire, although he will sometimes wear a Latin American-style shirt. In Funkadesi, the black and South Asian elements are the primary axes on which the group presents itself, and members with more marginal racial and ethnic identities are less visible in the sartorial realm. Former saxophone player Kristin McGee, a white woman, once asked Sharma what she should wear and he jokingly replied something Norwegian, since that is her family's ancestry. In addition to what would likely read as comically unhip to an audience, this costume would definitely not reflect the musical heritage McGee represented in the group: namely jazz and African American creative music. A clear visual for nonblack or nondesi members is not as readily apparent within the African–Indian binary and the racial categories built into the culture economy.

One band member deemed the group's emphasis on racial and cultural promotion "theater," a fitting moniker as they do actively stage the encounter between races and cultures in their performances. This characterization might suggest that the ethnically attired members are putting on atypical costumes in order to emphasize their difference. Yet all identity is performed. Is a heightened identity performance any less "real" than an everyday one? How do we determine what is a "regular" or "exaggerated" identity performance? When Funkadesi members don clothes that express their backgrounds, they present "musical personae," characters related to their offstage identities, often with certain elements highlighted or altered (Auslander 2006). The members' decisions to wear certain clothes and speak, sing, or play in a particular manner are shaped by their performative goals, but also encouraged by a space welcoming of racial and cultural difference and allowing them to more fully express their identities than they might feel comfortable in the rest of their daily lives.

What becomes problematic is when the performative distance is collapsed: when musicians' clothing or sonic output is received as a natural and predestined outgrowth of who they "are." This collapse of everyday and aesthetic performance can be exploited as a means for visual/sonic difference to stand in for social or political presence in civic art spaces. Funkadesi is the exception to the rule given the segregated demographics of Chicago, but they have been wielded as representatives of the city through various gestures of civic inclusion, spokespersons for an integration that does not (yet) exist.[22] Performative images of unity are not substitutes for the real thing.

Further, industry executives and audiences view racial/cultural markers as having varied appeal. Funkadesi and presenters (including critics and promoters) often bring the South Asian—especially Punjabi—elements to the fore. Sharma still occasionally plays the *sitar*, but *bhangra* takes center stage at their shows. Maninderpal Singh confirmed this shift and told me that, while he had played the *dhol* some before Funkadesi—the foundational instrument in *bhangra*—he began to study it specifically to incorporate it into the group's repertoire. When Hindi-singing, ethnically Tamil vocalist Pavithra temporarily left the group, she was replaced with Basati who is Punjabi.[23] And, in concert, the audience is called on to engage the desi elements more than others represented. Inder Singh will call out to "all of the Punjabis in the house," generally the only group hailed from the stage. And basic *bhangra* moves and vocal *bols* (rhythmic syllables) are demonstrated to the audience, who are then asked to join in.

The group has not necessarily made these choices to cater to the growing *bhangra* fad, especially given that they have several Punjabi members. But it is also possible that the promise of the exotic in Indian imagery and the wide-scale promotion of *bhangra* within the contemporary culture industry factor into what the band's audiences positively respond to. The highlighting of the "desi" in Funkadesi is also sometimes out of the group's control. In one instance, they were presented at a Mervyn's vendors fair in California unknowingly under the event title "Mervana." As Sharma told me, the band played an opening set that included some of their signature elements, such as a percussion processional, and were well received by the audience (and well paid: the group made twice their usual corporate gig rate for only a fifteen-minute performance). After leaving the stage, however, the television spokesperson for Mervyn's came out onstage wearing four arms, sporting a *bindi*, and doing a send-up of a Hindu goddess, saying things like, as Sharma remembers, "how cosmic and groovy." Despite how the group defines itself, Mervyn's sought them out for their Indianness.[24]

As the South Asian elements of the group's presentation are accentuated, blackness is minimized. In a quote they proudly display in emails and on their website, then Senator Barack Obama proclaims, "There's a lot of funk in that desi!"[25] While certainly a winning endorsement, Obama's statement confirms blackness as only qualifying desi.[26] Instead of the meeting of musical cultures, the band's output becomes weighted toward an image of South Asian music supported by blackness. Yet Funkadesi's history is greatly marked by the contributions of important African American jazz and creative musicians, including former members Byard Lancaster, Ari Brown, and Meshach Silas, and current members Kwame Steve Cobb and Abdul Hakeem. Further, their sound is heavily steeped in Afro-Caribbean and Afro-Brazilian traditions. Because of the longstanding cross-racial familiarity with African American and other African diasporic culture in the United States, these elements are sometimes taken for granted or read as the cultural default in Afro Asian settings.

The marginalization of blackness in Funkadesi's presentation can be seen clearly in a moment when the band came face-to-face with the upper echelons of the popular music industry. On a Wednesday in August 2005, I received a mass email from Sharma stating: "BE A PART OF HISTORY: Funkadesi's debut on MTV Desi!" MTV had recently launched MTV World, a conglomerate of several networks targeted at Asian American youth, also including MTV Chi (Chinese) and MTV-K (Korean). These networks are a clear example of the conflation of Asian—in this case, Asian *American*—and the "world" (i.e., not the United States). Funkadesi was to be taped for the channel at a party held in conjunction with a meeting of the Islamic Society of North America. The party was called "The Candy Shop"—a reference to rapper 50 Cent's latest hit single by the same name. And, much like a larger circuit of parties catering to young desis around the city, this event promoted a chic, sexy, and cosmopolitan version of South Asian American identity.

A friend and I arrived at the party's location—a northwest suburban Holiday Inn—a little after 11p.m. The event was being held in two adjacent meeting rooms, one side featuring a large refreshment stand selling alcohol and, appropriately, candy. The other side featured the stage, filling a third of the room and standing several feet off the ground. A banner announcing "Funkadesi" in large letters hung on the wall behind the stage. And both rooms were packed with approximately 200 desis ages 18–23, with a few whites and blacks the same age interspersed. Everyone milled around in the dark room, chatting and dancing to hip hop and *bhangra* tracks spun by several DJs.

A little after midnight, Funkadesi took the stage and the MTV Desi cameras came out to shoot the band with the audience looking on. But as soon as the band started, the crowd thinned as many of the youth moved to the concessions room. At one point, Sharma shouted "do the rap" to singer Pavithra, perhaps to find something to engage the youthful and waning audience. She began to rap in Tamil, but the exodus continued. The Funkadesi sign fell, ending up in a crumpled pile on the floor. Finally, about fifteen minutes into the set, the event closed down after a fight broke out in the concessions room. Less than two years later, MTV took the World stations off the air, claiming they underestimated the cost of running them.[27]

Talking later with Pavithra, I learned that this was not a planned Funkadesi gig: "That was all staged, the whole thing." MTV Desi had wanted to do a small feature on the group and, because they did not have an upcoming gig, the band scrambled to find an event that would provide a workable audience. But why did they not find their "fans" there? First, there was an obvious generational divide. Pavithra said: "We felt so old there. Honestly, those were kids. They were kids and they just wanted to drink and have fun.... I think all they needed there was a DJ to just dance and get high. You know, they were not ready for us over there. And that fistfight!" It is important to remember that the band has and continues to play for other primarily South Asian events. These shows, however, are generally for older or more mixed-age crowds, or more racially/ethnically mixed venues. "Desi" as a racialized audience/market was not enough to bridge the cultural divide between youth and middle-aged adults.

And neither was the music. There is not one South Asia unmarked by age, nor is there even one Afro Asia unmarked by genre. The attempt to merge Funkadesi's sound with this crowd was derailed by differing aesthetic tastes. The primary music featured on MTV Desi was contemporary pop such as *bhangra*, hip hop, and other sample-based music—its own Afro Asian blend. Funkadesi chose this preexisting party because it was the only option available on short notice. They hoped that they could make use of the publicity opportunity from MTV but, unfortunately, do not play the kind of music the youth wanted to hear.

Interestingly, as the young desi crowd thinned out near the stage, what remained was a smaller crowd of older, more ethnically mixed individuals—fans of the band but not a part of the ISNA conference. The band clearly has an audience and the desi youth at the Candy Shop were not it, despite presumed racial similarity. This incident points out the futility of using race as a determinant of cultural tastes, as well as what might be lost if Funkadesi were only able to perform as a South Asian band. And while MTV's (and the band's) intentions were not necessarily to force Funkadesi and the desi youth audience onto one another, it still had the effect of erasing their blackness and interracial identity within the taped segment.

Timothy Brennan suggests that black popular music is the only true *world* genre as it is one of the few forms actually listened to widely around the globe (Brennan 2001). As I showed in Chapter 2, popular discourse on globalization often ignores blackness as an image of globality or includes it only within the unmarked category "American." Similarly, the popular discourse on world music does not always recognize African American forms as music of color, but rather as generalized "Western" pop and rock. While world music discourse tropes Asian music as from "out there," Funkadesi shows that it is actively produced "right here." In reality, while "black" and "world" are figured in opposition to one another, Funkadesi and even the Candy Shop DJs' fare illuminate how they are closely integrated, neither one existing without the other.

The question of black visibility and audibility arises due to a slippage between race and culture in world music (and multicultural) discourse. In Funkadesi, varied African and African American expressions are collapsed into "funk," a generalized referent for blackness. The range of South Asian traditions—popular, folk, and classical—become "Indian" when interpreted through a sono-racial taxonomy. In this instance, not only are forms with very different sounds and social histories conflated but the broader subcontinental influence on the styles is also overlooked (Punjab is, after all, in both India and Pakistan). Even more so, the industry's racial taxonomy does not line up with the cultural history of traditions presented. Despite the African roots of Caribbean and Latin American traditions, they have been classified as Latino or Hispanic in the racial taxonomy of the culture industry, therefore resonating as a separate entity from the group's black material. Funkadesi exposes the difficulty for interracial bands to adequately make themselves legible within inflexible multicultural categories. After all, "funky desis" as a label allows for the coexistence of multiple cultures but only gives name to one racial category. Yet the group forges ahead and tries to create an extra-musical vocabulary that can allow for unity and diversity to exist together. One way in which they have found success is by emphasizing play over discourse—letting the performative power of music speak for itself and construct embodied experiences of hybridity and interracial conversation.

Rehearsing Utopia

Multicultural arts spaces present diversity through racially segmented infrastructures, often leading to racially segregated audiences. In Chicago, these dynamics exacerbate already extant partitions between racial and cultural communities, despite its wide-scale diversity and designation as a "global city." Funkadesi was formed to mitigate these separations through the creation, performance, and consumption of Afro Asian music. Their sono-racial collaborations draw on racialized images—specifically of blackness and Indianness—to create musical expressions of interracial unity-through-difference. The loosening of criteria for racial and cultural authenticity explored in Chapters 1 and 2 forms the foundation for Funkadesi's redefinition of racialized traditions in dialogue. The projects I discussed in previous chapters are based on illuminating cultural similarities between differently racialized forms. Funkadesi is similarly based on similarities founder Rahul Sharma heard between several Indian, African American, and Afro-Caribbean musical styles. But it has also become a space in which broader, irreconcilable racial and cultural forms are embraced and articulated to create Afro Asian music that has its own unique profile distinct from—but still connected to—the traditions that feed into it. They produce music that is more reflective of lived multicultural realities and offer localized insights into urban racial dynamics of post-1965 "browning" among the U.S. populace.

Funkadesi's sono-racial articulation stretches beyond their music due to the public and private spaces they have cultivated for intercultural and interracial engagement. In contrast to racially segregated spatialization between and within Chicago music venues, the group forges temporary spaces that offer opportunities for more substantive interracial engagement than available in the city on a whole. Their work resists discursive and physical separation between "black" and "world" music as enacted in the culture industry, even as they sometimes employ these labels to make their work legible. Finally, they argue for the redefinition of what an audience or community can be, especially showing that they can exist beyond singular racial or ethnic groups. In fact, Funkadesi's work demonstrates that community is not an a priori formation, but rather something that requires intention and work to build and sustain. The Afro Asian sites that result are imperfect, however, and sono-racial articulation is challenged by artists' competing desires, audience's perceptions, and culture industry imperatives.

If, as Dolan suggests, utopias reflect a frustration with current dynamics and the desire for something new (2005, 38), Funkadesi's Afro Asian ventures are a clear critique of the present. And while the group struggles with finding a balance between difference and unification in their music, they create spaces in which these tensions can be worked out among group members, the traditions they merge together, and their surrounding communities. In doing so, they provide tangible spaces in which the diverse population of Chicago can push past its segregated dynamics to explore new racial formations. Functioning as "simultaneously *musicus* and *cantor*, reproducer and prophet," Funkadesi keys us into the racial dynamics of contemporary society while simultaneously speaking against it (Attali 1985, 12). In the small ruptures of utopia that emerge in moments of performance, Funkadesi listeners are able to feel fleeting moments of a better, more integrated United States-to-come and practice how they will live in it.

4

Sonic Identity Politics
Fred Ho's Afro Asian Music Ensemble

"You know karate or kung fu?,"
the small black boy asked me,
his eyes in round amazement, as
I paid the brother for two bean pies.
"This the first time you ever meet
a Chinese?", i asked.
He shook his head affirmatively,
his eyes never leaving me.
"Well, young warrior, it's like
this: all chinks know kung fu like
all niggers can sing and dance. Are
you hip?"
The boy smiled his understanding.

As-salaam Alaikum.

(Ho 1975)

Although whites are elevated within the existing U.S. racial structure, it does not exist solely because of them nor do they perpetuate
it alone. U.S. dominant culture was for a time created by and for white
people. But as the popular culture industry got cooking, nonwhite people
consumed its products and eventually produced them as well. Dominant
culture is like a house built by whites—with the labor of nonwhites—that
we all now inhabit and maintain. The hegemonic success of the system
is evidenced in how deeply entrenched racial and cultural definitions
and stereotypes are in the minds of people of color. Fred Ho's poem demonstrates the awkward Afro Asian encounter that results from a young
black boy's preconceived notions of Asian/Americans fueled by a popular
culture diet of martial arts films. Just as whites, people of color engage
one another through racialized aesthetic tropes. When person-to-person

contact is not an option—or even sometimes when it is—sonic and visual images of Otherness become the mode of interaction. Yet Ho's poem also indicates the potential to shift this dynamic by calling out stereotypes, drawing connections between them, and illuminating how they foster oppression across racial lines.[1]

In the previous chapters, I looked at ways in which sono-racial collaborations are formed through tangible negotiations between people sharing space with one another and a desire to explore interracial affinities. Here, I would like to take a closer look at how racially marked sound functions in Afro Asian settings. I am especially interested in how instrumental sounds and their combination can present sonic stereotypes, as well as strategies that might resist this reception. The perpetuation of racist discourses through sound can come about from the ways in which they are employed, but also because of the previous meanings the sounds carry with them into new settings. The dawn of the twenty-first century requires a renewed focus on how music signifies within a modern world inundated with information. What exactly happened to the music of marginalized people that once threatened revolution when embraced by the culture industry? Was it the music that changed or the structures through which we hear it? This chapter presents Afro Asian musical endeavors motivated by answering these questions through explicit antiracist politics.

These questions are even more pressing for interracial artists because, as we have seen, once engulfed into the sono-racial taxonomy, their boundary-breaking projects are often simplified and conventionalized by what I call "sonic identity politics." Since the 1990s, scholars have detailed the ways in which multiculturalism evolved from a radical practice into a dominant political agenda. As this process unfolded, multiculturalism became a "theoretical paradigm of difference ... obsessed with the construction of identities rather than relations of power and domination, and, in practice, concentrate[d] on the effect of this difference on a (white) norm" (Carby 1992, 12). Scholarly criticism of identity politics indicates the tendency for politicking to be overdetermined by an individual's singular element of disenfranchisement (blackness, queerness, disability, etc.), as well as the increasing focus on inclusion and representation rather than material structural change. Thus, "hegemonic" (liberal and corporate) multiculturalism became a problematic rallying point for people of color because it works against coalition building, ascribes too close a correlation between race and culture, and can present marginalized identities—rather than actions—as automatically radical.

The musical counterpart to identity politics is the assumption that sonic representation of Otherness is equivalent to political engagement or enfranchisement. Sonic identity politics operates as a hegemonic discourse in which singular sounds come to stand in for entire groups of people through fixed and essential representations of race and culture. Artists, presenters, and institutions purvey these sounds with limited historical contextualization and predetermined political functions (e.g., all black music is rebellious). These gestures often originate from an attempt at advocacy, but place harsh limits on what a sound—or the people it represents—can be. Sonic identity politics is, in effect, the multicultural cooptation of cultural nationalism, which works to disconnect rather than keep intact links between music, historical and cultural context, and political efficacy.

In order for Afro Asian music to effectively support the formation of interracial identities and community, representational structures must be redefined in ways that resist these dynamics. This change is made possible not just by combining black and Asian sounds but in shifting how they are represented, severing singular racial attachments, and letting styles more freely influence one another. Chinese American composer and musician Fred Ho was one artist who worked to do just this.[2] Starting in the 1980s, he created what he called "new American multicultural music" in order to challenge well-entrenched sonic colonization. In compositions blending jazz with non-Western forms, he created new grammars for presenting racialized sounds and attempted to resignify their dominant meanings. Following Paul Robeson a half-century later, Ho's music highlights the importance of reviving traditional practices as a strategy for antiracist expression and finding racial and cultural solidarities across these reclamations. The progressive potency of his work lies in the ways in which multiple traditions work together to shift the shared context in which they reside, an intervention into the de-radicalization of hegemonic multiculturalism.[3]

The process of creating and performing Ho's music generated spaces for interracial conversations between him, his multiracial collaborators, and audiences. At the same time, his project was sometimes thwarted because the sounds he employed—the "words" to his grammar—were overwrought with racial and sometimes racist meaning. Like many Afro Asian artists, Ho struggled to have interracial conversations with a multicultural vocabulary. In the process, he often established his own sonic hierarchies that posed certain sounds as inherently radical, replicating the essentialism of the discourses he opposed. Examining his work, it becomes clear that sonic identity politics are alive and well in Afro Asian performance, even as the identities expressed may be new.

Sonic identity politics present a challenge to artists who wish to employ culture toward social change. My goal, however, is not just to diagnose the multicultural problem, but to show the particular mechanisms of cooptation through which it operates. Focusing on instrumental sounds, I will discuss several examples of Ho's musical and theatrical work and detail strategies he used to give fresh meaning to sounds that differed from their existing racial connotations. I will highlight how he actively cultivated a style steeped in antiracist and material politics, disrupted sonic stereotypes to push beyond the multicultural celebration of diversity, and resisted co-optation through perpetual innovation. Because minority artists are in an ongoing tug-of-war with an industry built to conventionalize them, they cannot simply seek representation. Rather, to produce truly politically efficacious work, they must actively work to preempt multicultural strategies of containment through what I call "radical interracialism."[4]

Sonic Identity Politics

It is hard to believe that multiculturalism was once a progressive movement founded in order to bring more attention to people of color and their associated cultures. Despite its roots as a tool to diversify curricula, corporate spaces, government, and the media, multiculturalism is now often criticized for producing the very sociopolitical fissures it was originally meant to address. Many hegemonic multicultural projects stop at the moment of inclusion: official government recognition (liberal), perhaps, or appearance in an advertising campaign or television show (corporate). And in order to manage inclusion, multicultural projects often employ "an idea of culture wherein culture is bounded into authentic zones with pure histories that need to be accorded a grudging dignity by policies of diversity" (Prashad 2001, 61). Thus, instead of growing interracial and intercultural knowledge and camaraderie, hegemonic multiculturalism has maintained or even heightened social divisions.

As the predominant racial system in the United States from the 1990s on, multiculturalism found particular success when paired with neoliberalism (Omi and Winant 1994). Neoliberalism is based on the tenet that an unbridled capitalist market will eventually grow the global economy and result in the erasure of socioeconomic disparities.[5] Multicultural policy operates with the understanding that the representation of racial difference within the market or civic sphere is evidence of more substantive social or political inclusion. In both cases, participation in the economic or representational system is seen as the solution to social ills. Further, since the language of multiculturalism has been co-opted by dominant voices, the "deployment of seemingly antiracist or postracist language" has even been used "to legitimate U.S. global power and the unevenness of capital accumulation," again ignoring the material concerns of people of color (Melamed 2006, 20). Through its alignment with neoliberalism, multiculturalism has shifted from radical to conservative, becoming, in the words of Vijay Prashad, "a principle for the regulation of social life from above" (2001, 40).

The expression of identity as a political tool was an important component of premulticultural movements for social and political uplift in the early and mid-twentieth century. Black activists such as W. E. B. Du Bois and Marcus Garvey both began from a point of highlighting the unique identity-forming experiences of black people even as their political projects diverged dramatically, projects that others continued into the 1950s and 1960s. In the 1960s and 1970s, other racial minorities, women, and queer movements began to center their politics on the definition and expression of nondominant identities (I cover this historical terrain in more detail in Chapter 1). The resurrection of lost cultural elements was viewed as a source of pride and representational power in conjunction with material quests for civic rights, human rights, and enfranchisement. But as multiculturalism was co-opted and identities codified within a limited system, identity politics lost focus on tangible redress of material inequities, perpetuating the extant racial system under the guise of "diversity."[6]

I see three primary ramifications of identity politics in the culture industry. First, images of difference proliferate at the expense of space for antiracist work that addresses, among other things, political-economic disparities. Artists of color are celebrated in festivals, for example, while their communities are neglected in civic spending. Second, racial markers are seen as evidence of cultural difference. Surface representations of diversity are celebrated even though there may be little concrete cultural dialogue hidden behind colorful costumes and performances. New communities are sought out as audiences in order to capitalize on new markets rather than strengthen local sociopolitical resources. Third, traditions that are represented are often culturally decontextualized and dehistoricized in order to fit an unbending mold of authenticity. Living traditions are frozen into simple, repeatable bites for a consuming public. In all, linking visible and audible difference to specific cultural behaviors maintains a racial status quo and system of oppression. Performers who do not ascribe to predominant sono-racial images find themselves at a loss in garnering attention and securing bookings.

Multicultural arts spaces have adopted a "color-blind" mentality in which culture is performed instead of race but, paradoxically, in ways that focus on phenotypic difference as evidence of culture. Performers who highlight racial identity, antiracism, or other strident politics are deemed too controversial for civic festivals or tourist spectacles. Artists of color who eschew politics and operate under a rubric of culture, education, or heritage preservation are foregrounded, infusing performance spaces with exotic sounds and tamed brownness. White performers of music of color experience mixed fates: in some instances, they are embraced more readily than musicians of color; in others, they are seen as less authentic. In many ways, the multicultural treatment of difference is not unusual in the long history of the U.S. culture industry; proponents simply use "culture" rather than "race" as an operative identifier.

I argue that Ho's "new American multicultural music" performs an example of radical interracialism that challenges the representational fallacies of sonic identity politics. *Recentering* the U.S. sono-racial landscape, he shows that representation in assimilationist models means traditions are not allowed to exist on their own terms in ways that are politically functional. *Resignifying* racially marked sounds, he illustrates the ways in which fragmentary inclusion does not address structural concerns. And by *remaking* musical traditions, he reveals the ways in which de-historicizing and de-politicizing musical culture results in feel-good sounds with no substance. Ultimately, his work illuminates the contrast between representing Otherness and true antiracism.

Making Music Antiracist

Ho recognized the futility of assimilation as a source of racial uplift and the inability for people of color to ever fully assimilate in the first place. Born in 1957 to Chinese immigrant parents in Palo Alto, California, he noted at a young age how teachers told his white classmates not to play with him on the playground because of his race (Smith 2013, 192–193). He began to connect his own experiences of racial ostracism to those of blacks when a junior high school teacher had him read *The Autobiography of Malcolm X*, and his subsequent political and musical evolution was greatly shaped by black nationalism. He joined the Nation of Islam for a brief time, even changing his name to Fred 3X. When he moved to New York City in 1981 to pursue a career in music, he gravitated toward stalwart figures of the Black Arts Movement such as Amiri Baraka (with whom he did several panels and performances) and musicians like Archie Shepp and Hamiet Bluiett.

Ho also participated in the West Coast Asian American jazz scene, itself inspired by Chicago's black nationalist–influenced Association for the Advancement of Creative Musicians (see Chapter 1). He worked with several Asian American artists who espoused cultural nationalist and antiracist agendas, such as Jon Jang and Francis Wong. A primary concern of this musical circle—primarily East Asian/American men—was how to articulate politicized Asian American identities through sound, which often led to experimentation with Asian forms and traditional texts. Ho's first encounter with an Asian tradition grew out of his political organizing in Boston's Chinatown, where he helped found the Asian American Resource Workshop shortly after college.[7] There, he learned Chinese traditional music and notation, eventually forming a folk singing group made up primarily of immigrant workers. As he began to participate in the West Coast Asian American jazz scene, Ho drew on this experience and researched uniquely Asian *American* forms to add to the mix. Much of his music focused on the expression of marginalized identities as a tool toward progressive political mobilization. He furthered this work in non-musical forums, including mobilization for leftist political campaigns, community-based activism, ecological causes, and writing numerous books and articles on arts and politics.[8]

As I discussed in Chapter 1, a common thread running through the Afro Asian/Third World movements that inspired Ho is the recovery and embrace of non-Western, nonwhite, and nondominant culture as central to combating imperialism. As jazz drummer Max Roach claims, "Culture is the final nail in the casket of exploitation. After you bring the army in and you conquer a place, it's too expensive to hold that with an army. So the next step would be to take the culture of the oppressors and impose that on to the mentality of the people who've been conquered physically" (1980, 16). Cultural reclamation can be a powerful political move, but its efficacy will be impacted by how and into what spaces nondominant culture is recouped. David Theo Goldberg suggests: "Implicitly underlying the theoretical politics of identity . . . stands the standard of integration, of monovalent center and plural peripheries, even as identity formations and their attendant theoretical debates have helped to clear a space in which incorporative political movements could emerge more clearly" (1994, 13). By operating with a politic of inclusion, people and communities of color strive to be a part of the prevalent racial system and, in so doing, fit themselves into historically racist structures rather than working to dismantle them. Sonic identity politics operate in the same way, as artists work within the racial taxonomy of the industry and strive to fit stereotypically expected sounds. Even in scenarios in which artists cross sono-racial boundaries—such as minstrel performers or Elvis—these transgressions are made pointedly and enforce the entire system through essentialist discourse. Despite a proposed anti-establishment pretext, these acts retain a white/Western musical center and limit or heavily mark the space available to music and musicians of color.

In his music, Ho contests this cultural domination by employing nondominant forms in representational structures that shift the locations of the margins and center. His work merges Black Arts Movement–inspired jazz; Chinese, Japanese, Korean, and Filipino folk and classical styles such as Beijing opera, *p'ansori*, and *kulintang*; West African drumming; and Asian American immigrant traditions such as Cantonese opera and wood-fish head chants.[9] These forms appear in his repertoire as entire songs, melodies or rhythms, instrumentation, and lyrics in non-English languages. His Afro Asian Music Ensemble's (AAME's) *The Underground Railroad to My Heart* (1994), for example, includes arrangements of the Filipino folksong "An Bayan Ko (For My Country)," Tibetan "Kang Ding Love Song," and Chinese "Lan Hua Hua (Blue Flower)." The album also includes "Bambaya," based on a talking drum piece of the West African Dagomba people, and "Joys and Solos," an original piece that features the *sona*, bass, and drum kit in a free jazz context.[10]

Ho's cultural canon includes traditions not typically given space in dominant U.S. and Western society. Nonwhite and non-Western traditions predominate and thus form the cultural default in his pieces. But the diversity of these forms is quite unusual even by multicultural standards; in fact, it is rare to find *kulintang* or Tibetan music, for example, in typical multicultural events catering to a mixed audience. Further, the African, Asian, and diasporic forms are multiple in their appearance: rather than a monolithic "Asia" or "Africa"—or "Asian" and "black"—Ho's work presents an audio portrait of the multiplicity within these broader designations. And a major goal of his work is to place these traditions in musical conversation. One ensemble Ho formed for this kind of interaction is the Monkey Orchestra, a group that started in 1989 to play the score for a staged martial arts saga, *Journey Beyond the West: The New Adventures of Monkey*. The ensemble featured eleven players from all over the world and the music incorporated jazz, Chinese folk, and Chinese classical instruments and musical material. The orchestra's roster included crossovers from Ho's AAME, additional jazz horn players, and Chinese instrumentalists playing *pipa*, *erhu*, and *sona*.[11] Rather than uncovering innate connections between musical traditions—as in some of the other Afro Asian projects I have explored—Ho says he believed the Monkey Orchestra established a dialogue between traditions that do not have inherent similarities.

A major project of original (radical) multiculturalists was to work against cultural homogeneity—specifically Eurocentrism—through the expansion of canons, media, and curricula (Prashad 2001, 63; Chicago Cultural Studies Group 1994, 114). But, as Peter McLaren argues, "Conservative or corporate multiculturalism refuses to treat whiteness as a form of ethnicity and in doing so posits whiteness as an invisible norm by which other ethnicities are judged" (1994, 49). As shown in Figure 4.1, multicultural policy requires nondominant people and culture to assimilate toward a dominant white center and fit into an enduring core–periphery structure. Ho's radical interracialism, however, does not turn marginalized traditions toward a white/Western standard. Bringing together world traditions, his work de-centers the Western musical canon, both classical and popular. Non-Western traditions form the core, providing a foundation and new point of reference. His *A Chinaman's Chance*, for example, is the first U.S. opera ever written and performed in Mandarin (also Cantonese

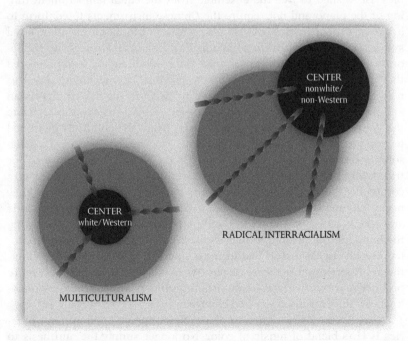

Figure 4.1. Multiculturalism versus radical interracialism. Graphic by Domini Dragoone.

and English), displacing German, Italian, English, and other European languages as the lingua franca of the genre. Important is that this piece is not Ho's reproduction of a Chinese opera form; the story and aesthetic are of the United States and highlight the lives of lesser-represented citizens.

Ho's predilection for establishing new aesthetic standards is a clear link to Black Arts Movement (BAM) politics. LeRoi Jones (Amiri Baraka) expresses this central conceit, saying, "Because the majority of jazz critics are white middle-brows, most jazz criticism tends to enforce white middle-brow standards of excellence as criteria for performance of a music that in its most profound manifestations is completely antithetical to such standards; in fact, quite often is in direct reaction against them" (1967, 15–16). Like the BAM New Black Aesthetic, Ho's new American multicultural music proposes a different set of musical touchstones. In addition to the Monkey Orchestra, he formed several other groups in order to experiment with how different combinations of instruments and traditions can create new sono-racial systems, including the Asian American Art Ensemble (to explore pan-Asian expressions), the Brooklyn Sax Quartet (cofounded with David Bindman as an experimental blend of saxophones), and the AAME (combining elements and players from the other projects).[12]

What these ensembles share is a space in which whiteness no longer functions as the aesthetic mold into which nonwhite traditions must squeeze. In the Monkey Orchestra, for example, Ho pointedly did not include a piano, which is a standard element of contemporary jazz ensembles. He wished to free the ensemble from the equal temperament tuning of the piano and not require the Chinese instruments to conform to a Western tonal framework. He also wrote music based on other tonal systems—particularly from the Middle East—and had an extensive collaborative relationship with saxophonist Hafez Modirzadeh, who pioneered the "chromodal" system of saxophone playing. This technique involves new fingerings that allow a musician to perform pitches from Persian and Arabic scales on the saxophone, despite its construction to replicate the Western diatonic tonality. Ho similarly bends the culturally ingrained techniques of other Western instruments, such as writing a percussion solo for drum kit and Chinese percussion in "No Home to Return To" or translating polyrhythmic Ewe drum parts into an arrangement for jazz combo in "Gadzo." Key to Ho's work is that he has not created one new norm, but multiple environments in which the center constantly shifts and adapts based on the project and players involved, further contesting the multicultural presumption of "a fixed 'we' or 'us' at an unshifting center" (Goldberg 1994, 16). Instituting a singular center in a radical interracial project could replicate disparities of center and periphery. A more productive corrective is to create structures that provide variety and ongoing possibility for discovery and change.

Aiding in the deconstruction of simple dominant-subdominant binaries is Ho's blend of music of color. No longer simply the antithesis to whiteness, African American music is instead situated alongside a host of world traditions that exist not only in response to oppression but also to express strength, pride, and creativity and promote community. In addition, African forms are presented as living traditions with their own unique histories, not just the precursors to African American styles. And bringing Asian and Asian American music to the center of his repertoire proclaims it as an important component of U.S. American culture with its own radical history. As I discussed in Chapter 1, "Asian" music and racial identity are often depicted as romantic and apolitical in dominant discourse. Ho, however, frames these forms as political within the racial landscape of the United States, through their nondominant aesthetics, precolonial origins, or advent in the context of marginalization (especially new Asian American styles). Also, unlike in many black–Asian musical encounters, jazz is not merely a vehicle for Asian American content in Ho's work: both sides of the Afro Asian equation are active partners in antiracist conversation and Ho explicitly invokes what he sees as jazz's historic radical race politics, which I will discuss to a greater degree later on. Whiteness—represented in the European classical and U.S. popular canon—is placed to the side of this conversation as blackness and Asianness speak directly to each other.

Ho is a consummate composer, but his ability to successfully bring so many styles into dialogue is due to the expertise of his longtime collaborators, especially the members of the AAME. Many studies of Ho focus on his music as a direct expression of his biography, especially his cultural heritage as Chinese American.[13] His work is more complicated than this single cultural position, however, and the artists with whom he collaborates greatly shape his product. The group's personnel have shifted over time, but the members during the bulk of my fieldwork were David Bindman (white, tenor saxophone); Wes Brown (black, bass); royal hartigan (white, percussion); Masaru Koga (Japanese American, alto saxophone); and Art Hirahara (Japanese American, piano).[14]

Bindman and hartigan both grew up in the Northeast and worked with several African American jazz musicians while still in high school, including, in Bindman's case, Bill Dixon and Milford Graves. Bindman, hartigan, and Brown met one another when they were music students at Wesleyan University. Wesleyan features an extensive jazz studies curriculum as well as a separate ethnomusicology and world music performance program. The trio was thus able to receive jazz training from Bill Lowe, Bill Barron, and Ed Blackwell alongside West African percussion and rhythm from Abraham Adzenyah and Freeman Donkor. hartigan eventually wrote his dissertation on cross-cultural rhythmic practices.[15]

Koga and Hirahara are younger than the others but had similar musical training. Koga grew up moving between countries including Japan, West Germany, and the United States, eventually studying music at San José State University (SJSU). Much like Wesleyan, SJSU is known for its strong world music performance curriculum and Koga took advantage of this in addition to his jazz studies. He also learned various percussion traditions, studying with hartigan (who guest-taught there). Currently performing and teaching saxophone in the Bay Area, Koga also plays percussion with an Asian American samba group, SambAsia, thanks to his intercultural training. Hirahara studied piano performance and composition at Oberlin and the California Institute of the Arts and worked in the Bay Area until moving to New York City in the late 1990s. Both Hirahara and Koga began their professional lives amidst the West Coast Asian American jazz scene and play in Asian Crisis, an ensemble dedicated to exploring pan-Asian musical dialogue and consciousness, often featuring pieces that denounce anti-Asian violence and racism.[16]

The AAME biographies reveal two complementary points: lives that have been lived interracially and the presence of intercultural musical knowledge on an individual level. The players display a politics of de-centering white/Western formations similar to Ho's, having sought out non-Western practices and musical conversation with people of different heritages and perspectives. This aesthetic mixture is not, however, based on essential racial or ethnic ties, but rather a common desire to cultivate marginalized traditions. Like the Funkadesi members detailed in the the last chapter, AAME members' training and interests reject industry-derived categories that relegate jazz and world music to separate production tracts, revealing through embodied experience the ability for these forms to reside together in one ensemble or one person. And because multivalence is the norm in the group, they reject a simplified identity politics that links their singular heritage to the sounds they produce. At the same time, they do represent homogeneity in the realm of gender. As I will discuss later, the lack of space for nonmale voices within AAME projects limits the progressive reach of some of their musical and political goals.

The AAME's push on limited notions of cultural or racial identification is keenly expressed in their concert attire, what Ho called "Afro Asian formal." Performing at the Brooklyn Academy of Music Café in 2005, for example, Ho and Bindman wore dress slacks and shirts with vests made of shimmery Chinese fabric, Hirahara a hand-me-down *hambok* (Korean formal shirt) given to him by Ho the day before, Brown and hartigan multicolored *dashikis*. The musicians wore clothes that represent the diversity of the musical cultures they perform, but do not necessarily correlate to their own backgrounds or the forms they personally play. In essence, members represent a collective Afro Asian identity rather than "lean[ing] on narrow nationalist frameworks" (Prashad 2001, 64). The group contests racist assumptions that a person who looks or dresses a particular way will possess a certain cultural skill, make a certain sound, or have market value because of their performed heritage.

Ho counters sonic identity politics by fostering tangible spaces for expression that do not conform to dominant images, which can also lead to broader discourse that contests racial authenticity and stereotypes. Still, there are limitations to the championing of Third World traditions in his work, especially as he imposes a new set of values in place of those he opposes. First, some of the traditions he employs actually reflect elite institutions, cultural hierarchies, and imperialist histories of their own. The *erhu*, for example, was a Chinese folk instrument that was embraced

Figure 4.2. Fred Ho sporting "Afro Asian formalwear." Photograph by Joshua Bright. Courtesy of the photographer.

in the early twentieth century as a classical instrument and its practice is now codified in conservatory training. Likewise, jazz has variously been attached to dominant agendas in its evolution in relation to U.S. politics (I will return to this point). And Japanese popular culture—a key element in Ho's mix—has long been a colonial presence in a number of Asian countries. An all-encompassing embrace of the Third World can miss some of these subtleties, and granting traditions political value simply because they stand in contrast to Western traditions can promote the replication of colonial binaries.

Further, while Ho and other AAME members did study and perform Western classical music at some point in their lives, they eventually eschewed it and often speak about Western popular music with condescension. This complete dismissal of all white/Western styles can essentialize Afro Asian into a solely oppositional stance. The notion of Afro Asian culture has the potential to disrupt simplistic cultural binaries by breaking down the monolithic "subaltern." But investing this union with inherent radicalism only allows it to function as a singular, nondominant block. Despite their politics, Ho and his collaborators were all educated in elite Western institutions. The ways in which these musicians have moved within a variety of musical worlds—rather than a flat-out rejection of the First World—actually demonstrates a more complex lived experience. Ho's desire to counter dominant patterns had him standing at a distance from his surroundings. Wanting to break from the mold of assimilation and Anglification, he was both of the West and apart from it. Despite his racial and ethnic background, his longing for a sense of history and culture performed an "American" identity long built on such a search. So it is no surprise that his valuation of Afro Asian traditions also leaned toward the romantic.

In the fall of 2008, Ho was an artist-in-residence at the University of Wisconsin-Madison, hosted by the University Arts Institute's Interdisciplinary Arts Residency Program. He taught a self-designed course, "Revolutionary Afro Asian Spoken Word and Performance," that culminated with a presentation—*Revolutionary Earth Music: People and the Planet Before Profit!*—featuring his students and the AAME. Performed before an audience of several hundred, the show was an unfolding of intergenerational Afro Asian sharing and collaboration. The performance that produced the most buzz of the evening was "The Dance of Crane/I am Korean" by Youn Jung Kim, a theater student from South Korea. This piece was a new *p'ansori* written and performed by Kim and accompanied by hartigan on the *buk*, a traditional Korean drum. Initially, Kim was going to perform her piece in English with a contemporary spoken-word delivery, but Ho challenged her to delve into her heritage and do something that resonated more with her Korean identity. Kim rose to the challenge and delivered a performance that kept the audience enraptured. Most amazing about this feat was that Kim had never before studied or performed *p'ansori* and very quickly absorbed the form by listening to recordings. Ho was ecstatic about the performance, saying he had been waiting his whole life to find someone in the United States who could create new *p'ansori*.

Kim's ability to produce such a powerful piece is a testament to Ho's teaching. She describes the class as "the most precious experience and opportunity in my life" and says, "from this class, I found the reason to seek my ethnic background, learn my cultural background." But Kim's transformation also highlights the ways in which Ho codified what constitutes a radical aesthetic. He asserted his belief in the greater value of Third World identity, experience, or language onto Kim and, while she did delve into her cultural background in more depth, it was in a way that reproduced his cultural nationalist model. Who is to say that the choice of a different aesthetic—from a different Afro Asian culture or a dominant one—could not produce a personal transformation in her? This blind reliance on the Korean form perpetuates a discourse of sonic identity politics even though in service of personal and political change. In seeking to preserve his version of radicalism, Ho effectively confined the aesthetic elements that could represent these politics.

Yet simultaneously, the Kim/hartigan duet shows the progressive potential of Afro Asian exchanges. It would have been impossible for Kim to do this performance without hartigan's presence. *P'ansori* requires the interchange between vocalist and drummer and, thanks to hartigan's previous study of Korean percussion, he was able to provide the support Kim needed to fully perform her piece. Through the combination of hartigan's cross-cultural training and a collective desire to innovate traditional culture, the audience was treated to a work that connected to specific cultural roots but in a non-essentialized way.

Ho created music that places Afro Asian cultures at the center and argued that players could legitimately take part based on their identity, ability, or experience. Foregrounding non-Western and nonwhite traditions, he addressed power differentials left unchanged by previous multicultural projects and produced new criterion for cultural value in U.S.-based arts spaces. Unlike hegemonic multiculturalism, he did not ignore race in the service of culture. Rather, he made both distinct and valuable, important because he distributed his music within a signifying system built on sono-racial categories. Cultural recentering only goes part of the distance toward radical interracialism, however, because recentered sounds carry with them dominantly defined connotations. While Ho used what he considered to be radical forms in his work, it is specifically through the ways in which he used them that we can recognize additional progressive strategies.

Resisting Sonic Stereotypes

In proposing a new sound for U.S. American music, Ho said he was "looking for anything that is so foreign and impulsive [repulsive?] to the western mind." But in order to locate this aesthetic–political position, he also relied on the marking of sonic difference. He employed racially codified sounds to indicate cultural groups, selecting particular sounds based on the piece's programmatic content. One example is "No Home to Return To," in which Chinese opera percussion sonorities indicate the heritage of the piece's subjects. Another example is *All Power to the People! The Black Panther Suite* (2003), in which a wah-wah heavy funk guitar joins the AAME as an expression of the black urban environment of the Black Panther Party. Multiculturalism relies on the legibility of difference between margin and center although, purportedly, to different ends. Therefore, it is the story told about this relationship that can express a particular political agenda. Especially since Ho's performance of marginalized culture at times took place within dominant venues such as the Guggenheim, Carnegie Hall, and the Brooklyn Academy of Music, the question becomes: How can this story serve a transgressive function and what does it take to decipher what that is?

The multicultural margin-to-center imperative leads to the decontextualization and fragmentation of music of color. "Ethnic groups are reduced to 'add-ons' to the dominant culture" and are invested with synecdochic notions of authenticity that highlight their Otherness and difference (McLaren 1994, 49). In sonic identity politics, this dynamic is perpetuated through the limited incorporation of racialized sounds into the dominant palette. Instrument timbres or melodic fragments are painted onto the surface of a mainstream musical bed that is more familiar to dominant listeners. The problem with this dynamic—beyond the simplification of music of color—is that these snippets are then invested with meanings derived from the dominant culture and prevented from speaking on their own. They come to operate as sonic stereotypes even when possessing some aspect of cultural verity.

I would like to propose here the strategies one might use to draw critical distinction between music that serves an agenda of sonic identity politics versus radical interracialism using Ho's stage production *Deadly She-Wolf Assassin at Armageddon!* as an example. In this piece, Ho resignifies nondominant instrumental sounds not only through their inclusion in the score but also by experimenting with novel ways of contextualizing them. Giving new voice to these sounds in combination, Ho intercedes in stereotypical structures that limit the effectiveness for nondominant sounds to challenge listeners' expectations.

She-Wolf is a martial arts epic loosely based on *Lone Wolf and Cub*, a popular Japanese *manga*, television, and film series from the 1970s. The original follows the journey of a rogue samurai and his toddler son as they travel feudal Japan working as assassins-for-hire. Ho and playwright Ruth Margraff's piece tells a newly created story of the Lone Wolf's forgotten daughter, stolen at birth by a rival clan and trained as the ultimate weapon to destroy him. *She-Wolf* updates and builds on the *Lone Wolf* narrative, examining the concept of "the traitor" and its contemporary ramifications in the era of globalization. Ho and Margraff unabashedly trade in camp and spectacle over a simple narrative framework.[17]

The 2006 production I discuss featured a cast of ten, a mix of actors, dancers, and martial artists, many of whom had training in two or more of these areas. The dialogue was spoken entirely by a Narrator who changed her voice to personify the various characters. The rest of the cast employed stylized pantomimic gestures that coordinated with the Narrator's lines. The spoken text served as a guide through the narrative, but the plot was primarily propelled through martial arts sequences that made up a majority of the stage time. All of the action unfolded over a spare set—a black box with several cloth banners hanging along the back—with props that mostly consisted of the performers' stage weapons. Brightly colored costumes made the actors stand out against the setting, complemented by sharply focused lighting.

Music is the driving force of *She-Wolf*, underscoring the spoken narration and moving to the fore during beautifully staged fight sequences. As in Ho's broader work, the score draws from a canon centered on Third World traditions. The instrumentation of the score is keyboard, drums, bass, alto saxophone, *shakuhachi, fue,* baritone saxophone, and 21-string bass *koto,* and the music combines the style of Japanese music theater with funk grooves and free improvisation.[18] Ho also employs Japanese and jazz melodic motifs: a descending three-note line in traditional Japanese *iwato* mode and ascending pattern built on a blues/pentatonic scale (Ho 2006a). The music pays homage to the original *Lone Wolf and Cub* film scores that blend Western orchestral film scoring, Japanese instruments such as *taiko* and *shakuhachi*, and jazz/funk-influenced guitar and synthesizer riffs.

At first glance, *She-Wolf* appears to be a typical Orientalist fantasy. The piece is set in Japan at the end of the Tokugawa period (mid-nineteenth

Figure 4.3. She-Wolf's Sister (Mika Saburi), the Narrator (Marina Celander), and She-Wolf (Ai Ikeka) in *Deadly She-Wolf Assassin at Armageddon!*, Mandell Theater, Drexel University, Philadelphia, 2006. Photograph by Jordan Rockford. Courtesy of the photographer.

century) at the turn from feudalism to modern capitalism. According to Ho's program notes, the era heralds "the ominous arrival and contact with The West," resulting in "traditional values becom[ing] diluted, distorted, corrupted, perverted and inverted" (2006a). This setting is one that presents a foreign and temporally distant Japan, hardly seeming pertinent to contemporary politics. The Orientalism is enhanced by stage elements—most notably costumes—that display the requisite embroidered fabrics, fans, and even beard and eye-patch of the Fu Manchu-like Iyagu (modeled on *Othello*'s Iago). The show also hinges on an exotic femme fatale lead character who serves to further a feminized representation of the East. Adding to the spectacle is the foregrounding of martial arts and the iconic yet often stereotyped samurai.

The choice of the *koto* and the Japanese flutes in the score draws a sono-racial connection between these instruments, their sounds, and the cultural setting of the story. The show opens with a flourish in which the Japanese instruments and drum kit are predominant. This ornament repeats several times, accelerating until indistinguishable from one another, similar to a common traditional Japanese rhythmic motif. Thus, before we hear any "jazz" or see something other than the Lone Wolf's son playing with a red ball, the resonant plucking of the *koto* and airy timbre of the flute become an aural synecdoche for a feminine "Japan."

In my field research in 2006, audiences responded to the Japanese sonorities as foreign or unusual. At a performance of selections from

Figure 4.4. She-Wolf (Ai Ikeka) and Iyagu (Takumi Bando) in *Deadly She-Wolf Assassin at Armageddon!*, Mandell Theater, Drexel University, Philadelphia, 2006. Photograph by Jordan Rockford. Courtesy of the photographer.

the score at the Brooklyn Academy of Music's BAM Café, the first time *koto* player Yumi Kurosawa played, there was much shifting around as the primarily white audience tried to catch a glimpse of what instrument was producing the sound. After the concert, an older white woman approached Kurosawa and told her how much the *koto* "added" to the music. In both instances, it is clear that the instrument produced a sound that stood out from the rest of the ensemble and in a way that preserved its foreign connotations for a non-Japanese, or non-Japan-knowledgeable, audience. It is also notable that Kurosawa stood out as the only female player in the band, further mapping *koto*, femininity, and Asianness onto one another.

Unlike a multicultural performance, however, the goal of *She-Wolf* is not the simple parading of Asian difference within the theater. Ho and Margraff employ the setting of the original stories as an allegory of the post-9/11 world and to critique the gender politics of the samurai film genre. While the Rogue's embrace of "the cold-blooded capitalist way of 'professional for hire'" seems counter to Ho's socialist leanings, his liner notes contend that the feudal aristocracy stands for the gilded class of the contemporary West and the Rogue and his son are revolutionary figures "disgraced [by the ruling class] and who in turn discard social position and proprieties" (2006a). Three super-warriors hired by the Shogun to take down the Rogue form a triumvirate exposing the fatal flaws of the capitalist military-industrial complex and are all, in turn, defeated by the Rogue: Bok Mei Lotus, a Chinese sell-out to the Western economy and mentality; Colonel Ulysses Sam Armageddon (i.e., USA), the Western super-warrior debonair in his knack for exterminating people of color; and Qaseem the Killing Machine, a black, transnational figure embodying both Islamic fundamentalist blowback and "race traitor" blacks, a character "who once profited from the slave trade of his people" (Ho 2006a).

Despite the creators' thematic ideas and desire to speak to local concerns, the Japanese sounds that accompany the story are marked within the existing sono-racial taxonomy as foreign. Ho spoke to this in an email:

> *koto* is a problematic instrument for complex scores as it is a non-diatonic instrument; to play it diatonically requires difficult if not impossible fret [bridge] reordering; therefore its intrinsic character as a mostly modal instrument offers very difficult challenges, likewise the *sona* which has great limitations with diatonic music.... The orientalism is almost BOUND by the character and limitations of the instruments which are modal in nature and not diatonic. To recontextualize them means a major challenge given their physical sonic character.

While there are many examples of the *koto* being used in diatonic contexts, Ho accurately reveals the ways in which physical characteristics of instruments must be altered to "fit" into non-native cultural contexts. The tonality—and I would add timbre—of instruments are the substance of sono-racialization and are difficult to escape. The very features some listeners may hear as evidence of the exotic are ingrained in construction and formal features. The *koto* is the *koto* because of its particular timbre and tunings, and the sounds it produces hold a variety of meanings for listeners depending on their racial, cultural, national, and musical backgrounds.

Sono-racial meaning only exists within a system of reception. When sounds are used as synecdochic representations of people or cultures in dominant Western culture, it is done so with a particular listener in mind; namely, a white one. Snippets of cultural material are not employed to make meaning for the people whom they represent, but rather to represent them to a separate audience. People of color have been historically excluded from this intended audience, but they have and continue to make up a significant portion of the mainstream market. On occasion, it is true that a white creator will attempt to connect to a population of color through ignorance and stereotype, but as studies of minstrelsy have explained, these performances are typically more about self-definition.[19] In cross-minority situations, a creator might not imagine a white audience but still employ the same types of images since they are a part of the representational system for all. So, if a person of color employs a stereotype of another, they are giving energy to a racist taxonomy that marginalizes nonwhite people. But moving too far away from these racial expectations can mean lack of legibility and thus no representation at all.

The racialization of sound in the U.S. cultural economy is not just the attachment of a label; it is a process of being enfolded into an entire sono-racial complex over which the dominant culture holds significant control over representation. Thus, when the center embraces the margins, it determines how they are presented. The racial meanings of sounds repeatedly reinforced by marketing and other industry framing are so ensconced within the popular imaginary that many listeners in the U.S. cultural milieu are unable to tell stereotype from cultural reality. Yet the music of *She-Wolf* is a specific nod to the aesthetic of the original series. So in what ways must the music operate in order to oppose an Orientalist reading in the United States?[20] How exactly might the presence of non-Western musical traditions in Ho's music differ from white/Western-initiated world music "fusions," in which ethnic sounds are foregrounded for their exotic purposes but with little substance?

First, the *She-Wolf* score resists sonic identity politics in that the Japanese instruments do not "sit on top" of the jazz score, but are closely woven into it alongside the other instruments. An Orientalist use of *koto* might have the instrument play a melody while the other instruments provide rhythmic and harmonic support, highlighting its timbral difference.[21] In *She-Wolf*, the Japanese instruments are integrated into the ensemble, shifting between the foreground and background like the others. For example, the listener's sono-racial expectations from the score's opening *koto* and flute flourish are soon thwarted when, in a pause, the baritone saxophone intones an ascending fourth and is then joined by keyboard, *koto*, and percussion. As the first fight unfolds, the ensemble launches into a heavily jazz-influenced vamp while the *fue* player takes up the alto saxophone for the remainder of the scene.

Second, while the Japanese instruments are employed to signal geography, they are not only linked to Japanese characters or Asian performers. This point becomes highlighted in a fight sequence between the Rogue and Colonel USA. In this moment of American ego and prowess, Ho places the *koto* central in the ensemble. Supporting a white character played by a white male actor with this instrument severs the sono-racial link. This serves dramaturgically as well: the *koto* becomes almost an echo inside USA's mind, a memory of the millions he has slaughtered. Ho conceived of the *koto* as supporting USA and some of the other characters not because of its acoustic exoticness, but because it could stand in for electric guitar, in the case of USA, and Chinese timbres for Bok Mei Lotus. He did not, however, feel that the *koto* fit for Qaseem, believing an *oud* would be more appropriate and because the Arabic mode he chose for the theme required too difficult bridge movements for the *koto*.

The Qaseem choice reveals the ways in which Ho is still tied to *instrument*–culture determinism even as this is tempered by his openness to the *koto* representing other cultures beyond Japanese. Further, despite his desire, the sono-racial connotations of the *koto* trump its ability to fully signify as electric guitar, meaning it simply reads as a *koto* supporting a white character and actor. While there are limits in sono-racial signification, technical choices can support the process of resignification. For example, the amplified *koto* signal could have been run through an effects pedal, the distortion disrupting its timbral properties.

Third, Ho's use of *koto* and *fue* suggests that there is more than one way to be sonically Asian. McLaren suggests that in left-liberal multi-culturalism's embrace of cultural difference, "it is often that there exists an authentic 'female' or 'African-American' or 'Latino' experience or way of being-in-the-world, rather than historically or politically contingent" (McLaren 1994, 52). In *She-Wolf*, however, the *koto* has a range of sonic positions. Kurosawa, for example, was called upon to improvise in several sections, a technique not central in traditional *koto* repertoire, especially not in a jazz aesthetic.

But is the range afforded the Japanese instruments also reflected in the presence of jazz? While the *koto* and *fue* are well integrated into the ensemble, sono-racial assumptions and Ho's own musical foundation relegate jazz to the default position. In this sense, the African American music is unmarked and could be taken as a generalized jazz base for the Japanese sounds. While the ensemble still performs their particular brand of free jazz, in the presence of the Japanese sounds and with little other context, this tradition does not come to the fore in the same way the Asian sounds do. For many U.S. audiences, Japanese sounds are a foreign addition and jazz the familiar domestic sound they are accustomed to. What mitigates this dynamic is the presence of a majority of nonwhite bodies among the cast. Ho employs people of color to create a space in which the "mainstream" cannot be read as white.

Unlike some of his other productions, however, the *She-Wolf* casting is a bit more conservative. In past shows, the performing ensemble had greater racial and ethnic diversity and roles were often cast with actors who did not "match" the character's racial/cultural background. In *Journey Beyond the West*, one role was even tag-teamed by multiple performers varied in race/ethnicity, gender, and body type. The *She-Wolf* cast was mixed—six of the ten cast members were Japanese, two Asian American, one black, and one white—yet no roles were cross-racially cast. The Japanese and Asian American actors played the Japanese characters, the white actor played Colonel USA, and the black performer Qaseem. This casting, in effect, reflected body–culture determinism by, for example, placing Asian bodies—even non-Japanese ones—into those roles. These casting choices worked against some of the progressive strides made by the score.

At the same time, the actors' bodies were employed to different political ends beyond mere expression of identity. Allowing for this racial essentialism in casting made Ho and Margraff's overarching political message more legible. It also meant that the one black actor was placed in a drama-turgically powerful position. While a number of the other characters are shown as weak and provincial, Qaseem is depicted as cosmopolitan and on more equal physical and intellectual footing with the Rogue. Some of the actors did move in and out of multiple roles as well. The actors play-ing Colonel USA and Qaseem appeared in other moments of the show as ensemble ninja and samurai alongside Asian actors. Thus, these two were not solely constricted to their racially determined lead parts. Further, all of the characters were voiced through the female, mixed Asian/white body of the Narrator. Much like in the solo performance work of Anna Deavere Smith or Sarah Jones, the Narrator served as a common ground for the expression of multiple identities and conflicting viewpoints. Zooming out to look at the entirety of She-Wolf's brown cast, we see that whiteness is made to fit into this world rather than function as the norm. Colonel USA's white privilege and historical specificity are highlighted and marked in the same way as the other super-warriors. And jazz is not the "American" sound attributed solely to him but for everyone to make use of.

Martial arts set the standard for movement in the production, a departure from the primacy of modern dance, ballet, and realism-based acting on U.S. stages. Choreographer Tsuyoshi Kaseda combined Japanese sword techniques, Chinese martial arts such as *wushu* (his specialty), and even elements of *capoeira* into She-Wolf's staging. The use of martial arts is apropos to the *Lone Wolf* stories, but also an important movement vocabulary Ho incorporated into previous stage works such as *Journey Beyond the West* and *All Power to the People! The Black Panther Suite*. For Ho, martial arts film consumption and training in the United States are not a mere Orientalist fascination but a space for Afro Asian community building.[22] The employment of martial arts in She-Wolf was also influenced by contemporary use of these forms in popular media. In one moment, for example, the Rogue fights three opponents and their movement shifts from real time, to slow motion, and back to full speed at a key moment. This bit of staging is a theatricalization of the "bullet time" effect employed extensively in the trilogy of *Matrix* films and indicates the wide-ranging palette Kaseda employed to dramatize the story.

The presence of female performers in a martial arts show based on physical strength is an important move. Of the cast, four were women: Ai Ikeka (She-Wolf), Mika Saburi (She-Wolf's sister and ninja/samurai), Takemi Kitamura (the Boy and ninja/samurai), and Marina Celander as the Narrator (a nonfighting role). In fight sequences, the female performers were incorporated with the males and, by the end, all of the adult male characters were killed off, with only the She-Wolf and Boy still standing. This choice is another critique of the original stories: while the narrative of the *Lone Wolf and Cub* stories deals with the Rogue avenging his wife's death, the films themselves are full of misogynist imagery much in the vein of Blaxploitation films of the same era. As I have discussed elsewhere, Ho and Margraff make several gestures that critique these dynamics in the original series (Roberts 2013). What is important to note here is that She-Wolf incorporates female performers into nontraditional roles and features the voice of a female playwright even as the show's discursive politics retain some normative intersections of race and gender.

How exactly can one tell the difference between radical interracialism and sonic identity politics—Orientalism and primitivism from Afro Asian? If a progressive reading of She-Wolf depends on the viewer's background knowledge and degree of analysis, is it even possible to label a performance one or the other? The images that will fan the flames of Orientalist desire in one audience member are the very ones that might connect with someone of that culture or with greater understanding of their meaning. This is particularly complicated when dealing with aesthetics that are meant to be pleasurable in their original cultural context—fans, lanterns, or *koto*, for example. Is it not valid for a non-Asian viewer to appreciate them? How can we know through what lens—racist or otherwise—an audience member is experiencing a performance? If we cannot ascertain an artist's cultural or personal identity merely from their racial status, it follows that we also cannot make similar assumptions about audience members.

Perhaps the creator's background or intentions provide the necessary information as to the political drive of a piece. But, in the case of *She-Wolf*, what even gives Ho or the others cultural ownership of the material? The director and several performers are Japanese, but neither Ho nor Margraff is. Why was Ho's use of these forms not Orientalist? In some cases, Ho had no personal connection to the people or cultures he used, drawing them into his projects but not necessarily forging broader or bi-directional conversation. The pan-ethnic coalitions formed in recent Asian American history do not exist on a widescale in Asian countries.[23] What gave Ho the right to Japanese traditions and say over how they are reformulated within his pieces? Ho responded to these types of questions by positioning himself as connecting to the political and emotional intent of the traditions, rather than a cultural essence. But his voice and interpretation of them still stand in for those of insiders. Despite Ho's anti-imperialist goals, it was his privileged position in the West that allowed him access to myriad styles and the power to render them at will.

Ho's reliance on musics of color, especially in dominant cultural spaces, also opened up the possibility for misinterpretation. Many reviews of his work highlighted his or the music's Asianness with titles such as "An East-West Meeting of the Minds," "Putting the Ming in Mingus," "Horn Dynasty: The Varying Sounds of Asian American Jazz," and "It's a Real Kick: Composer Fred Ho Uses Martial Arts to Jab at Other Art Forms."[24] These statements paint Ho and his work as Other to the United States, and simplify and conflate vastly different traditions into a singular performed Orient. Further, these critics draw links between Ho's Asian visage, assumed cultural heritage, and the sounds of his ensemble despite the fact that he only came to knowledge of Asian musical traditions as an adult. Ho's work is not a simple fusion of East and West, but a combination of multiple Eastern, Western, and other styles—an amalgamation meant to trouble these very binaries. The Orientalist dynamic expressed in these titles mark him solely as a foreigner.

Yet Ho often did legitimate himself and his collaborators through their personal histories. His writings, interviews, and introductions at performances heavily employed his biography as an authenticating device, detailing his experiences with racism and connections to black nationalism.

Placing so much emphasis on his personal background, even though it is not the subject of his compositions, opened up the possibility for critics and audiences to re-inscribe identity politics onto his "Chinese jazz." There is room for growth in critics' and Ho's abilities to parse out the fine but nonetheless important distinction between understanding and experiencing oppression and having an innate relationship to it because of racial or cultural categorization.

The Afro Asian identity Ho proposed was unbound from biology, and based on antiracist, anti-imperialist, and even anticapitalist action. In this way, interracialism becomes a performative stance rather than an innate, fixed social category. Afro Asian performance is both a way of creating work and a mode of active reception. Ho approached this notion in his conception of "soul" as an aesthetic. He said, "It's just not about notation. It's really about how to interpret these melodies. And the stories inside these melodies. It's not just you gotta play this bend here or you gotta do this kind of drop or fall or lift here. It's not about this kind of pitch alteration there. It can't be dissected in that type of way, it has to be understood from the point of view of meaning." Musical politics does not reside in the replication or reception of codes, but in actively infusing a performance with the desired ethos and politics. "Expressive culture is both a musical and sociological phenomenon," Ho said. "You have to live it. You don't have to be genetically of it. But it's an understanding, it's a consciousness, a sensibility, ethos." Understanding the hardship of the people who forged these traditions and the intention to right these injustices form the political backbone of radical interracialism.

Innovating Culture

"Living" Afro Asian musical production means focusing on what a sound *does* rather than what it *is*. In this way, culture and politics are innovative processes versus material endpoints. The tendency for hegemonic multiculturalism is to control progressive culture by managing and containing it as it is embraced into the mainstream. Proponents select less progressive forms to promote in dominant culture, place limitations on their significations, erase their resistant historical roots, or crystallize them into static, consumable objects. Similar dynamics play out when music of color is swallowed by the culture industry, either as diversity tokens or because a song or artist happens to catch the broader public's fancy. Traditions (and invented traditions) are paraded as authentic artifacts of a singular culture and, generally, each culture is only allotted one style. Spanish music is performatively glossed as flamenco, Cuban or Puerto Rican as salsa, and Polish as polka. These forms are presented devoid of historical or political context, or with attention to historical preservation rather than contemporary performance style. And they are often promoted in a celebratory fashion that champions how they spice up rather than challenge dominant culture and the status quo. This cultural dilution is not always intentionally meant to depoliticize its content, but rather to make it more market-ready: cultural performance becomes something that is repeatable (even if the given artists change), predictable, consumable, and able to be produced through existing tangible and representational infrastructures.

Numerous scholars have discussed the manifestation of similar issues in the jazz world. Since the mid-twentieth century, jazz has been in various ways embraced as quintessential U.S. American culture. As certain pockets of the tradition have been institutionalized, questions have arisen about its continued ability to function as a space of resistance or counterdominant expression. Some note the conservatism that has accompanied the promotion of jazz as U.S. classical music, with Jazz at Lincoln Center a popular example.[25] Locating himself in the free jazz lineage of the Black Arts Movement, Ho drew on its roots in black nationalism and its performative heart of establishing new sonic vocabularies to create music he saw as resisting institutionalization. Jodi Melamed proposes "race radicalism" as "the attempt to rupture how race as a sign has been consolidated with the cultural, ideological, and social forces of liberal movements and to reconsolidate race as a sign with the cultural, ideological, and social forces of worldly and radical antiracist movements and the critical perspective they generate on race as a genealogy of global capitalism" (2006, 9). Ho attempted to forge such a politic by defying the commodification of black music as attached to essentialized— and de-politicized—notions of blackness. Instead, he promoted the historical radicalism of many of these forms as illuminated in the free jazz tradition.

What is typically called "free" or "out" jazz emerged in the 1950s and 1960s. While the form cannot be reduced to a singular aesthetic or lineage, there are several features shared among early practitioners. Free jazz was an extension from bebop in which artists, in part or whole, lost the rhythm section or even the notion of a steady pulse, experimented with forgoing chord changes or using modal harmonies, revived collective improvisation, and played with parameters of timbre and texture. For practitioners in what George Lewis calls the "Afrological" stream of the form—including artists in the Black Arts Movement and Association for the Advancement of Creative Musicians—the freeing up of time and tone was a decisive choice to move away from European-influenced structures, and improvisation was an important hallmark of the break away from formal rules and notions of "works" in contrast to process (G. Lewis 1996, 93). Lewis describes how "AACM musicians challenged the use of jazz-related images to police and limit the scope of black cultural expression and economic advancement. Through their music and in interviews, AACM musicians constantly challenged racialized hierarchies of aesthetics, method, place, infrastructure, and economics that sought to limit their mobility of genre, method, and cultural reference" (Lewis 2004). Some free jazz artists aligned their aesthetic experimentation with black nationalist politics as they sought to create forms that expressed specifically African American points of view and build a sense of heritage and pride.[26]

Ho located a radical political voice in free jazz and sought to reinvigorate jazz practice by employing those ideals in a new era. If adherence to strict racial and aesthetic boundaries is part of the preservationist bent of multicultural policy, Ho's music contrasts this tendency for he worked to remake what is considered traditional through an ongoing process of cultural innovation. Thus, he called on free jazz techniques and texts, but purposefully changed them as a means of honoring their historical and political roots. Rather than replicating a free jazz *sound*, Ho performed the free jazz *search* to create new sounds.

One way in which Ho innovated was by updating pivotal pieces from the free jazz canon. "Momma's Song" is one example, an adaptation of Archie Shepp's "Blasé" (1969). The original piece is based on a subdued instrumental foundation over which Jeanne Lee speak-sings poetry that deals with images of interracial sexual violence. Restrained for most of the ten-minute piece, the ensemble opens up in the final moments when a harmonica duet and horn scream transform the covert pain of the poetry into musical form. Ho rewrote the classic accompanying riff from an evenly measured 4/4 to an off-kilter 5.5/4. Over this groove, he opens with a baritone saxophone solo that immediately injects the piece with the energy and volume of the original's endpoint. The ensemble then drops down to a more reserved tone and vocalist Jennifer Kidwell speaks new words, astutely punctuated by hartigan's drumming.

Ho commissioned poet Christine Stark to write the text, which explores historical cycles of misogynist violence much like Shepp's version. The new poetry continues where the old left off, turning Shepp's tale of a singular violation into a lamentation for how women across the globe are harmed by masculine violence:

> Daddy pushed pushed pushed
> into you
> ripped skin
> his pistol dick shot your womb
> one two three four times
> five times
> you screamed
>
> Daddy was
> the black robe man with a gold and silver cross
> the trapper
> the hunter
> the tree cutter
> the animal trader
> the soldier man
> the earth digger...
>
> Momma
> i saw what Daddy did
> 100 200 300 400
> 500 years ago last night

the moonlight so white
the crushed wings of a dragonfly glistened
blue and purple on the black tar road

(Ho 2010a, 5)

Stark describes how men harm women with their bodies—the focus in Shepp's version—and through institutions like the military-industrial complex, church, and ecologically harmful industry.

Rather than paying tribute to Shepp and BAM by redoing the original, Ho and his ensemble retain its tone and thematic core in text and music. At the same time, they update it with new sonic images and references to contemporary, but historically linked, issues. The AAME actually covered the original "Blasé" for a time (as "Blasé Redux"), but "Momma's Song" shows the further outgrowth of their evolution of the piece. The new version also offers the possibility of healing that the original does not:

I wandered over roads
found bits of me floating
under the moon
met raped babies
talked to spirits of murdered mommas
until my mind came back to me
my mind came back
the mommas and babies
told me to sing
sing my girl
sing for us...

now I sing strong
the fishes swim to the sea
the trees crawl toward the sky
their heart shaped leaves
fed by the sun
momma's love momma's love
I sing I sing
the trees watch
the sky listens
the owl
the crickets
the fox
the muskrat
the beaver
the birds
I saw I saw I saw momma
I saw what daddy did
I have the blue purple wings of the dragonfly
I fly

I glisten
translucent
momma I am your pain your shame your voice
momma I sing truth

(Ho 2010a, 9–10)

In this version, the horrors of the past uncovered in Shepp's original are met with a means for transformation as Stark (and Kidwell in performance) gives voice to the silent Momma as an antidote.

"Momma's Song" and other AAME works showcase extended instrumental techniques as another nod to the group's free jazz roots. Ho forged tremendous personal ground on the baritone saxophone, pushing its range through use of the altissimo register and employing various percussive sounds thanks to his strong embouchure. AAME members also stated one of their primary reasons for joining the ensemble was the high level of musicianship Ho and their colleagues demanded. As in "Momma's Song," Ho frequently used complex rhythms, including meters less frequently found in the Western classical and popular traditions, such as 7 and 9, polymeters (the combination of or changing between meters), and polyrhythms derived from traditions such as West African drumming. These techniques present a musical challenge to players and listeners. As AAME saxophonist David Bindman told me, these explorations in meter and form are a way of creating an aural space "where one can hear differently."

One long-term effect of capitalism as manifested in the popular music industry is the de-skilling of the listener, engineered to appreciate a limited palette. Ho's use of compound meters is a sono-political rejection of the 4/4-dominated Western classical and popular canon, and an act of aesthetic resistance by encouraging listeners not to conform to a system bent on, as he felt, dumbing them down. The first time I interviewed Ho, I mentioned Funkadesi (see Chapter 3), and he asked, "Are they all 4/4?" using it as a measure of Funkadesi's musical and political clout. Of course, duple meter is found in many Third World traditions—and Ho's own work—but he found it important to explore metrical and other formal choices as a potential site of revolution. Creating music to encourage listeners to hear differently is one way of fostering a more open sense of the possible, culturally and politically.

But the degree to which tradition should be transformed did not go unchallenged among Ho's collaborators. Ho and drummer royal hartigan had a longstanding disagreement over how traditional non-Western rhythmic patterns should be incorporated into their work. For example, Ho's "No Home to Return To" begins with an opening percussion solo that he prescribes should evoke the sense of being trapped in the hull of a ship. In the November 2008 performance at University of Wisconsin-Madison, hartigan performed the solo making heavy use of Chinese opera woodblocks and gongs, at times incorporating the kick drum. He told me that he played several standard *jingju* patterns in their typical form, although he did not perform them in their usual order. Ho was not pleased with the performance because he felt hartigan adhered too strictly to the opera tradition and did not achieve the necessary feeling for the piece. Ho emphasized that he wrote the introduction for a "hybrid kit," meaning one that does not function solely as Chinese opera or a jazz kit, but would become a space for both voices to reside. Yet hartigan resisted pushing too far from the standard patterns because he did not feel he had enough ownership over the *jingju* form to decide when to change it. He believes that world musical cultures, particularly folk cultures, often serve an important social and religious function in their societies and should not be played without permission or altered.

The stakes for Ho's innovations versus hartigan's are different given their racial/ethnic backgrounds, and hartigan's sensitivity is in no doubt due to negotiating his whiteness in relation to the forms he plays. However, when I asked Ho if he thought that hartigan would be more harshly judged for pushing traditional styles, he said, in true Ho fashion, that this was "his problem" and a symptom of white guilt. Again, we see an example of Ho's idiosyncratic criteria for aesthetic and political creation. This discussion elucidates some of the tensions that mark the unfolding of his musical theorization: its actualization by musicians with different identities and opinions. Rather than restricting the group's output, this creative tension was an unavoidable part of the process and allowed for the development of rich, multivalent music. Ho wrote "No Home," but in the moment of performance his ideas met hartigan's and they were mutually compromised. Ho said the AAME's work is "a process, it's a communal endeavor, it's about community building. It doesn't happen overnight, doesn't happen in one gig. It happens over a protracted amount of years." The Afro Asian negotiation of aesthetics and politics is an ever-unfolding forum ripe with disagreements, not a momentary or easily realized union. And while this conversation takes place onstage in the moment of performance, it is also forged through intense backstage conversation. The rehearsal room and social spaces become sites of embodied cultural transmission and change.

With that said, the ways in which whiteness manifested in the AAME are particularly complicated. Ho contested the mainstream commodification of jazz by presenting it as a racialized and specifically African American form. Historically, as the music was institutionalized and began to enter elite cultural spaces, more white players performed it, sometimes excluding blacks from ensembles or venues.[27] Even now, when jazz is embraced as "American," its blackness is often downplayed or silenced. This tendency has played out repeatedly in the history of African American music in which mainstreaming disenfranchises black artists of their culture, even if unintentionally (Garofalo 1994). The flipside to this patriotic embrace is that pointedly marked blackness—sonically or otherwise—is often ascribed elements of disrepute, in line with perceptions of "cultural" dysfunction in nonwhite populations, with black music posed as "a distorted development, or a pathological condition, of the general American culture" (Myrdal quoted in Melamed 2006, 8).

Ho is explicit about jazz's origins and what he views as its politically radical roots, and he pays much homage to its black innovators.[28] Yet while Ho promotes the tradition's blackness, he does so through an ensemble of multiracial—including white—voices. One important piece of this jazz radicalism is the challenge to the dominant image of who and what an authentic jazz musician is. On the first day I met the AAME, our discussion quickly turned to the myth of the quintessential jazz player. Members argued that New York has a great industry for jazz, but that it is weighed down by constructions of the proper jazz player as a black male. The group had encountered musicians (although a minority) who are prejudiced against nonblack players. They also dealt with promoters who felt black faces would sell to bigger audiences. Bindman told me that a black venue tried to cancel a gig by the Brooklyn Sax Quartet—himself, another white musician, a black player, and Ho—because of their mixed membership. However, as they already had ticket sales, they ended up playing to an appreciative audience. Bindman suggested the jazz musician stereotype also hurts black artists. There are quite a few young black players, he said, who do not know anything about the history of the music beyond their narrow path of study. He gave the example of seeing a black trumpeter perform who was not doing a very good job. But the white people in the front of the audience were "giving him a lot" because of his race, not helping the trumpeter to improve. With these essentialized practices marring contemporary jazz the AAME modeled how to promote African American radical heritage without assuming only black people can inhabit these politics.

The omission in the band's conversations about essentialist racial frameworks is the intersecting workings of gender. Like the AAME, the major voices and proponents of BAM and many black nationalist movements were men. As Stephen Ward contends, "During the mid- and late 1960s, overt calls for black women to recede into the background in deference to male leadership were tied to the ostensibly revolutionary objective of reclaiming 'black manhood'.... But this metaphor and the male-centered political framework that it represented could be, and too often was, used to silence and discipline the activism of black women" (2006, 124–125). Ho's coming into racially conscious adulthood was indelibly impacted by the masculine-centered discourse of these discussions. Asian American activists of the 1960s and 1970s frequently performed black masculinity as a way to counter emasculating racist discourses (Maeda 2009). Ho in many ways embraced similar gestures in arguing for Asian American male strength and sexual identity. But while helpful for articulating nondominant notions of Asian masculinity, the focus solely on masculine prowess neglected female subjectivities. This is even more glaring in Ho's claims to represent a "matriarchal socialist" political agenda (Ho 2009). As I have detailed in other work, Ho's representations of feminine concerns end up replicating misogynist discourses by posing his singular, masculine voice as the spokesperson (Roberts 2013).

Thus, "Momma's Song" in some ways rings hollow in its feminist propositions. The lack of female instrumentalists replicates the historical lack of women involved in free jazz scenes and jazz in general as nonvocalists. Just as in "Blasé," a female voice is superimposed over male instrumental improvisations to give credence to their sentiments. This use of a feminine sound is similar to the sonic identity politics of race I critiqued above. Presenting culture—in this case, "women's" culture—in such a manner is a conservative adherence to a history of free jazz stuck in time. Ho did collaborate with female writers, dancers, singers, and actors, and in a few cases featured female instrumentalists. In the years after I completed my research, he also began to mentor female composer Marie Incontrera who now leads two of his ensembles, The Green Monster Big Band and the Eco-Music Big Band. For the most part, though, Ho was more concerned with the presentation of race and Afro Asian culture than championing female musical representation or musicians.

Ho and the AAME drew on the performative politics of free jazz as an invocation to continued evolution. Originally, the tradition was meant to resist the sonic status quo by asserting sounds that were beyond what was considered "black" or "jazz" by the dominant culture. But as eras and musical discourse change, so must revolutionary music. As Salim Washington suggests, "The perpetual avant-garde is about a certain attitude toward constant innovation, motivated in part by a desire for greater justice in the world" (2004, 30).[29] Keeping this spirit alive is less about replicating sounds from earlier moments and more about re-creating the intention behind creating those sounds. It is a core of radicalism that has been central to the musical and political lives of the AAME. "Jazz is a verb," Ho said; it is not a thing but a lifetime built on bucking critics, building revolutionary consciousness, and resisting commodification and objectification. This definition of jazz disavows identity politics that deterministically proclaim it and other African American musical forms as revolutionary simply because they are linked to black people. Ho's merger of free jazz with Asian forms retained this heart by further opening up the sounds that can be included as part of African American tradition and by recognizing that the crossing of racial boundaries is required to contest hegemonic multiculturalism. As Ho's legacy unfolds, there remains room for his colleagues to continue to explore ways to innovate their work to address new political necessities.

Inextricably Bound

The point of this chapter has been to tease out the sonic dimensions of multicultural debates that play out in interracial arts practice. I also want to suggest the difficulty in changing these dynamics when discourse is so structured by entrenched racial understandings (in this case, sono-racial triangulation). Musicians of color are challenged in their efforts to produce radical culture by a reception system and sono-racial taxonomy built on simplification and difference. We can infer Afro Asian performativity through artist choices that resonate with particular political stances. But these selections will never be foolproof antiracist strategies, for performances are as multivalent as the viewers that receive them. In the end, Afro Asian artists—with explicit political aims or not—constantly inhabit a space between sonic identity politics and radical interracialism: with every progressive gain they must continually remain innovative in order to stay ahead of the banalizing tendency of dominant culture. Performers must recognize the tenacity of this dynamic and present work that consciously and perhaps extra-musically frames their output in ways to resignify their dominant meanings.

Can the performance of identity still be radical in the twenty-first-century United States, when hegemonic multiculturalism and postracialism dominate popular discourse on race? Ho's embrace of music of color stands in contrast to the former's incorporation of identity and rejects the latter's covert white supremacy.[30] Instead of inviting marginalized traditions into the mainstream, his repertoire creates a new center and shifts the dominant–subdominant relationship. And by presenting culture as an evolving entity, his music contests multicultural logic that seeks to preserve and contain difference through fragmented and ahistorical representations. Ho's work exposes audiences to new timbres, instrument combinations, temperaments, modes, rhythms, languages, and subject matter, in all cultivating an appreciation for pushing beyond the status quo. Of particular note—in comparison to cases I have previously detailed—Ho made an effort to spotlight jazz as sono-racially black, and many of his musical and written works laid out his belief in the form's historical lineage of counterdominant social and aesthetic resistance. When he combined sono-racially Asian sounds with jazz, as in *She-Wolf*, some of the same slippage of "black jazz" to generalized "American jazz" I have mentioned before could occur. Ho, however, developed additional projects focused solely on (free) jazz legacies and used extra-musical framing to try to keep its racial contours present.

Ho hoped his music would lead listeners to think outside of existing musical contexts and translate these thoughts into actions that can fight oppression and domination. But to what extent these sounds translate into a political call-to-action greatly depends on the particular audience member. Listeners are crucial to hearing counterhegemonic possibilities, and in the next chapter, I will discuss what skills audiences might develop to cultivate radical interracialism as a mode of reception. Like-minded listeners might see in Afro Asian music a reflection of their own desires, spurring them on in their own political pursuits, while to others it may offer a temporary aesthetic diversion or simply pique their curiosity. In the end, Ho's work reminds artists of color that it is ignorant to think that the presence of their work in the mainstream alone—or remuneration—will have a political effect. Rather, radical music must work to stay ahead of the status quo and actively critique it.

5

Toward an Afro Asian Theory of Critique
The "Addictive" Case

I t was 2002 and a war was raging. The United States had recently begun operations in Afghanistan and was poised to invade Iraq. But the war I speak of was waged on civilian lines. In April, black R&B singer Truth Hurts released "Addictive," the first single from her debut album *Truthfully Speaking*. Having previously worked as a back-up vocalist for several major hip hop and R&B artists, this album was a chance for Truth Hurts to become a star in her own right. Released on Dr. Dre's Aftermath label, the album featured support from Dre, DJ Quik, Hi-Tek, and Timbaland, a virtual pantheon of contemporary black popular music makers. "Addictive" was massively popular, breaking into the top 10 on charts in the United States and United Kingdom, and holding the number nine spot on the Billboard Hot 100 (Kusnur 2002a). Unfortunately for Truth Hurts, it was not her own voice that attracted so much attention. The song's accompanying track featured a sample of "Thoda Resham Lagta Hai," sung by Bollywood veteran Lata Mangeshkar. "Thoda" originally appeared in *Jyoti*, an all-but-forgotten 1981 film, and was written by prolific Bollywood composer Bappi Lahiri. The merger of Hindi film song and R&B in this transnational and trans-temporal duet proved infectious and "Addictive" has remained a staple of urban, rhythmic, and top 40 playlists for over a decade.[1]

In "Addictive," sonic blackness and Asianness/Indianness circle around one another. The song starts with Mangeshkar's voice singing "kaliyon ka chaman / tab banta hai," higher and faster than in her original recording.[2] Shortly after, Hurts's voice enters, singing vocable moans to accompany Mangeshkar. The two voices contrast in timbre: Mangeshkar sings in the high, nasal, lyrical style of Bollywood, while Hurts vocalizes in a low, chesty tone that sits somewhere between speaking and singing, typical of singers working on the cusp of hip hop and R&B (e.g., Mary J. Blige). Even when sounding together, the two voices never seem to occupy the same sonic world due to their distinct styles and the distortion of the sample.

The instrumental elements contrast the vocals as the Bollywood sound is molded onto a hip hop scaffold. With a low bass groan, the track drops

153

in under the voices, primarily composed of a bassline, kick drum, tambourine, and a sample from B.T. Express' 1974 recording "Do It ('Til You're Satisfied)," which prominently features open conga hits that emphasize the backbeat.[3] The additions to instrumentation and textures typical in hip hop signals an attempt to timbrally emulate the sampled song. Elements present in "Thoda"—namely the drums and tambourine—are repositioned within a hip hop rhythmic framework, sonically "matching" the original but metrically distinct. In all, "Addictive" draws on the sonic palette of Bollywood to create an exotic and sexy statement in hip hop.

Despite the importance of "Thoda" in the sonic profile of "Addictive," after Mangeshkar opens, Hurts takes over and the Indian vocalist fades to the background for the remainder of the piece. Truth Hurts sings about a male lover and their roller coaster relationship: "We fuss, we brawl, we rise, we fall / He comes in late but it's okay" because "he's so contagious" that their union survives. The sampled portions of "Thoda" discuss a flower garden in which costly objects such as gold and silk sit alongside glass, a metaphor for love as both beautiful and bittersweet. The two vocalized narratives both deal with the pleasure and pain of relationships, but Truth Hurts gets to tell a complete story while Mangeshkar is left to repeat: "thoda resham lagta hai / thoda sheesha lagta hai / heere moti jadte hain/thoda sona lagta hai."[4] Edward Said argues that imperialism creates "an accepted grid for filtering through the Orient into Western consciousness" and the Orient is made unimportant as the Occident speaks for both of them (1978, 6). In a similar fashion, Mangeshkar's agency is limited in "Addictive" and she is presented as needing a translator in order to come into the West.

"Addictive" was not the first hip hop or R&B song to sample South or East Asian sounds, but it was one of the most popular and circulated widely. This profusion was due, in part, to its accompanying video, which compounds the song's Orientalist tendencies. While "Addictive" sonically indexes India, video director Philip G. Atwell places Truth Hurts and other black revelers in a pseudo–Middle Eastern nightclub full of lavish carpets and ornate light fixtures. The setting mirrors the party at a bar or club that is the locale for many a hip hop video, but with added foreign decor. The cast wears typical uniforms: jeans, skirts, slinky tops, and high heels for the women, baggy jeans, polo tees, and button-down shirts for the men. In addition, female dancers sport gauzy fabric, henna, and coined hip scarves, while performing choreography emulating belly dance and Indian classical dance. The song and video together collapse South Asia and the Middle East into a singular, fictive Orient. These images are not "simple reflections of a true anterior reality, but composite images which [come] to define the nature of the Orient and the Oriental as irredeemably different and always inferior to the West" (R. Lewis 1996, 16). "Addictive" can be read as a contemporary minstrel attempt through which Truth Hurts and crew assert their Americaness by homogenizing and performing the Other through generalized representations of the East. At the same time, the Orient is layered onto visual and sonic trappings of urban blackness, two racialized Others rubbing together in a setting that is both fantastical and utterly banal in some U.S. cities.

The Orientalism in "Addictive" might have received only a passing nod in the odd tale of a resurrected Bollywood relic-cum-U.S. pop hit. Yet soon another story began to emerge. "Addictive" producer DJ Quik had sampled vocals and accompaniment from "Thoda" without permission or compensation. Composer Lahiri and Saregama, the Indian label holding the copyright for the song, filed litigation against Dre's Aftermath Records.[5] Lahiri called the case a "war for the Indian composer" and charged Truth Hurts and DJ Quik with practicing "cultural imperialism" (Bhattacharyya 2003, Kaufman 2003). Many voices from the press followed suit, decrying Hurts and her colonizing ways. By the spring of 2003, the Indian parties had successfully won an injunction to stop sales of *Truthfully Speaking* unless they were stickered with Lahiri's credit. Yet the staying power of "Addictive" had been unleashed: at least five documented producers across the world have created new versions of the song or its track, including Lahiri himself (Marshall and Beaster-Jones 2012). These remixes specifically emulate—or even sample—"Addictive" rather than drawing directly on "Thoda." Despite the much-publicized legal battles, the black–Asian blend in Truth Hurts's song inspired producers with its aesthetic and signifying potential. Few of these subsequent versions offer credit to Lahiri, Saregama, Dr. Dre, DJ Quik, or Truth Hurts.

In this chapter, I explore the ways in which discourses of sono-racial triangulation generated in the United States operated in the global context of the "Addictive" case. In particular, I look at the shared cultural space occupied by elite U.S. and Indian popular artists and how "Addictive" reveals their cosmopolitan connections rather than disconnection. How

Figure 5.1. Truth Hurts and dancers performing "Addictive."

did a simple case of intellectual property rights become a heated racial and cultural battle? And why—among all of the iterations of "Thoda"— did "Addictive" become the sole target of legal action and critical derision? A large part of the answer lies in the discourse of sono-racialization that insists African American and Indian popular music could only come together through foul play. The music war was made possible by an investment in maintaining this discourse, even when it ignored the realities of the situation. Observers of this case and its participants operated through a lens of black–Asian difference that could not account for the interpenetration of the involved artists' cultures and industries. Racial/cultural separation became the hallmark of respectable music making and "Addictive" the monstrously hybrid progeny of Bollywood and hip hop miscegenation. Yet the song was popular for precisely these reasons: a variety of listeners found something of themselves or their desires reflected in the piece. Knee-jerk critiques of cultural imperialism based on East–West binaries missed the nuanced ways the song revealed interracial and intercultural yearnings and the limitations of the sono-racial system.

Several other scholars have criticized the Orientalism of "Addictive."[6] I believe these concerns are valid but that they do not paint the full picture, one in which multiple racial stereotypes were mobilized in service of monetary gain. In a 2012 article, Jayson Beaster-Jones and Wayne Marshall begin from a similar point of criticism and go on to discuss the explosion of remixes spurred by "Addictive." They claim that the global proliferation of subsequent tracks "unsettle easy charges of appropriation, whether cross-cultural or illegal, as well as notions of ownership, whether national or personal" (Marshall and Beaster-Jones 2012, 2). Tracing the "Thoda" melody that DJ Quik revived, they argue for the usefulness of the "Addictive" affair in revealing the methods and transnational conversations of remix artists across the globe.

I agree that looking to the cultural work that "Addictive" does is beneficial, although I take a different path than Beaster-Jones and Marshall. My critique of the song's resonance will focus on its illumination of sono-racial discourses, revelation of interracial and intercultural conversations, and catalyzing of new ones. After all, despite the court case, Hurts's song and unabashedly Orientalist video remained on the airwaves and were consumed nationally and internationally with aplomb. At the same time, her work fell victim to attacks by journalists and bloggers who drew on well-worn stereotypes of black and Indian music to determine what had gone "wrong" in the sampling and denounce the African American artists. "Addictive" is definitely the discursive coming together of blackness and Asianness, but in what follows, I argue that it also has the potential to be an Afro Asian performance that does antiracist work by disrupting racially triangulating discourses. Seeing this possibility requires a shift in reception, one that differs from both a romantic celebration of musical universality and automatic cries of racism, neither of which fully account for the realities of how people make and use music in a complex world.

To get at this idea, I will develop and model what I see as an Afro Asian critical theory. Many scholarly analyses of cross-racial interaction and cultural exchange replicate the very multicultural traps I detailed in the last chapter, conflating race and culture or posing sounds as synecdoches for groups of people. An Afro Asian critique can avoid these pitfalls by illuminating the problematics of the sono-racial system and allowing (or looking) for signs of interracial promise such as shared experiences or understanding, joint counterhegemonic gestures, and non-essentialist representations. In other chapters, I have described "Afro Asian" as a way of being musical, a way of shaping space, and a way of promoting anti-racism. Here, I pose it as a mode of reception: how one hears and interprets music with an ear toward interracial dynamics. Listeners perform their own sono-racial collaborations with Afro Asian music that can reveal varied and potentially lesser heard meanings within it. Afro Asian critical theory is tuned to specifically reveal dynamics missed in clichéd, and now hegemonic, dominant-subdominant analyses and poised to pinpoint progressive political potential amidst racial faux pas. Reading multiple discourses of black and Asian marginalization together, this theory can illuminate how they are both subjugated within triangulating paradigms as well as ruptures in this framework.

I will first delve into the particulars of the "Addictive" case and discuss how the artists and popular critics framed the conflict. There were certainly "misfires" in the sampling and ensuing litigation that opened the door to charges of artistic impropriety. But I will show that these indiscretions were hyperbolized into a metonymic war that drew on assertions of Asian music as foreign and highbrow and black music as domestic and lowbrow. Attempts to spotlight the racism of Hurts and associates relied on misunderstandings of the racial system and Indian cultures, in effect producing the very Orientalist discourse being railed against. In contrast, I will perform an Afro Asian critique of the case in order to illuminate how the framing of the affair as purely antagonistic neglected points of interracial and intercultural connection the song offered artists and listeners, and failed to challenge the sono-racial system.

Music Wars and MTV

Lahiri and his legal team employed rhetorical images of war in their presentation of the "Addictive" case in court and the popular press. The framing of the copyright infringement as a racial, cultural, and economic battle was an inflammatory gesture meant to garner attention and spark outrage. The effectiveness of this campaign was enhanced by statements made by other artists involved in the case and several voices from the United States and international press that perpetuated the story. Without denying the legal questions around the sampling, I contend that the portrayal of the case as a war of racial/cultural wrongdoing is one *interpretation* of the case, which relies heavily on notions of black–Asian difference.

Even as Lahiri toned down his vitriol once Saregama became the official plaintiff in the suit, the notion of interracial and intercultural antagonism proved too provocative to die and continued to circulate in discussions of the case. This story is worth exploring in depth, as it reveals the gaps that must be overlooked in order to hold tightly to a narrative of sono-racial triangulation.

While claiming his songs have been stolen before, Lahiri says he merely noted it and moved on (Bhattacharya 2002). But post-9/11 international tensions and the worldwide prestige of Dr. Dre made "Addictive" a promising case in which to exact reparations. The charge of "cultural imperialism" suggests the sampling was both an act of theft and colonization. Sampling "Thoda" was not simply a musical or financial transaction but one in which the U.S. artists were asserting their dominance over Bollywood artists. In a press release, Lahiri's team called "Addictive" a "flagrant disregard, and disrespect, for [their] client's religious beliefs, culture and ownership of the copyright," claiming some of the lyrics "are obscene and offensive, and cause extreme offense, to the company's owners and to the sensibilities of many Hindu and Muslim people" (Davis 2002a). It was therefore morally wrong and culturally insensitive for the U.S. artists to sample the song because they possess different standards of behavior. Invoking language of religious difference specifically alluded to post-9/11 "Islam versus the West" constructions, further abstracted when Lahiri, instead of naming individuals, claimed he would "take legal action against *the Americans* for recycling [his] song" (quoted in Bhattacharya 2002, emphasis mine).

Lahiri's claims came at an opportune moment in black popular culture. Shortly after 9/11, there was an explosion of hip hop recordings featuring East and South Asian idioms used to create exotic, romantic, and pleasurable sound palettes. The so-called War on Terror created renewed interest in the East among Westerners, especially in the navel-gazing United States. Artists including R. Kelly, Redman, Missy Elliot, and Timbaland drew on samples of Asian musical styles, instruments associated with Asian cultures, and visual images in their songs and music videos, often in generalized Orientalist combinations. Claire Sponsler suggests that individuals often commit "acts of cross-cultural poaching" in order "to imagine alternate possibilities for selfhood while also negotiating anxieties about racial, gender, and national differences" (2000, 3). It is clear these black artists were exploring a generalized East through the racial and cultural language gathered from dominant discourses.[7]

These visual and sonic acts of sampling stand in contrast to hip hop from the 1980s and 1990s, in which artists referenced local racial tensions with Chinese and Korean immigrants. Ice Cube's 1991 "Black Korea" is one example, a song denouncing "chop suey ass" Korean shop owners for racially profiling black customers and threatening a nationwide boycott. The song's language is incendiary, angry, and speaks volumes about interracial misunderstandings, economic inequality, and debates over immigration in late-twentieth-century Los Angeles. By contrast, post-9/11 references to Asian people were based less on domestic reality and more on international fantasy, such as in R. Kelly's 2003 "Snake." In this song, Kelly commands: "Move your body like a snake, ma," the dancing snake a metaphor for the addressed woman and also presumably alluding to his penis. In the video, he sits in a militarized desert setting, playing a *sitar* as veiled brown women dance suggestively. The video setting patently references the U.S. military occupation of Iraq and reflects fascination with the exotic people that might live there.

"Addictive" draws on similar images of the Middle East (by way of India) and in several ways supports Lahiri's war metonym. "Thoda" is placed into the context of a hip hop song, a popular form fed by U.S. corporate enterprises. U.S. popular music presents a telling imperialist image as it sweeps across the globe with what Douglas Little calls the "peculiar blend of ignorance and arrogance that [has] characterized U.S. [foreign] policy" (2002, 2–3). Sampling "Thoda" furthered the U.S. imperialist project, turning it into a Third World drum machine for Truth Hurts. (We can, of course, discuss the ways in which the music industry similarly colonized African American practices, which I will get to shortly.)

This imperialism plays out more specifically in the track given that, according to Lahiri's legal team, DJ Quik "literally superimposed [his] own drum track and lyrics over [Lahiri's] beat" (quoted in "Indian Composer" 2002). Listening closely to "Addictive," one can indeed hear the presence of "Thoda" in the background throughout, offering a hazy texture to Quik's incisive beats. Like other sampling situations, rather than a collaborative endeavor in which Mangeshkar might have herself responded to a track with fresh vocals, Quik determined what she would say, when, and the tempo and pitch, the source material altered to support the new song's content. What is more troubling is that in "Addictive," Mangeshkar functions less as a singer and more as an instrument on the track. Her voice was captured, chopped, and forced into new sonic environs and arrangements much like a sampled drum hit. The supposed unfamiliarity of her expressions was manipulated to fit into a format that would be more readily accessible to an assumed hip hop listener. Truth Hurts replicated this exoticization, saying that when she first heard the track, she thought, "Man, I've never heard anything like this," reflecting a sense that DJ Quik discovered a new sound that did not exist until Westerners came to find it (quoted in Remé 2002).

DJ Quik took aesthetic liberties in shaping the sampled sounds that are typical with hip hop producers, but his inability to acknowledge the human specificity behind the sounds he manipulated showcases a cultural myopia. Quik stumbled upon the Bollywood film on television one day, heard the song, and, liking it, hit record on his VCR. Yet he claimed he had no idea how to go about finding the original composer, assuming an unbreachable cultural and geographic divide (Salomon 2003). Dr. Dre's legal counsel confirmed this perspective, saying that their clients "didn't know how to find the owner of the track" (Davis 2002b). These statements were attempts to justify the sampling through a spatialized Othering discourse, portraying hip hop and Bollywood—the United States and India—as disconnected worlds despite the fact that *Jyoti* was circulating through media channels that allowed DJ Quik to hear it. But hearing does not necessarily mean understanding. Dr. Dre described "Addictive" as "a drum track, bassline and this Indian girl singing" (quoted in Remé 2002). Mangeshkar, however, was in her fifties when she recorded "Thoda" and in her seventies at the time of "Addictive."

Dre's comment is seemingly based on a lack of familiarity with Bollywood vocal aesthetics: the airy, playful, and high-pitched vocals could possibly sound more youthful to an uninitiated ear.[8] Having seen the film might not have helped either, given the fact that a younger actress lip-synced to Mangeshkar's vocal, as is typical in this genre. Mangeshkar's advanced age aside, there is something pejorative and dismissive in Dre's statement, as if the singing is something simple, nonspecific, and, again, akin to the track's instrumental components. In this sense, Mangeshkar was present as a voice and racialized body but not as a fellow artist or industry-mate. Nina Sun Eidsheim has shown that voices are "choreographed" to produce "socially imposed" sounds, which are then frequently read as inherently linked to the racial identity of the performer (2012). Thus, while voice does not represent the essence of a person's race, because of the shaping of voice—internally and externally—to fit into genres with sono-racial conceptions, a link between sound and body is instantiated. Dre's remark is an apt demonstration of the link he and assumed listeners will make between Mangeshkar's voice and a female Indian body, a result of a sono-racial system that stretches well beyond individual prejudices he might hold. More problematic is that he only heard the Bollywood singer's voice as a body rather than a human with aesthetic and extra-racial agency.

Coverage of the "Addictive" case by popular journalists in the United States, United Kingdom, and some in India reproduced the cultural imperialism narrative, often relying solely on statements from Lahiri's legal team. In an online article for *BBC News*, one of the lawyers is quoted as saying, "It's our opinion that the label [Aftermath] simply took it for granted that Hindi music was something they didn't need to pay for, that it could be used simply at will" (quoted in "Indian Composer" 2002). In an online column for *Pop Matters*, Chris Fitzpatrick described the case as an example of U.S. music producers "finding ways to pillage the 'third world' for material" (2002). Most of the reporting in professional outlets did not offer their own commentary, as did Fitzpatrick, but nonetheless used the legal team's claims as hooks for the story. A few journalists and amateur bloggers presented a more varied response to the case, which I will detail shortly.

Lahiri had much evidence to justify his charge of cultural imperialism and insensitivity. But were these the only engagements possible between East and West? Many negotiations that allow for individual agency within sociopolitical crises are overlooked in a world of 30-second news bites, while events that are the biggest, create the greatest fear, or spur consumption are promoted systematically by those that control media images. Thus, in the United States and Western media, "war" becomes *the* intercultural (and interracial) performance, a "metonym" for all East–West interaction—what George Lakoff describes as a "general principle … needed because one cannot list all the examples" (1987, 78). Members of the press, world political leaders, scholars, and others employ the war metonym by using discourse that separates and polarizes cultural and national entities. I do not suggest that this conception dictates our thoughts or actions, but that its proliferation must influence our experience. When we hear "war," it conjures images of drone strikes, improvised explosive devices, force-feeding at Guantánamo, and suicide bombers. Because these tropes do not capture the full reality of the war experience— or broader international engagements—they are more specifically a stereotype, a representation based on partial images of a whole and used to make quick judgments about a person or event (Lakoff 1987, 79). The result of likening the "Addictive" affair to war is a preconstructed narrative of greed, dominance, and bloodshed that breeds fear of interracial and intercultural interaction and breaks down communication.

Performing Antiracist Critique

An Afro Asian critical theory can provide additional lenses through which to consider complicated cases such as "Addictive" without resorting to appraisals that are all "good" or "bad." Theories of spectatorship have delineated the active nature of reception in performance, as well as the ways in which individual subjectivities influence what and how something is received.[9] An Afro Asian mode of reception can further the interracial projects discussed in previous chapters by modeling how to engage a performance in ways that disrupt the dominant racial taxonomy, illuminate voices unheard in mainstream discourse, and counter racism. For much of the industry's history, U.S. popular music journalism (and early scholarship) assumed listeners to be part of a young, white "mainstream" (Mahon 2004, 159).[10] While this may have been the target or assumed audience, a variety of people have consumed popular culture precisely because it is dominant culture. These listeners take in the material but often filter it through different experiences and racial outlooks. For example, drawing on Steven Feld's notion of "interpretive moves," Louise Meintjes suggests that the different sociopolitical positions of South African listeners informed their evaluation of Paul Simon's *Graceland* album in relation to the racial politics of apartheid (1990, 49). Interpretive moves are the means through which listeners link formal musical features to accumulated sociocultural experience and "give meaning to sound for particular listeners and social sets of listeners, at particular historical moments" (Meintjes 1990, 49). Because Afro Asian music signals a shifting listenership and the juxtaposition of varied aesthetic discourses, it requires fresh criteria for interpretation. Afro Asian critique can model these new interpretive moves.

This method is akin to doing a queer textual reading but in service of antiracist goals. A hallmark of queer studies is the analysis of texts with an eye and ear toward formal, thematic, or contextual residues that are evidence of the queer subjectivities of creators or intended audiences.[11] Doing an Afro Asian critique similarly argues that subjectivities and experiences are influential to how a text or performance is created and received. A piece can be radically interracial when its content specifically states so, but it can also potentially function as such when informed by a creator with those beliefs or using methods that displays these politics. The point of Afro Asian critique is not, however, simply to call out how it reflects Afro Asian or other interracial identities and politics, anymore than a good queer reading is not "a project of simply seeking and marking homoerotic presences" in texts (Somerville 2000, 137). My method is an attempt to show how shifting our perception might open up alternative understandings that change the terms on which we enact and consume future interracial engagements. Afro Asian critique questions the very foundation of racial categories that are employed to mark and interpret musical exchanges.[12]

Afro Asian criticism can illuminate radical interracial tendencies in several ways. First, performances are read against dominant receptions. When an audience member subscribing to a reigning ideology experiences a piece, they will typically interpret it in so far as it adheres or does not adhere to this agenda. An Afro Asian critique draws out ideas that are distinct from the norm and works against the preservation of the status quo. It also hails those who harbor these counterhegemonic ideals. The experiences and perspectives of marginalized audiences are not accounted for in the formation of dominant paradigms. In fact, in some cases, dominant ideologies are specifically constructed against those of marginalized populations. Afro Asian criticism illuminates the alternative ways a nondominant person might experience a text. Rather than showing "new" perspectives, however, this method reveals points of view that already exist but are lesser known in the dominant public sphere. It therefore not only shows these perspectives but also acknowledges the people who hold them.

Beyond simply revealing nondominant viewpoints, Afro Asian critique also seeks to encourage their production. At this point, it is worth returning in more depth to Eidsheim's work on voice and race, for it specifically accounts for the role of the receiver in the production of racial knowledge. She describes three layers of a vocal performance: (1) the singer's actions, (2) the effects of the actions or outcomes of the actions (including but not exclusively sound production), and (3) how they first two layers are mediated by a listener "based on her experiences, values, and beliefs" (2012, 23–24). Thus, sound enters the social realm through interpretation in which the listener greatly informs its meanings. Part of doing Afro Asian criticism is thus revealing what some of a listener's presuppositions might be and how this impacts the work that an interracial project will do in the world. But it also recognizes listening as an action unto itself, suggesting that listeners have the ability to alter how they hear interracial sound. Analyzing how blackness has been historically heard in the voices of American opera singers like Marian Anderson, Eidsheim states:

> The prevalent ability to detect acousmatic blackness, or racialized vocal timbre, demonstrates that listening does not connote passive reception of information and is not a neutral activity. Rather, in listening we participate in social processes both embedded in and producing cultural forms. Consequently, no ear is innocent. Each cochlea curls around its past, and this past resonates with the present.... Only by educating ourselves about the complex set of practices that constitute listening can we emerge from layers of perception molded by the values, ideologies, fears, and desires carried by our forebears and liberate our hearing from the cultural commodity of blackness. (2011, 665)

I find these words astute as they argue it is the responsibility of the audience—in addition to the artist—to shift long-held sono-racial structures. As I showed in several cases throughout this book, placing the onus for radical sound only on the producer neglects the ways in which artists rely on someone hearing their work for it to do anything at all, much less anything counterhegemonic.

As part of intervening in the politics of listening, an Afro Asian critique can establish new criteria for evaluating the success of a work. Dominant success might be based on adherence to established aesthetic trends, the promotion of conventional political agendas, or the volume of sales in a capitalist mode of production. But the Afro Asian project is the promotion of counterhegemonic values and cannot be assessed through this matrix; in fact, Afro Asian performances are often deemed unsuccessful in hegemonic terms. The bashing of "kumbaya" multiculturalism has become de rigueur in dominant discourse, and critics and scholars often cannot determine the differences between projects that operate as diversity displays furthering the status quo versus those that disrupt it.[13] Afro Asian criticism requires analysts to hold social and political knowledge attuning them to criteria that distinguish multicultural performances from those that operate differently at deeper levels.

To begin, these projects need to be evaluated based on their promotion of antiracism rather than maintenance of the existing racial system. This means efficacious Afro Asian work will also generally incorporate sounds and sonic relationships that break from established sono-racial categories. As I highlighted in Chapter 4, the Black Arts Movement is one model of an attempt to define a new sono-racial profile for blackness, one that stretched beyond sonic stereotypes as well as the Western art tradition as an aesthetic standard. Similarly, Afro Asian music not only questions dominant portraits of black and Asian music, it also creates new sonic combinations that cannot be represented in extant sono-racial terms. Critics must educate themselves about these aesthetic desires and their political intent, shifting their expectations in order to interpret and comment on Afro Asian projects.

Afro Asian (and other interracial music) is also about bringing together people from varying backgrounds and perspectives. An Afro Asian critique understands the importance of community building toward the formation of radical interracialism and includes this as a marker of success. It might also give more weight to this potential over the production of innovative sounds or high record sales, in some instances making the motivation of action paramount over aesthetic concerns. This criticism also accounts for alternate readings of the employment of the concept of *unity* in these racial projects (see Chapter 3). Pluralist thinkers take particular umbrage with the profession of unity in multicultural projects, seeing this dynamic as homogenizing and exclusionary. Indeed, unity has served as an important rallying point for notions of U.S. American identity that excluded people of color and other marginalized populations: "To 'hear America sing' has come to imply a specific kind of listening, a listening that is nationalist and tuned into the frequencies of cultural consensus and univocality, keeping minoritized voices quiet, or audible only by proxy" (Kun 2005, 30–31). Afro Asian criticism intervenes in this hegemonic project, not by denying the efficacy of unity, but rather by reframing it to mean something other than assimilation and unanimity.

Afro Asian criticism can also help to grow a tradition by defining new or revealing existing audiences. When sales alone are not taken as a sole indication of success, the ability of an artist to reach new audiences—in community spaces, festivals, or other venues—becomes an important variable in addition to, or instead of, the consumption of CDs or merchandise. This is key in disenfranchised communities where performances or workshops might be offered for free not because of their worth, but because of lack of community funds. The "consumption" of a musical product is thus redefined as engagement and appreciation. Criticism that focuses on these aspects can be useful to artists who are seeking to do community organizing through music rather than make it big on the charts, helping them to understand whom they are playing to. Of course, some Afro Asian artists are of more elite backgrounds or come from different cultures than some of their listeners. Informed criticism can thus also be a means for artists to learn about who is consuming their work, their expectations, their use of the music, and their desires.

Clearly, what I am calling here an Afro Asian critique can more generally be considered a radical interracial one. "Afro Asian" is a useful label, though, in that it signifies a broader history of counterdominant politics. It is a marker bearing the sociopolitical weight and residue of Afro Asian antecedents discussed in Chapter 1, part of which is the notion of an ever-expanding politic. Rather than limiting what can be examined, this method uses a particular set of racial dynamics to open up broader ways of evaluating any cultural production, especially those that are interracial and intercultural. The thornier part of this endeavor is allowing for the possibility of new perspectives without limiting interpretation to a singular path. Afro Asian criticism must remain dynamic and hold as part of its makeup an intention to continually reexamine its foundations and the social, political, and economic landscapes in which performances take place. In response to the technique of queer reading, some have questioned the value of illuminating the influence of a creator's identity over their work, criticizing these endeavors as deterministic. Similar criticism is also leveled at scholars doing antiracist work: that what they produce is moralizing, subjective, and pushing a particular political agenda. Work that adheres to the status quo, however, also holds a political stance, one often stated much less openly. Afro Asian critics are not afraid to say that racism has been a harmful enterprise. Neither do they shy away from calling out racially conservative practices as less productive in establishing an egalitarian public sphere, or claiming antiracism to be a positive social force. Afro Asian criticism calls into question the ways in which the promotion of objectivity serves a dominant agenda specifically designed to discredit claims for minority enfranchisement.

You Can't Handle the Truth

In many ways, this book has been one long example of Afro Asian criticism. My point in using this method to examine the "Addictive" affair is specifically to show that the potential for interracial dialogue or identity formation exists in scenarios that are not consciously progressive in their conception. By looking and listening in a new way, it becomes clear that, amidst the copyright battle, Truth Hurts's song inspired a number of potentially positive sociopolitical results that cannot be overlooked as part of its life. Litigants used racially charged language to stand in as evidence for monetary grievances because of its power in dominant discourse steeped in political correctness (the hegemonic multicultural counterpart to antiracism). My Afro Asian critique of the case reveals this conflation of race and economy and asks how the song can instead illuminate unrecognized social identities, forge interracial relationships, and express antiracist politics.

Aside from Lahiri's comments about the inappropriate lyrical content of "Addictive," none of the other involved artists have ever claimed to dislike its aesthetic or thematic images. Singer Lata Mangeshkar allows, "I don't mind what they've done. They haven't tampered with my song. They've retained my voice as it was recorded and have rapped over it" (quoted in Ferrao 2002). The discourse of Orientalism asserts "that the imperial encounter pitted an active Western intruder against a supine or inert non-Western native" but in reality "there was *always* some form of active resistance, and in the overwhelming majority of cases, the resistance finally won out" (Said 1993, xii). A notion of one-sided appropriation or domination denies the agency of both involved parties, seeing them as objects in part of an all-engrossing, nonvariant system. How might the semiotics of

"Addictive" be taken in a different interpretive direction? Can the juxtaposition of Mangeshkar and Hurts's voices tell a different story?

Sampled Mangeshkar starts the song singing about the flower garden and then Truth Hurts joins, stepping into the scene set by the Hindi vocals. Though unintended, the pleasure and pain shared by these women are palpable. The sampled "Thoda" lyrics say it "takes a little silk / it takes a little glass" to indicate the hurt one must endure for the joys of a relationship. Truth Hurts sings, "he breaks me down / he builds me up / he fills my cup / I like it rough." Both songs feature a woman knowingly engaging in unions with a patriarchal sting, continuing because they also find satisfaction. The Mangeshkar sample features longer vocal lines and phrases, while Truth Hurts sings in a gruffer and more staccato voice. In form, the two voices perform a geographically and temporally displaced duet. In alternating moments, one voice sings words, while the other shifts to vocables that accent the lead voice. The two never approach melodic or linguistic unison, instead weaving a polyphonic texture that fleshes out the sparse hip hop track. The sample of Mangeshkar is, however, pitched a half-step higher than the original, adding an edge of urgency to her voice. This by-product of speeding up the original track results in Mangeshkar's vocals better supporting the less figurative, in-your-face rawness of Truth Hurts.

In order for this dialogue to be understood, a listener must be able to understand English and Hindi and possess some familiarity with hip hop and Bollywood conventions. This is not a far-fetched profile, but one very much extant in India and the Indian diaspora. Because of the strong presence of the Bollywood song, "Addictive" offers several points of identification for these listeners. Manasi Singhal, for example, describes driving with her mother and their surprise and excitement at hearing a Bollywood song on a hip hop station ([accessed] 2003). Critic Chris Fitzpatrick dismisses the presence of "Thoda" in the new song, saying it provides the average American a way to "feel magically sexy, dancing in a club to the 'forbidden,' 'risqué' sounds of a faraway 'foreign' land like India, even when almost all of those people have no idea what is being said in the song" (2002). But who are "those people" that do not understand the Hindi lyrics? There are plenty of Hindi speakers in the United States, not to mention those who will hear the song around the world. A variety of listeners might understand the intertextual dynamic of "Addictive" and will not just cast Lahiri's composition to the background.

As for the accompanying track, the original song actually bares similarities to hip hop instrumentation and orchestration. Both are driven by drumbeats accompanied by a subtle bassline. Lahiri's song also features sforzando chordal string "hits" and syncopated percussion riffs to accent Mangeshkar's vocals, both hip hop staples. These features—not just the exotic appeal of "Thoda"—certainly piqued DJ Quik's interest. The "Addictive" track consists of a long sample from Lahiri's piece and retains the same harmonic movement from those segments. Quik echoes Lahiri's piece by making use of newly created tambourine and supporting flute melodies, instruments employed prominently in Lahiri's song.

Several Orientalist hip hop tracks that followed "Addictive" solidified the sound of the flute into a trope for Indianness, including R. Kelly's "Snake" and Timbaland and Magoo's aptly named "Indian Flute" (although this "flute" is actually a Colombian *gaita* sampled from Totó La Momposina's "Curura"). In the case of "Addictive," the flute and its placement in the background texture of the track suggest more of an attempt to embellish the sample with instrumentation drawn directly from it.

There is no question that using Lahiri's track without permission was unethical, and it is part of a long history of music pirating in both East and West. Joanna Demers claims that hip hop producers have increasingly turned to non-Western samples due to the high cost of licensing Western recordings (2006). Artists select tracks more obscure in the West and hope that the companies that own them are defunct or so out of touch with Western pop culture that they do not discover the use of their material (Demers 2006, 103). Interscope's approval of the sample without clearance is a symptom of this trend and speaks to larger questions about how to allow for open creative processes without sacrificing appropriate compensation. Demers's comments focus on the U.S. context, but it turns out that Lahiri was also known, before the "Addictive" affair, as a composer who frequently "lifted" songs from around the world to make into his own hits (Sharma 2010, 251). In researching the "Addictive" case, I have also come across multiple websites with long lists of U.S. pop songs that were remade or sampled by Hindi artists, many without permission, and quite a few by Lahiri.

Sampling proliferates in many cultural directions in twenty-first-century popular music, providing a digital record of the kind of musical borrowing or alternative conceptions of cultural ownership that is a part of many traditional forms. The notion of a singularly owned musical statement is not a temporal or cultural universal and has challenged artists from a variety of styles to limit or obscure these conversations as their work becomes commodified.[14] Some artists actively denounce the copyright system as a hindrance to creativity and a way to force cultural practice into a consumer model (McLeod and DiCola 2011). The idea that the "music war" could be "won" or that the "Addictive" trial would "solve" this sampling phenomenon is as false as the idea that a war with bombs and ground troops will resolve political issues.

We should not neglect to criticize the Orientalist gestures of Hurts and her collaborators, but we must also examine the racial and racist discourses used to denounce their sampling. It is interesting to note the mainstream media's distinctive treatment of black hip hop samplers from a white artist such as Girl Talk. While black artists—and Indian remix artists—are repeatedly dragged out as unimaginative thieves in the popular press, Girl Talk is critically acclaimed for his entirely sample-based oeuvre and Robin Hood championing of Fair Use.[15] Further, Lahiri and his team claimed that the black music denigrated the Indian content, especially in his claims that Hurts's lyrics would offend Hindu and Muslim listeners.[16] This sentiment was echoed when writer Chris Fitzpatrick likened Hurts's Orientalism to a "pole-greasing stripper" labeling herself an "Exotic Dancer" [sic] in order to appear magical and sexy, a misogynist statement with subtle racist undertones (2002). Other accounts made a point of "revealing" Hurts's legal name to be Sheri Watson, as if she were a criminal operating under an alias. That Hurts—not DJ Quik or Dr. Dre— was the target of these attacks is telling. Despite having the smallest hand in the sampling debacle, Hurts became the scapegoat because she was the face (or voice) of the song. But the feminized nature of the racist comments suggests it is particularly her sexually excessive black femininity that sullied the sampled song.[17]

In contrast, critics often described Lahiri's song as one of sophistication or even mistakenly as Indian classical music. In reality, the song was a popular song and, in the original film, sung by a deceptive call girl—not a virtuous bride. Beaster-Jones and Marshall suggest that the "Addictive" "video's stereotypes are not so far from eroticized *tawāyaf* [courtesan] representations in Hindi films" (Marshall and Beaster-Jones 2012, 3). The critical maelstrom that ensued over "Addictive" pitted two different portrayals of female sexuality against one another and valorized one over the other simply because of racial difference and misperception.

Framing the trial as a battle between black and Indian music neglected the true conflict, not one of representation but of money. In reality, all parties profited from "Addictive." It was a major success for Hurts, by far her biggest success even in years since. Lahiri declared, "I feel very proud because no Indian composer before has made it to the US and UK top 10 charts. It's a proud moment for Indian music and for the Hindi film industry" (quoted in Bhattacharya 2002). Instead of reveling in the pride of cultural representation, however, Lahiri released his own album of song remixes, *Bappiwood Remixes* (2003), which included a version of "Thoda" under the title "Kaliyon Ka Chaman." He also toured the United States, capitalizing on the success of "Addictive" (Demers 2006, 103). And while Dr. Dre's legal counsel claimed he did not know how to find the original track's owner and thus did not credit Lahiri, copies sold in India supposedly *had* credited Lahiri presumably as a way to increase sales (Kaufman 2003). Due to the popularity of the song, Truth Hurts was asked to perform at the 2003 Zee Gold Bollywood Awards in New York. Kamal Dandona, chairman of the awards, said having Truth Hurts perform was a coup and that, since she brought Bollywood to mainstream America, they were bringing her to Bollywood ("Nightingale" 2002). The symbiotic exchange is evident here, but inviting Truth Hurts into an Indian setting also allowed for the continued evolution of the meaning of the song and the cultural exchange it fostered. "Addictive" thus bridged audiences, cultures, and industries through shared consumption and enjoyment.

Further complicating this scenario is the 2002 remix of "Addictive" by producer Harry Anand and released by Universal Music India. Despite initial statements to the contrary, Anand admitted that this song, also retitled "Kaliyon ka Chaman," was based on the Truth Hurts version, although it did not sample it (Marshall and Beaster-Jones 2012, 6). Universal agents approached Anand to do the piece, indicating their recognition of "Addictive"'s popularity and a desire to extend the revenue-producing capacity of the black–Indian mixture even more, again without obtaining permission. The video for "Kaliyon" most clearly situates it as descended from "Addictive": a group of Indian women wearing jeans and skimpy tops perform belly dance moves in the same choreographic formations as Truth Hurts's video. In "Kaliyon," the original gestural images from the "Addictive" video contribute to an unintended self-Orientalization by the Indian artists, reproducing the U.S. artists' conflation of South Asia and the Middle East. It is worth mentioning that there are some unverifiable Internet sources[18] that claim "Addictive" was derived from "Kaliyon," more evidence of the complicated circuits of remixes and how they come into various listeners' lives. Rather than arguing for which came first, the more important point is that multiple parties wanted to claim ownership over the lucrative musical and visual material.

Journalist Narendra Kusnur reflects the more lighthearted sentiment of a lot of the Indian and desi press, stating, "THE music world can be really funny ... a song whom nobody knew, a song which was a complete flop when it was released two decades ago, a song which even the film's director and music director had forgotten ... this tune has now become a rage in the West. But never mind—that's showbiz, folks [sic]" (2002a). Several producers subsequently created remixes based on "Addictive," some of whom credit that song or others in its lineage, and others who do not (Marshall and Beaster-Jones 2012). This flurry of activity led Kusnur to write, "I kept imagining what would happen by the month-end. Would I be bombarded with 50 more versions of Thoda Resham Lagta Hai? [sic]"

Figure 5.2. Meghna Naidu and dancers performing Harry Anand's "Kaliyon Ka Chaman."

(2002b). Kusnur's statements—and Singhal's above—are not lamenting cultural violation but finding humor in the overlap of mediascapes (Appadurai 1996) that can turn arcane pop ephemera into digital age sensations.

Approaching "Addictive" in this manner shows how the reliance on the East–West metonym simplifies the interpenetration of the global South and North and the cosmopolitan circulation of people and media. The intersection of Orientalist, neo-primitivist, and gender discourses creates a space in which subject positions are not easily demarcated or stratified, illuminating points of resistance against dominant powers on both sides of the sampler. In her study of nineteenth-century European women's roles in creating imperialist representation, Reina Lewis shows that they sometimes contested but often colluded with male artists (1996). But, she notes, "since all subjects are the product of more than one discourse, the ascendancy of different discourses may differently complexion the relations of power and knowledge" (R. Lewis 1996, 43). In the case of "Addictive," the multiple dynamics of race allow for the black artists to be imperialist or create Orientalist representation at the same time that they are subjugated in domestic and global racial taxonomies. The black artists are wedged in an in-between space as both colonizer and colonized, revealing the monolithic Occident to be a fictive construction. At the same time, Lewis claims, "for Said ... Orientalism is a homogenous discourse enunciated by a colonial subject that is unified, intentional and irredeemably male" (1996, 17). My attention to the gendered contours of the sono-racial debates suggests that black and brown femininity became a specifically potent site for the inscription of black–Asian difference by primarily male actors, suggesting the Orient is no less monolithic than the Occident.

The third verse of "Addictive," rapped by guest MC, Rakim, is a good example of the way the song, while Orientalizing India, calls out the impact of U.S. imperialism on the home front. In his 1987 "Paid in Full," Rakim says he might reject his youth as a "stick-up kid" and search for a "nine-to-five," ultimately hoping he can make music as his source of income.[19] Rakim recalls this earlier song in the "Addictive" rap by employing the same opening line, "Thinking of a master plan." He then diverges in sentiment, detailing his narcotics career riddled with "drug wars trips to jail and shootouts" and celebrating the love and support of his woman in these ventures. No longer considering the corporate route, he vows to quit the game after "another hundred mill." Rakim's reference to the war on drugs calls up the U.S. government venture that simultaneously targets marginalized populations within and outside of the nation. The shift in his chosen mode of economic uplift indicates an early-twenty-first-century economic context in which the hope of a nine-to-five job is fleeting for young men of color, especially in the face of more lucrative shadow economies. Rakim's casual reference to multiple incarcerations also reveals the disproportionate impact of the prison system on people of color in which going to jail is commonplace or expected (Alexander 2010). Presumably not intended as a political statement, Rakim's verse nevertheless speaks to these sociopolitical realities for Occidental blacks.

By proclaiming themselves victims in this other war, the "Addictive" participants occupy a position that stands in opposition to the state. As in the case of Paul Robeson in Chapter 1, Bill Mullen's "Afro-Orientalism" is apt here. This discourse employs dominant Orientalist images in the service of nondominant aims or in attempts to build interracial solidarities. More specifically, the "Black-yellowface" of this particular song "works as a conduit through which Asian ethnic representations—however distorted—stand in for a naïve sense of a romanticized culture positioned outside of the Otherness of Blackness" (Whaley 2006, 193). In "Addictive," there is a dual longing on the part of the creators: to escape to an exotic locale and temporarily inhabit an identity that is not (fully) blackness. The sampling of non-Western music by white artists like Deep Forest, Enigma, and David Byrne mirrors colonial dynamics because of the racial and power differentials. In "Addictive," while power differentials exist, they are complicated by a racial discourse that does not so easily align. This is not to say that black Orientalism is justified, only that it might serve as a step toward identification rather than Othering (Sharma 2010).

We can read "Addictive" as a violent interracial violation that proves we will never see eye-to-eye with the Other, or we can look at the various doors DJ Quik's overzealous indiscretion opened for transnational communication. What was the investment in portraying the affair as a war when there was obviously something else going on? Why was Bollywood music cast as something utterly foreign and hip hop as a lowly, deviant art form? And why would few critics acknowledge the popularity of the song in the United States and India? These responses are reflections of how racial triangulation deeply rooted in the U.S. popular music industry carries over into international arenas, in fact proving the U.S. cultural imperialism Lahiri lamented in the proliferation of domestic racial discourses. Songs and other cultural productions can further or intervene in this project. Each reader or listener possesses a personal agency that allows them to read for or against dominant ideologies. But the metonym of war does not allow this space for fluid and thoughtful critique. Rather, our only narrative choices for "Addictive" are, as laid out by critic Chris Fitzpatrick: (1) akin to "mutilations by landmines, refugee camps, resurfacing warlords and drug lords, suicide bombers, occupations" or (2) serving as a "reassuring sedative to the average American viewer, conveniently leaving out" the fore-listed horrors (2002).

The Promises and the Problematics of Interracial Music

Performing an Afro Asian critique of "Addictive" illuminates multiple criteria for success by revealing the many sociopolitical employments of the song. Different listeners have varied interpretations of the text and the musical traditions it brings together. The song presented a stereotyped vision of "the East" amidst the intensifying War on Terror. Its black creators performed U.S. Americanness in their Orientalist evocations, while simultaneously reviving a Bollywood song so off the radar that even its composer did not remember it.[20] Multiracial pop and hip hop listeners consumed the song in the United States and abroad, earning Truth Hurts the status of a one-hit wonder (so far). And the song ratified existing communities as desi consumers used the song to fashion a sense of home within the diaspora. In the process, new audiences were defined at the intersection of hip hop and Bollywood as it became clear that the two styles both appealed to black and South Asian consumers believed to be separate, as well as a specific audience of diasporic Indians interested in pieces that employ them both. Music producers capitalized on the song's interracial and intercultural appeal in order to further their careers, latching onto the key elements and remixing them into new tracks.

Of course, blind celebration of problematic exchanges is unproductive. The discourse of war—while extreme—did make known the pitfalls of black–Asian endeavors that appear to forge new paths while drawing too heavily on outdated sono-racial taxonomies. The extant critical reads of "Addictive" focus on black–Asian musical difference, perpetuating racial and cultural separation in the broader sociopolitical realm. Afro Asian criticism does not deny colonially defined difference—it discusses this difference, unearths why it exists, and reveals the ways in which this discourse is incomplete. But this chapter is not simply about how blackness and Indianness are represented in contrast. My underlying point is that anti-Asian and anti-black racism will never be a means to sociopolitical liberation, and using racism to fight racism will always undermine the quest for cultural legitimacy.

Further, in "Addictive" and similar cross-racial and cross-cultural intellectual property cases, money and ego came before a desire for conversation and mutual education. Are these the values we want held up as central to the national and international communities built around music of color? The conflation of intellectual property and cultural ownership in analyses of the sampling in many senses enforced the sonic identity politics I revealed in Chapter 4, suggesting that people "own" culture simply because they are of a racial category (or other identity marker) attached to it. At the same time, the "Addictive" case raises questions about the politics of music of color and the limits of black–brown alliances amid cultural misunderstanding and commerce.

In the end, we can read "Addictive" as a violation that proves we will never see eye-to-eye with each other. But this move only solidifies antagonism and eliminates potential for positive connections—and reasons for artists to be more careful in the future. We must complicate our arguments and open our minds to imagine the possibility of good amidst the difficulties of interracial exchange, and Afro Asian studies offer narratives that help move us beyond simplified negatives and romantic positives. Cultural production and political economy are connected but do not always move parallel to one another.

The danger of the cases in *Resounding Afro Asia*, and in the book itself, is placing too strong of an emphasis on U.S. racial dynamics. In continued conversation, we must be careful to not let U.S. voices eclipse alternate perspectives on race and sound. The ultimate challenge to continued Afro Asian, Third World, and other anticolonial projects is that people of color living in the First World are so entrenched in dominant systems that they actively construct the hegemonies that perpetuate their colonization. Interracial music has the potential to place these global conversations back into U.S. societal discourse. That is, if we are willing and able to hear it.

Conclusion
Red Baraat and Other Reverberations

N ot long after their 2012 White House debut, Red Baraat released their second album, *Shruggy Ji* (2013). The record debuted at number one on the Billboard World Music chart and launched the band on a two-year world tour, with performances at major festivals and venues including the Monterey Jazz Festival, Bonnaroo, TED, and the Olympic Games (Red Baraat 2015). The Afro Asian project that had shortly before broken onto "the" national stage was now an indisputably international phenomenon, bridging black, Asian, "American," and "world" in their hybrid declarations. This group seems a fitting end to my tale, a younger/newer group of artists that has matured in the jazz and world music scenes—and spaces in between—rife with inter-racial and intercultural engagements. Their meteoric rise in the music industry and large national and international fan base indicate one possible future for Afro Asian and other interracial music (which is not to say that many of the older artists in this book are not continuing to develop their own projects).

Yet Red Baraat's career also indicates the persistence of racial discourses that limit the freedom of artists of color. While onstage the band performs the wonders of interracial and intercultural encounter, leader Sunny Jain says there's a "dark part of it, as well" (quoted in Red Baraat 2015). Jain explains the title track of their 2015 release *Gaadi of Truth*

> is addressing the hard realities of traveling and all the work that's involved in getting from show to show. The hardships of going through TSA at the airport—one of our guys, Sonny Singh, is a Sikh, and he always gets harassed and patted down a lot more than anyone else in the band does, because of his turban. We have two African-Americans in the band, and we'll be driving in the South and get pulled over by a cop with some nonsense reason. And the constant thing of people remarking on the multi-ethnic makeup of the band, or me being asked questions like, "Where are you from?" "I'm from Rochester, New York." (quoted in Red Baraat 2015)

Figure 6.1. Red Baraat. Photograph by James Bartolozzi. Courtesy of Sunny Jain.

Jain's language is telling. While acknowledging the group's multiracial profile and how their music is a place to work through its ramifications, he also expresses exhaustion with the persistent racial fascination and questioning. He seems impatient for a moment when structural racism and the microaggressions of essentialist thinking no longer cloud the band's operations.

The "colorization" of the United States (Chang 2014) has led us to a paradoxical state: while supposedly in a post–civil rights era of openness and equality, we experience the continued plague of racism, sexism, homophobia, and xenophobia. How is it that we can see and hear so much diversity around us—on our televisions, city streets, the Internet, and iTunes—but still not, in Rodney King's infamous words, "just get along"? Obama's election launched widespread discussion of the possibility that we are living in a "postracial" society, even while it is clear that racial conservatism continues to rear its ugly head. Jain's comments express an understanding of the still pressing need for basic antiracist changes in how U.S. society operates, officially and in people's daily lives. His words are especially relevant in a moment of national debate sparked by multiple high-profile murders of young black and brown people by law enforcement officers, a conversation that is highly polarized along racial, political, and generational lines.[1] Jain's simultaneous longing for the ability to simply make music is also apropos to many citizens'—especially younger generations'—increasing frustration with our inability as a nation to make significant headway on these racial questions.

This book has used popular music as a space in which to take stock of where we sit in relation to race in the contemporary United States and see where we might be going. I have examined Afro Asian ensembles as sites of *sono-racial collaboration* between people and sound, analyzing the ways in which black and Asian/American musicians form relationships across racial lines and use music as the primary vehicle through which to do so. In the process, I exposed the ways in which sound can be wielded as both an expression of one's identity and a tool to connect with others by supporting their identity productions. In particular, I claim that it is possible for members of one race to productively contribute to the expressions of another, although there are more or less effective ways of doing so. The cases presented here make clear that successful sono-racial collaboration requires an open mind, a willingness to understand experiences different than one's own, a desire to learn new ways of communicating across lines of difference, the ability to question how the self fits into broader sociopolitical structures, and a readiness to work against the power dynamics they engender. Afro Asian projects reveal productive strategies for forging and sustaining interracial community as well as the challenges, competing desires, successes, and shortfalls that are a large part of the process.

These multifarious expressions resist and reproduce prevailing racial dynamics in popular music discourses and spaces. Throughout this book, I detailed how the music industry has been influenced by broader racial segregation in the United States, as evidenced in part by *sono-racial triangulation*. Just as blacks and Asians have been jointly racialized, so are musical styles deemed "black" or "Asian" in contrast to one another. In particular, black music is appreciated as homegrown national culture despite also being viewed as a source of moral pollution. Asian music is held as more sophisticated and respectable, yet perpetually foreign. These categorizations are not merely mapping a racial lexicon; they are part of a racist system that perpetuates white domination through segregation and stereotype.

Races jointly constructed can also be jointly dismantled, however, and Afro Asian music can counter sono-racial triangulation not by "transcending" race through color-blind logic, but by calling out racial structures and harnessing race in ways that work against more limited frameworks. Brandi Catanese argues for racial "transgression" as a more productive antiracist strategy, one that "exposes the moral limitations of transcendence as a viable strategy for social change by acknowledging the histories of social location that people wear on their bodies and that inform all of our interpretive frameworks" (2012, 22). Rather than leaving behind our "racially mediated reality"—were that even possible—we might be better served by actions that "violate," "offend," or "disobey" extant racial patterns (Catanese 2012, 21). Through mixing of racialized sounds and, sometimes, explicit extra-musical politics, Afro Asian artists increase the opportunities for people of color to establish counterdominant formations.

In particular, Afro Asian music confounds a culture industry and society based on racial divisions because it cannot be reduced to monoracial categories. Yoko Noge's music is neither black nor Japanese, but something else that sits between the two. Funkadesi's audiences do not fit a profile that "matches" only one racially marked genre or scene. Fred Ho's work sounds new racial centers in which multiple racialized forms become musical touchstones. And "Addictive" proved that artists and audiences do not strictly adhere to segregated categories in how they listen and consume music. Of course, even with the acknowledgment of racial mixture, artists must still work against the Othering discourses that treat their work as a new or passing fad. In the cases I examined, it is clear how hard it is for artists to hold onto complex identities in the face of longstanding sono-racial divisions and, despite their best intentions, this goal is sometimes thwarted. For bands seeking wider recognition—national and international—the pull of the legible label can be strong.

In response to industry (and scholarly) assumptions that a group's racial and ethnic makeup directly gives rise to their hybrid music, I point out the mixture of heritage, affiliation, and aesthetic license that leads to each of this book's ensemble's production. In doing so, I argue for a model of the relationship between identity and its sonic expression as less deterministic and more a result of multiple markers (race, culture, gender, class) and impetuses (community building, antiracist politics, entertainment). Despite the *body–culture determinism* prevalent in how music is marked in the popular music industry, I claim that being of a given race does not mean one produces a particular cultural expression. Recognizing the range of sounds a given artist can and does make leads to a better understanding of how musicians in the United States have historically worked across racial lines. The interracial musical abilities of the musicians I discuss here transcend the limitations of multicultural discourse that conflates race and culture.

Afro Asian projects, then, operate within multicultural frameworks while pushing on their limitations. Hegemonic multicultural policies and industry spaces pose visible racial markers as evidence of deeper cultural or political representation, a concept that can also be extended into the acoustic realm. For example, as I have described several times, public arts festivals are a particular hotbed of multicultural discourse, promoting parades of racial and ethnic imagery accompanied by little substantive insight into their cultural underpinnings, (subversive) histories, or the political-economic circumstances of the people who create them. Decontextualized and surface images of "culture," including instruments, melodies, and clothing, are incorporated into programs or venues that provide a representational platform but separate and attempt to make equivalent a wide variety of people and practices.

The artists I examine are caught in the tension between disrupting these dynamics and reiterating sonic stereotypes that perpetuate them. I refer to these two positions as *radical interracialism*—the employment of fluid cultural production to disrupt deterministic links to race—and *sonic identity politics*—a simplistic rendering of culture that results in the re-inscription of simplified racial markers. Many of the groups

I discuss in this project actively resist sonic identity politics because they perform musical traditions without divorcing them from their cultural meanings, other practitioners, and industries. And in all of their cases, traditions are actually included in their repertoire specifically because of their historical and political-economic resonances, not just their sounds.

The complication of countering sonic identity politics, however, is that artists rely on the same sonic vocabularies employed in standard multicultural rhetoric, which can easily slip into dominant simplifications. Because of the racial meanings we invest in sounds, countering these assumptions is not always as simple as a musician performing them cross-racially to the delight and political enlightenment of audiences. Funkadesi keyboardist Inder Singh, for example, cowrote the lyrics and composed the music for "Muy Cansado," a song from the group's third album that is partially in Spanish. He also sings lead on the song and, in concert, audiences see and hear a Punjabi man performing in Spanish, a disruption of body–culture determinism. In one performance I attended, I saw a group of twenty-something desi women look shocked and then giggle with disbelief at Singh's cross-lingual performance. These women's reaction reflects the difficulties of wrenching sounds away from their assumed origins. Even though Singh's performance makes clear that a desi body can embody nondesi cultural material, reading his singing as a juxtaposition is predicated on a notion of racial and cultural separation. A performance can be encountered through this hegemonic lens despite the intentions of the people who perform it, or even the best intentions of listeners. Thus, listeners may only hear Noge's "broken English" or Funkadesi's "ganja-induced" reggae grooves and not the more complex cultural processes displayed, or the ways in which the styles interact with other elements to form new meanings.

I suggest that Afro Asian artists are engaged in unfolding processes that reshape typical multicultural spaces and discourses. Examining Yoko Noge and collaborators, I demonstrated how musicians authenticate and legitimate their performance of non-heritage-related forms, as well as how these endeavors continue to be overwrought with essentializing discourses from within and without. The spatial politics of Funkadesi and their audiences became a means to understand how the intentional sharing of space pushes on patterns of venue racialization that support racial segregation in Chicago. In my read of Fred Ho's Afro Asian Music Ensemble (AAME), I argued that resisting these sono-racial discourses requires not only the joint performance of sonic identities but also a reframing of the larger system through which they are heard. The AAME's work becomes a space in which racialized sounds are performed within larger sonic frameworks that shift how the individual voices and instruments signify. And, finally, by reading the "Addictive" case for its radical interracial potential, I suggest that it is not only up to musical creators to change how sound expresses new racial possibilities, for listeners play a part in interpreting these politics.

While I argue for the continuity of broad distinctions between black and Asian music over the past century of the popular culture industry, my case studies also reveal more nuanced portraits of the black–Asian dynamic that can disrupt fixed multicultural categories. One basic distinction is the varied combination of cultural material that makes up the black and Asian portions of their praxis. While the sono-racial category of Asian music conflates numerous traditions into one grouping, for example, my case studies indicate very different and specific Asian and Asian American cultural, political, and economic experiences. Noge, for example, is a first-generation Japanese immigrant with strong ties to her home country. She continues to tour in Japan and thus circulates her work in the cultural economies of both of her national affiliations. While Noge is a more recent immigrant, the history of Japanese migration to the United States is one of the oldest of the Asian countries, a fact symbolically evoked in Noge's performances or perhaps read into her performances by audience members who do not know her biography. This older "version" of Asianness stands in contrast to the, generally, newer waves of South Asian migration to the United States illuminated by Funkadesi, Red Baraat, or the Truth Hurts case.

My analyses also illuminate the hybridity of what is glossed as black music, a racial category encompassing forms from beyond the United States and inflected by regional histories here. Funkadesi's performance of funk and reggae elements highlights the transnational African diasporic conversation evidenced in black music, as does Fred Ho placing both jazz and West African percussion into the "Afro" position. Even within specifically African American traditions, the jazz and blues scenes that form part of the Jazz Me Blues and Afro Asian Music Ensemble foundation profess unique marks from their separate locations within Chicago and New York City. The former city is a more playful and relaxed space of intercultural exploration, the latter a stricter locale that prizes aesthetic and political innovation alongside an economic bottom line necessitated by the higher cost of living and production.

The interaction of at least two nonwhite categories in Afro Asian performance makes it a productive site for understanding race not as so many labels on a chart, but as a multidirectional relationship. The majority of discussions of minority music making and studies of interracial and intercultural performance highlight a single racial/ethnic group and their relationship to a white majority. Examining interminority performances that disregard—or at least de-center—whiteness can complicate binary discussions of race and power. Vijay Prashad suggests that "there is little space in popular discourse for an examination of what goes on outside the realm of white America among people of color" (2001, x). Afro Asian performances show that people of color do much more in life than lament whiteness. Instead of relying on simplified theories that pose minority traditions as created solely in contestation of the white/Western "mainstream," I highlight the variety of political and artistic inspirations for interracial music making.

While racialized distinctly and coming from a multitude of cultural locations, I also posed the term *music of color* as a rallying point for non-white/Western traditions that share a lack of full representational freedom in dominant discourses. It is a formation that offers an alternative to the separation of "black" from "world" built into the music industry and provides a discursive means for artists to reclaim nonwhite/Western forms toward nonhegemonic ends. Music of color allows for people of color to draw from a collectively "owned" bank of traditions to further their individual and mutual ends. As an example, Asian American jazz pianist and composer Jon Jang claims: "The first Chinese music I heard was when Paul Robeson sang Chinese folk songs of resistance in Mandarin, when I was four years old" (quoted in Paget-Clarke 2000). The notion that multiply raced performers can further racial, cultural, political, and spiritual projects not directly related to their heritage is a powerful testament to the possibilities for extra-musical solidarity. And these coalitions need not require conformity: music of color, like people of color, can hold differences of race or nation in addition to or as part of a collective identity. Still, a case like Truth Hurts's "Addictive" is a reminder that there are limits to these formations, as black cannot fully stand in for brown or vice versa. Music of color must be continually interrogated as its fragile unity can easily slip into cross-racial mimicry.

As we engage artists that draw on multiple racialized genres, we glimpse the "origins" of forms that might eventually become as ingrained in U.S. culture as salsa or the blues. The question remains whether they will be able to exist in their interracial profile or be forced into mono-racial boxes. There are clear reasons to hold onto racial and cultural demarcations for music, especially in the face of imperialist projects that use art as a front for domination. But we must also ask why this investment remains so central in our contemporary aesthetic and political work. The height of contemporary progressive thinking around gender and sexuality is that individuals must be free to choose their own labels. Confining someone to one fixed category based on birth circumstances, body, or familial role is considered to be conservative. Why can't this be the same for cultural affiliations? Clearly, because of colonial legacies, there are historical reasons this concept has not been embraced. But the refusal to open up this possibility—or even ask questions of what it might require—is acquiescence to a system that derives power from determining for others who and what they are. Afro Asian music provides a space to consider the various implications and outcomes of these potential debates.

If the United States is indeed in a perpetual identity crisis around its racial composition, Afro Asian music can challenge what we hear as "American." Key to these endeavors is that they declare a world in which all of their attendant sounds can be audible indicators of U.S. Americanness. Performing both inherited and chosen racial/cultural identities, the groups I cover perform collective interracial identities based on unity-through-difference, actively challenging historic notions of national solidarity that ignored people of color, as well as ameliorative multicultural representations of racial groups as isolated entities that only engage with a white majority.

The unity I discuss differs from existing narratives of the melting pot or U.S. national "family." Josh Kun (2005) and Charles Hiroshi Garrett (2008) have shown that these tropes are based on notions of cultural conformity and exclude as much as they include, especially people of color and their practices. Both scholars' work remedies longstanding narratives of U.S. musical identity by presenting it as "not a seamless integration of traditions but instead a complex interplay of musical worlds, a sonic expression of the debates that characterized this era's discourse on race, class, and nation" (Garrett 2008, 13). Music of marginalized peoples has long offered an alternative vision of what it means to be U.S. American and provided a sonic basis to depart from dominant cultural paradigms.

Where I diverge from Kun and Garrett is that I argue for the continued utility of unity in new formulations of U.S. identity. Theorizing difference is important to combatting historic dynamics of assimilation, which has never been fully achievable by nonwhites. But discourses of racial difference have also been a means of defining dominant white subjectivity.[2] People of color come to know themselves not only in contrast to but also in conjunction with other racial groups. Through Afro Asian processes, artists showcase a model in which unity and difference inform rather than oppose one another. Instead of the static uniformity of previous national narratives, they present coalitions that are dynamic, each ensemble a laboratory in which cultural processes are rarely complete and mean different things to different people.

Looking jointly at blackness and Asianness complicates understandings of music and race in the United States, the myriad traditions these labels represent, and the variety of ways they come together. Afro Asian music is the expression of complex individual and group identities that reach across difference. It says we don't have to wait until a vaguely brown "super-race" emerges to "fix" the problem of race.[3] This music and the people who make it show how all raced people—meaning everyone—are agents in the shaping of racial discourse. At the same time, interracial performance (and research) requires a willful ignorance, the understanding that one is entering spaces and encountering traditions about which one may know nothing. But, as I hope I have shown here, the power of taking this step toward another human being is the foundation on which all potential for change—political, social, or spiritual—rests. Will we continue, again and again, to take this step?

Notes

Introduction

1. All Sunny Jain quotes and paraphrases are taken from a phone interview I conducted with him on November 27, 2012.

2. Obama has one parent who is black, the other white. His racial identity has been much debated during his presidency, with various voices arguing he is black, mixed, or even Asian American (based on the ways in which his life experience resonates closely with Asian American histories). See Yang 2008 on this last point.

3. Red Baraat's Jain and Tomas Fujiwara also toured as cultural ambassadors with the U.S. State Department (Jain [accessed] 2015, Fujiwara [accessed] 2015).

4. This "colorization" was the result of several changes in the second half of the twentieth century that shifted how race was lived in the United States. The Immigration and Naturalization Act of 1965 led to an influx of South and Southeast Asians and Central and South Americans of a wide range of classes. Also, by the mid-twentieth century, a variety of populations—not just black and white—were represented by multiple generations in the United States, from people having newly arrived to those whose families have lived here for decades. The 1967 *Loving vs. Virginia* decision struck down anti-miscegenation laws and ushered in increased interracial marriage. In 2010 interracial marriage rates had doubled since 1970, and 1 in 12 married couples were interracial (Morello 2012). Also, thanks to the civil rights movement and resultant multiculturalism, there has been an increase in civic voice for people of color, as well as the production of interracial coalitions among national and ethnic groups that previously considered themselves to be separate, the mobilization around Asian American unity being one example (Kondo 1997, Wei 1993, Wong 2004). Finally, technologies such as satellite television, air travel, and the Internet allow people to stay connected to their homelands or more easily encounter people and places beyond their experience.

5. Counterparts from outside the United States include Susheela Raman (U.K.), Afro Celt Sound System (U.K.), Delhi 2 Dublin (Canada), Talvin Singh (U.K.), Violons Barbares (Bulgaria, France, and Mongolia),

Fun^da^mental (U.K.), and Trilok Gurtu (who is originally from India and works extensively in Europe and North America).

6. See Fellezs 2011, Garrett 2008, Kun 2005, and Pacini Hernandez 2010. I will very shortly offer greater critical insight into the term "hybridity." For now, I employ it simply to mean cultural mixing.

7. "One box" refers to official forms, surveys, or censuses that require an individual to select only one racial category. Mixed-race advocacy and scholarship have heavily criticized the limitations of this way of accounting for racial identification. Michele Elam offers a productive summary of these arguments as well as an insightful push back in which she questions the political or social efficacy of checking more than one box, when "the census is an economic tool that was never meant as—nor should it be—a site for self-expression" (2011, 14).

8. Throughout the book, I distinguish between Asian immigrant and Asian American artists. At times, however, I use the designation "Asian/American" to indicate a fluid range of national and cultural identities between Asian immigrant and U.S.-born Asian American, which are all collapsed into the Asian racial category. In some cases, this designation better renders artists' complex and shifting understandings of themselves as Asian and/or Asian American, as the slash "affords the possibility of being both at once or moving between the two" (Wong 2006). Similarly, David Palumbo-Liu says the slash "implies both exclusion and inclusion" marking "*both* the distinction installed between 'Asian' and 'American' *and* a dynamic, unsettled, and inclusive movement" (1999, 1). Thus, aside from marking self-identification, my use of the slash also helps render the larger discourses of how "Asian" and "American" have historically dis/articulated, questioning the boundaries of both.

How to define and textually render Asian/American identities forms a significant portion of scholarly discussion of Asian immigrant and Asian American performance. Su Zheng distinguishes ethnically specific labels like "Chinese American" from the racialized "Asian American," a political moniker coined in the U.S. Asian American movement (2010, 12–13). Like Zheng, Dorinne Kondo (1997), Joseph Lam (1999), and Deborah Wong (2004, 2006), I avoid ascribing aesthetic criteria to Asian American music and instead embrace the term as an indication of the processes of Asian Americans making and listening to music.

9. The Third World movement refers to a mid-twentieth-century conglomeration of anticolonial and transnational gatherings, organizations, actions, and philosophies spearheaded by organizers and politicians in postcolonial nations in Africa, Asia, and Latin America, and people of color in Western nations (Prashad 2007). The Afro Asian movement was a subset of this larger endeavor specifically made up of representatives from African and Asian states. Both movements were conceived as alternatives to the geopolitical ultimatums of the First (NATO) and Second (Soviet bloc) worlds. I will discuss these movements and this historical moment in greater detail in Chapter 1.

10. My study looks at these musical exchanges in the United States, but there are many corollaries in other national and cultural contexts. The most obvious are interactions between blacks (African and Afro-Caribbean immigrants and descendants) and South Asians in the United Kingdom, historically jointly labeled "black" according to white British racial logic (Gilroy 1987, Mercer 1994). This same label was embraced as a politicized category in various British movements for social justice starting in the

1970s, although this usage grew less prevalent over subsequent decades (Bakrania 2013, 13, 206). A number of scholars have explored the sonic manifestation of the British black–Asian context, especially in *bhangra* and other Asian remix genres (Bakrania 2013; Sharma et al. 1996; Taylor 2007; Zuberi 2001). There is also a sizable history of encounters between blacks and Asians in the Caribbean, in some instances leading to the formation of mixed-raced communities. The musical resonances of these exchanges have been engaged by several scholars, some emphasizing hybrid practices (Manuel 2000, Guilbault 2007) and others the participation of South and East Asians in the production of black and Creole styles (Lipsitz 2007, Prashad 2001).

11. I use "race" to mean a taxonomy of sensorial characteristics that "signifies and symbolizes social conflicts and interests by referring to different types of human bodies" (Omi and Winant 1994, 55). The components of race—visual markers, sounds, smells, tastes, or tactile traits—are granted more or less emphasis based on shifting social and historical dynamics. And while they are ultimately discursive constructions, racial categories result in material consequences that tangibly affect people.

"Culture" consists of materials, beliefs, and behaviors that bind people into communities. Racial connotations are often attached to cultural features, just as people of a given racial group may share similar cultural material. But there is no inherent link between the two. Further, each of us belongs to a number of identity categories—by both inheritance and personal choice—that can coexist or conflict with one another. Chosen affiliations can even manifest more strongly because an individual wants to be a part of that community, a fact important in understanding the motives and problematics of interracial performance (Hollinger 2000, 121).

To keep these distinctions clear, I use "black" and "Asian" to indicate racial categories. These labels might be placed on sounds or people, but should always be understood as nongenetic (even though they reference the body) and based on sociopolitically constructed generalizations. I use these terms even when referring to music from non-U.S. traditions because, when performed in the United States, they are usually understood through the racial matrix prevalent in this country. To indicate lived practices and culture-based communities, I use "African American," "Asian American," or a specific national or cultural label such as "Japanese" or "Ewe."

12. Although sound and vision are the most studied, other senses can also communicate information about race. In *Virtual Homelands: Indian Immigrants and Online Cultures in the United States* (2014), Madhavi Mallapragada offers an example of olfactory racialization in a theorization of the association of the smell of curry with South Asian/American populations.

13. Michael Omi and Howard Winant suggest it is important to distinguish race from racism, as both have shifted through time. While racial projects can take a variety of forms—both constructive and destructive— a project is racist "if and only if it *creates or reproduces structures of domination based on essentialist categories of race*" (1994, 71, emphasis in original).

14. Much like Kim, I do not view racial triangulation as an exclusive or static formation excluding other racial groups, but rather as an abstraction of three elements from a larger racial field. For example, "Latin" as a sono-racial category plays an important role in the racial taxonomy of the industry, although this is beyond the scope of my book.

15. Asai 2005, Atkins 2001, Condry 2006, Fernandes 2012, Jones 2001, Sharma 2010, Sterling 2010, Stowe 2006, Thien-bao 2008, Wong 2004, Wong 2006, Yoshida 1997.

16. Hankins 2011, Robinson 2006, Whaley 2006. Hafez Modirzadeh's study of John Coltrane (2001) and Franya Berkman's work on John and Alice Coltrane (2007 and 2010) are exceptions in that they deal with black artists performing actual Asian practices.

17. Ho 2009, Ho and Mullen 2008, Wang 2006, Wong 2004.

18. "Radical" is my own term, meant to relate the birth of multiculturalism to multiple endeavors and ideologies of social movements of the 1960s and 1970s, including cultural nationalism, development of ethnic studies and other non-Eurocentric curricula, and platforms such as Black Power and Red Power. As an aesthetic antidote to white cultural dominance, multiculturalism grew out of these activities and shared an overlapping set of political goals (Chang 2014).

19. Chang 2014, Omi and Winant 1994, Prashad 2001.

20. Prashad 2001, Lowe 1996, Goldberg 1994, Guilbault 2011.

21. Chang 2014, Goldberg 1994, Lowe 1996, McLaren 1994.

22. Multiculturalism has also been a historically important tool for policy and governance in other countries, including Canada, Australia, Indonesia, and many European nations (Guilbault 2011, Hesse 2000, Taylor 2007). In more recent years, even countries that have long represented themselves as mono-cultural, such as Japan and South Korea, have erupted in debate around the presence of racial and cultural difference and how that factors into conceptions of national identity.

23. Prashad 2001, Wise 2010.

24. See Goldberg 1994 for examples of "critical" multiculturalism proponents.

25. While I highlight the ways in which race is assumed to give rise to culture, "body–culture determinism" can also refer to how gender or other bodily markers are similarly assumed to dictate behavior.

26. Kelley 1999, Prashad 2001.

27. To start, see Carby 1992, Goldberg 1994, Hollinger 2000.

28. Scholars of popular culture have proposed other terms to refer to the racial realities of the latter twentieth and early twenty-first centuries, including "post–civil rights era" to indicate the shift in black radical politics from civil rights/Black Power tactics (Neal 1999), "post-soul" to refer to aesthetic expansion in black expressions in this era (Neal 2002, Royster 2012), and "post-racial" to question racial essentialism (Touré 2011). I have chosen to riff off of "multiculturalism" as it provides a way to think between racial policy, cultural dynamics and arts institutions.

29. See the "Call and Response" collection of short essays in the Spring/Summer 2010 issue of *Ethnomusicology* to get a sense of this fraught debate (Volume 54, Number 2).

30. Jones [1963] 2002, Floyd 1995, Iton 2008, Kofsky 1970, Monson 2007, Murray 1970, Neal 1999, Neal 2002, Radano 2003, Ramsey 2003, Rose 1994, Saul 2003, Wagner 2009, Ward 1998, Werner [1999] 2006.

31. Asai 1995, Asai 1997, Bakrania 2013, Ho 1999, Lam 1999, Maira 2002, Sharma 2010, Wong 2004, Wong 2006, Zhang 1993/1994, Zheng 2010.

32. Scholarship on British South Asian musical identity and musical expressions has been an important counterpart to U.S.-based studies. See Sharma et al. 1996 and Zuberi 2001.

33. Awkward 2007, Fellezs 2011, Fellezs 2012, Flores 2000, Johnson 2013, Lipsitz 2007. Passing refers to someone of one identity category choosing to live—"pass"—as someone of a different category (Smith 2011).

34. Lipsitz borrows this term from Juan Flores who uses it specifically to talk about Puerto Rican interactions with other racial and ethnic groups in the United States. See Flores, "Que Assimilated, Brother, Yo Soy Assimilao: The Structuring of Puerto Rican Identity in the U.S.," *Journal of Ethnic Studies* 13, no. 3 (1985): 1–16.

35. Timothy Taylor makes a similar point about discourses around fusion music, showing how white artists are seen as individuals who create hybrid music, while people of color who do so are presented as merely the result of cultural mixture (2007).

36. Dagbovie-Mullins 2013, Daniel 2002, Elam 2011, Erai 2011, Ifekwunigwe 2004, Kilson 2001, Root 1992, Spickard 1989, Williams-León and Nakashima 2001, Zack 1993, Zack 1995.

37. Brennan 2002.

38. Fulbeck 2010, Gaskins 1999, Prasad 2006, Senna 1998.

39. Fulbeck 2010, Gaskins 1999, Kilson 2001, Moore 1995.

40. Maureen Mahon, in fact, argues that Kravitz's mixed parentage was often used by journalists as evidence of why he liked "white" music, rather than simply that a black person could like rock (2004).

41. Butler 1990, Goffman 1959.

42. Cruz 1999, Lott 1995, Malone and Stricklin [1979] 2003, Miller 2010, Pecknold 2007, Radano 2003. Deborah Pacini Hernandez's *Oye Como Va! Hybridity and Identity in Latino Popular Music* (2010) and Michael Rogin's *Blackface, White Noise: Jewish Immigrants in the Hollywood Melting Pot* (1998) also deal with the racial composition of the music industry, although they primarily focus on later periods of time.

43. Farrell 1999, Lancefield 2004, Moon 2005.

44. Lott 1995, Rogin 1998.

45. It is also worth noting popular styles such as reggaeton, which has been read as a "mix" of Latin and African American elements, despite a much more complicated history. See Rivera, Marshall, and Pacini Hernandez 2009.

46. Michele Elam's critique of mixed-race studies is an apt correlative to Hutnyk's argument (2011). She says many studies that celebrate mixed identity assume that having one race is somehow limiting and that race mixing is something new. She also criticizes a tendency to mark mixed-raced status as inherently progressive and believes that efforts to highlight people with these identities can sometimes separate them from other people of color.

47. Studies analyzing Western-non-Western or white-nonwhite encounters include Feld 1996, Fellezs 2011, Meintjes 1990, Steingress 2002, Taylor 2007. Benjamin Brinner's *Playing Across a Divide: Israeli-Palestinian Musical Encounters* (2009) is an exception in this body of work, productively using the sociopolitical environment of the Middle East to complicate notions of East and West. Deborah Pacini Hernandez's *Oye Como Va!* (2010) is another excellent study that queries hybridity in new ways, focusing on cultural mixture and racial definition *within* Latino popular musics.

48. Aarim-Heriot 2003; C. J. Kim 1999, 2000; Prashad 2000.

49. Joyce 2003, K. C. Kim 1999, Kurashige 2008, Lee 2002, Lie 2004, Palumbo-Liu 1999, Takaki 1993, Yamamoto 2002.

50. Jun 2011, Jung 2006, Lee 2011, Prashad 2000, Steen 2010.

51. Anderson 2013, Chang and Diaz-Veizades 1999, Gallicchio 2000, Harden 2003, Ho 2006b, Ho 2009, Ho and Mullen 2008, Horne 2008, Kearney 1998, Kurashige 2008, Maeda 2009, Mullen 2004, Prashad 2001, Raphael-Hernandez and Steen 2006, Watkins 2014.

52. To start, see Flores 2000, Fojas and Guevarra 2012, Kim 2008, Márquez 2013, Milian 2013.

53. The doctrine of hypodescent has stated that a mixed-race individual is assigned to the racial category of lower social status (Brennan 2002, Zack 1995). Historically, mixed-race people with any portion of black "blood" were assigned to the black racial category (Joseph 2013, 2).

Chapter 1

1. Other songs from the same era mixing black and Asian signifiers include "I Don't Care If I Never Wake Up" (1899), "Ching-a-Ling" (1907), "Li Hung Chang" (1898), "Ragtime Temple Bells" (1914), and "Wing Lee's Ragtime Clock" (1899) (Moon 2005, 131–132; Tsou 1997, 38–41).

2. The show parodied A Trip to Chinatown, a popular white-penned musical from the 1890s now remembered for the hit song "After the Ball" (Garrett 2008, 121; Moon, Krasner, and Riis 2011, 7).

3. Krystyn Moon indicates that "The Wedding of the Chinee and the Coon" was added to A Trip to Coontown specifically as a vehicle for Brown—one of the first black Chinese impersonators—to showcase his Chinaman character (2005, 135).

4. Cole and Johnson's last show, The Red Moon: A Sensation in Red and Black (1908–1909), tells the story of a mixed-race black–Native American woman and her efforts to navigate two different cultures. Krasner suggests the creators used "ethnicity as commodity" in this and other works by employing racial labels and colors as selling points of their own, as indicated in the show's subtitle (1997, 141–146).

5. Miller 2010, Pecknold 2007.

6. Examples of this seesaw immigration manipulation are the Asian exclusion laws of the late 1800s and early 1900s and the Bracero program for Mexican laborers in the 1940s.

7. The 1965 Moynihan Report (officially titled The Negro Family: The Case for National Action) is one example of how governmental discourses framed economic disparity between races as a product of cultural behavior versus structural inequity. Moynihan argued that blacks were a dysfunctional underclass with poor family structures and Asians model family-makers.

8. For more on the model minority stereotype, see Palumbo-Liu 1999, Prashad 2000, and Takaki 1989. Prashad, in particular, highlights how this representation is used as a "weapon" against blacks.

9. Although not the subject of this book, other racial groups were, of course, defined alongside black and Asian.

10. Sounds associated with white Appalachians and Native Americans also made their way into popular songs for this same reason (Moon 2005, 87).

11. At the same time, a popular black-owned label like Motown sometimes worked to dilute the blackness of their releases in order to make it more palatable to white consumers. "American music" thus became an ambiguous center toward which white and black artists both strived.

12. This dynamic can be found in other areas of mass culture as well. For example, in the fashion and visual art trends leading up to art deco in the 1920s, women stopped wearing corsets and designers used Chinese- and Japanese-influenced cuts and ornamentation to dress the new silhouette in exotic sophistication. In contrast, African, Polynesian, and Latin American patterns were used as a surface source of pattern and primitive emotional expression.

13. Robeson graduated from Columbia University with a law degree in 1923, but he ended his law career not too long after. He was dubious about his prospects for full advancement in the field, and when a white secretary refused to take dictation from him in his first position, it motivated him to turn away from that line of work (Duberman 1989, 55; Robeson 1978, 99).

14. These musical explorations were part of a larger study of world cultures on which Robeson had embarked, enrolling in the School of Oriental and African Studies in London in 1934. He was also an avid amateur linguist, eventually gaining some proficiency in Mandarin, Swahili, Zulu, Mende, Ashanti, Ibo, Efik, Edo, Yoruba, and Egyptian [sic] (Stuckey 1976, 101).

15. Tian Han and Nie Er wrote "Chee Lai" for the 1935 leftist film *Children of the Storm*. The song became popular in the resistance against Japan and was adopted as the temporary national anthem of the People's Republic of China in 1949. It remained popular in subsequent years, although sometimes performed with altered lyrics (Chi 2007).

16. In his account of meeting Robeson, Liu recognizes Robeson's politics as fighting "for black people and all oppressed people in the world" (Liu [1950] 2006). Liu does not, however, state that he himself is invested in furthering black-Chinese solidarity with the *Chee Lai* album.

17. Robeson's early stage roles often had him performing prevailing stereotypes of blacks. These productions included *Shuffle Along* (1922), *Taboo* (1922), *God's Chillun Got Wings* (1924), *The Emperor Jones* (1924), and *The Hairy Ape* (1931). Robeson began starring in Hollywood films in the 1930s, but grew increasingly uncomfortable with similarly problematic portrayals of blackness (Robeson 1978).

18. Robeson's formulations of "Asia" resonate with sentiments also expressed by W. E. B. Du Bois. Du Bois traveled to multiple Asian countries, wrote profusely about their histories and political shifts, and "consistently saw Asia as the fraternal twin to African—and African American—struggle for political freedom and cultural self-preservation" (Mullen and Watson 2005). In addition to nonfiction writings on Asia, he also composed the novel *Dark Princess: A Romance* (1928), which details the relationship of an African American man and Indian woman.

19. While I focus here on Robeson's Afro Asian philosophies, it is important to note that they were part of a larger evolution of his political beliefs over the course of his career, from black internationalism to Communist internationalism (Duberman 1989, 172–173; Steen 2010, 110).

20. Examining Nikolas Muray's nude photographs of Robeson, Hazel V. Carby illuminates how Robeson's body became a tool through which white U.S. society worked through gendered racial fears and desires (1998).

21. Robeson was, in fact, only 6'2" (editor's note in Liu [1950] 2006, 205).

22. "Chee Lai" lyrics and translation, as written in the album liner notes, are as follows:

Chee lai! Bu-yuan-tzo nu-lidi run-men,
Bar wo-men-di shur-ro
Tzo-chen wo-men sin-di chang-chung.
Chung-hwa-ming-chu dow liow
Tzui-way-shien-di shur-ho
May-go-run bay-po-cho far-chu tzui-how-di ho shun:
Chee lai! Chee lai! Chee lai!
Wo-men wan-chung Ee-sing,
Mow-jo di-run-di Pow-ho,
Chien jing!
Mow-jo di-run-di Pow-ho,
Chien jing! Chien jing! Chien jing!
Jing!

Arise, you who refuse to be bond slaves!
Let's stand up and fight for
Liberty and true democracy.
All our world is facing
The chains of the tyrants.
Everyone who works for freedom is now crying:
Arise! Arise! Arise!
All of us with one heart,
With the torch of freedom,
March on!
With the torch of freedom,
March on!
March on! March on, and on!

23. Liu even expresses in the album liner notes that of the traditional Chinese, Western-influenced, and "songs that combine Oriental and Occidental tunes," he believes the last "has the brightest future in China." He goes on to suggest, "Blended songs do not sound too strange to our ears, but neither do they have the weak and wailing quality of Eastern music. We do not wail today, for we know that our fate rests in our own hands." He thus equates typical white/Western ways of hearing Chinese music with the "Old China" he seeks to leave behind.

24. In a subsequent moment, a Mandarin-speaker attending a talk I gave on "Chee Lai" told me she thought Robeson's pronunciation was sound. Unlike my first translator, who was Taiwanese and did not know the song, this listener was from China and had a strong knowledge of the song. Therefore, it is possible that Robeson's enunciation is easier to hear if one is familiar with the words he is singing.

25. In 1956 he was brought before the House Un-American Activities Committee to testify in response to accusations of his alleged Communist leanings.

26. While I have chosen to use no punctuation in "Afro Asian," I render the conference name as it has been historically documented.

27. If not for the revocation of his passport, Robeson expressed interest in attending the Bandung meeting in 1955 (Duberman 1989, 388). In his stead, he sent a statement in which he proclaimed: "The living evidence of the ancient kinship of Africa and Asia is seen in the language structures, in the arts and philosophies of the two continents. Increased exchange of

such closely related cultures cannot help but bring into flower a richer, more vibrant voicing of the highest aspirations of colored peoples the world over" (Robeson 1978, 399).

28. Prashad notes that these international solidarities were framed primarily as "Afro Asian" in the first half of the 1950s, and by the latter half were spoken about more broadly as "Third World" and included Latin American and Caribbean nations (Prashad 2006, xxii).

29. See Maeda 2009, 73–96; Pulido 2006, 167–168; and Prashad 2001, 138. This influence extended back to Asia as well. For example, the Dalit Panthers formed in Bombay in 1972 and professed a relationship to U.S. antiracist struggles (Prashad 2001, 141).

30. "People of color" has not been unilaterally embraced among racially marginalized communities. The writer Janani expresses their discomfort at how the term erases differences such as class privilege, immigration histories, and other forms of color-based stratification that operate outside of the United States and in diasporic populations in the United States (2013). And Rinku Sen discusses the ways in which many immigrant and refugee communities in the States mobilize around cultural and national monikers rather than the racialized "people of color" (2007).

31. In my formulation, "music of color" can label both singular traditions and those used in tandem.

32. Brown 2010, Modirzadeh 2001.

33. Monson productively situates Coltrane's work amidst a larger exploration of non-Western music by his contemporaries.

34. Yusef Lateef's study and performance of a variety of East Asian, Middle Eastern, and West African instruments are another example of this stream of Afro Asian musical conversation.

35. As I discuss in other chapters, Sharma's work looks at South Asian American hip hop artists. Also worth mentioning here, but beyond the scope of my investigation, are studies of hip hop production in various Asian countries, especially Japan (Condry 2006, Fischer 2013).

36. Ho 2006b, Kato 2007, Prashad 2003.

37. See George Lipsitz's chapter "Crossing Over: The Hidden History of Diaspora" in *Footsteps in the Dark: The Hidden Histories of Popular Music* (2007) for more examples of artists and projects, both Afro Asian and interracial.

38. Fred Ho's interview with Bill Cole is an excellent introduction to Cole's performance of Asian double reed instruments (Ho 2008). In the same volume, Ho and royal hartigan offer a brief look at the influence of Chinese opera percussion on the development of the African American drumset (hartigan and Ho 2008).

Chapter 2

1. *Minyo* (or *min'yō*) is a general term for Japanese folksongs, traditionally featuring voice accompanied by *shamisen, shakuhachi* (flute), and/or drums (Broughton and Ellingham 2000, 145). Distinctive to the form is the marking of place, often evoking a sense of nostalgia for rural home life (Broughton and Ellingham 2000, 145; Hughes 2008, 2).

2. I conducted multiple formal interviews and had numerous casual conversations with Japanesque and Jazz Me Blues Band members. Quotes

and paraphrased information in this chapter are from these conversations unless otherwise stated. Formal interviews were held with: Yoko Noge (5/18/06 and 4/6/08), Clark Dean (7/23/07), Avreeayl Ra (6/12/06), Tatsu Aoki (10/4/07), Jimmy Ellis (6/8/06), Jeff Chan (8/22/07), John Primer (6/25/07), and Kaz Terashima (8/10/06).

3. The *shamisen* is a Japanese lute. *Taiko* is a general name for several different Japanese drums.

4. Atkins 2001, Fernandes 2012, Jones 2001.

5. For more on Asian/American negotiation of black–white racial dynamics, and these particular performers, see SanSan Kwan's "Performing a Geography of Asian America: The Chop Suey Circuit" (2011).

6. The HotHouse/Center for International Performance Exhibition (CIPEX) was founded in 1987 as a space dedicated to featuring performance artists and supporting community activism. When I refer to HotHouse here, it is as the physical space of its former location in Chicago's South Loop neighborhood. I discuss HotHouse and its history in greater detail in Chapter 3.

7. What Noge describes corresponds to a similar era of significant growth in Japanese jazz production and consumption (Atkins 2001, 222–223).

8. This method of music acquisition is almost as old as recording technology itself. For example, in the film *Wild Women Don't Have the Blues*, an oral history of female blues musicians, several artists discuss learning the blues from their parents' record collections. Separately, David C. Alan has discussed how Japanese American chanteuse Pat Suzuki described recordings as her musical "mentors" (Alan 2009).

9. Herd 2004, Wade 2014.

10. Unfortunately, Watson passed away before I was able to speak with him.

11. My designation also signifies on historical jazz formulations in which female vocalists were often not considered to be sidemen or musicians at all (Monson 2007, 339).

12. While some have questioned the continued salience of this term, I use "diaspora" here as what Brent Hayes Edwards calls an "interventionist" term (2001, 63). That is, it can speak to abstract memory of a shared origin, such as in Africa among blacks outside of the continent, and concrete differences within diasporic populations (Edwards 2001, 63–64). "Diaspora" has been used widely in scholarship on race and culture over the past several decades. The concept originally described the global "scattering about" of Jews from Israel, but has grown to incorporate issues of migration, immigrant identity formation, cultural circulation, and transnationalism within and between many different populations (see Slobin 2012 on the term's scholarly evolution). As the use of "diaspora" has expanded, it has also come to provide a general framework for dealing with dynamics of difference and marginalization within a society. Therefore, I find "diaspora" useful in speaking between race and culture inherent in the asymmetrical confrontation of "African/American" and "Japanese" and how both operate as markers of identity and heritage. Especially as this section deals with conceptions of home, diaspora provides a useful framework for engaging individual connections to a larger, geographically distant collective.

13. See Butler 2001, Edwards 2003, Flores 2009, Lewis 1995, and Rivera 2012 for theorization of diaspora beyond the singular. I take up this issue in greater detail in Chapter 3.

14. Noge graciously provided the lyrics and translation in 2008.

15. A reported 40 percent of Africans who were enslaved in the United States entered the nation through the port at Sullivan's Island, South Carolina. This so-called Ellis Island for blacks and written records of the enslaved people that passed through it indicate the fallacy of undocumented histories for many African Americans.

16. To be clear, I analyze here the Silk Road Chicago programming, linked to but not directly under the auspices of Yo-Yo Ma's Silk Road Project.

17. In the years since my primary field research, there has been a slight increase in representation of Asian/American artists in city-run blues and jazz spaces, in large part due to Noge and Aoki's efforts.

18. This embodiment of multicultural discourse becomes more apparent when comparing multiple Daley Plaza events. During my fieldwork, I attended numerous festivals there over several years, and on the majority of occasions the booths are arranged in the same layout of food, information, and crafts. Thus, regardless of what particular culture or cultures were represented, they were squeezed into the same arrangement as the others.

19. This point is even more complicated in that what I have described as "traditional" *taiko* ensemble playing is actually a twentieth-century formation. While based on instruments and techniques thousands of years old, Japanese musicians created modern *taiko* performance in the 1950s specifically to reclaim traditional culture in the wake of postwar modernity. Asian Americans adopted the genre starting in the late 1960s as a means of asserting a unique cultural heritage in the space of the United States (Wong 2006). Yoshihashi and Homma's musical grounding, then, is not in an ancient, foreign practice, but one central to the formation of contemporary Asian American culture. Their playing as accompanists references older Japanese styles of playing, although it counters "traditional" Asian American *taiko* practice in the United States.

20. A common link often made between black roots music and various Asian traditions is the use of pentatonic scales.

21. For example, a 2008 Miyumi Project show was called "East Meets the Rest." Covering the concert, *Chicago Tribune* critic Howard Reich's headline proclaimed: "It was a gamble, but East thrillingly meets West in Miyumi Project" (Reich 2008).

Chapter 3

1. Abu-Lughod 1999, Kun 2005, Longworth 2000, Sassen 2001.

2. A number of scholarly and popular writers have employed this term since the late 1990s to signal demographic shifts in the U.S. population, racial intermixing and subsequent mixed-raced progeny, and the proposed future shift of the country into a "minority majority" citizenry. See Rodriguez 2002, Contreras 1996, and Sundstrom 2008.

3. A more detailed breakdown is as follows: 32 percent black (including Hispanics), 45 percent white (31 percent non-Hispanic white plus 14 percent white Hispanics), 5 percent Asian (including Hispanics), and 3 percent from two or more races (including Hispanics). The ethnic makeup of the population is 28 percent Hispanic (of any race) and 72 percent have a non-Hispanic background (of any race). In 2000, 21.7 percent of the population was foreign-born; of this number,

56.3 percent came from Latin America, 23.1 percent from Europe, 18.0 percent from Asia, and 2.6 percent from other parts of the world (United States Census Bureau [accessed] 2012).

4. There are a few neighborhoods in which black and South Asian people coexist, including Rogers Park and the areas around Devon Avenue. These places indicate the smaller-scale locations of interracial possibility I discuss in this chapter.

5. I conducted multiple formal interviews and had numerous casual conversations with Funkadesi members. Quotes and paraphrased information in this chapter come from these conversations unless otherwise stated. Formal interviews were held with: Pavithra (3/16/06), Carlos Cornier (6/2/06, 3/29/09), Lloyd King (8/21/07), Rahul Sharma (8/25/04), Maninderpal Singh (8/20/07), and Byard Lancaster (8/12/07).

6. Founded in 1976, the Heartland Café is a restaurant, bar, store, and meeting house in Chicago's Rogers Park neighborhood. An active site of left-wing political organizing, Heartland has long featured speakers and musical guests on its small dining room stage.

7. Butler 2001, Edwards 2003, Flores 2009, Lewis 1995, Rivera 2012.

8. "Diaspora" is quite a diffuse term, as it is variously used to indicate racial, ethnic, and national groups, as well as communities with tangible links to a homeland (Chicago's South Asian population) and a more mythic sense of common roots (Chicago's blacks as part of the African diaspora). As in Chapter 2, I use this term here precisely for its ability to speak between groups we consider racially and others we consider ethnically. I especially wish to situate discussions of overlapping diasporas into the inevitable U.S. landscape of race, especially as the musical practices I discuss are actively read through this lens. Dealing with intricacies of overlapping diasporas means contending not only with the meeting of cultures but also how they are framed in racial discourse.

9. This list reflects the group's roster during my primary fieldwork from 2005 to 2009. Navraaz Basati and Pavithra did not typically perform together—they rotated the position of lead female vocalist a number of times during those years. Former band members include saxophonist/flutist Byard Lancaster (African American), saxophonist Kristin McGee (white), saxophonist/flutist Ari Brown (African American), guitarist Johnse Holt (African American), vocalist Radhika Chimata (Telegu), and percussionist Meshach Silas (African American).

10. *Tabla* are small hand drums used in a variety of South Asian musical styles. The *dhol* is a large double-headed drum used to accompany *bhangra*.

11. Here, I describe the recorded version of the song (the second track from *Uncut Roots*), but it is performed similarly in live performance. The main differences are the lengths of instrumental solos and slightly altered instrumentation.

12. An *alaap* is the slow, introductory section of a Hindustani piece. Unlike in traditional settings, Chimata's *alaap* is metered, as it unfolds over instrumentals with a steady pulse.

13. *Dun dun* (or *dunun*) are large, low-pitched drums used in West African percussion styles. Played with sticks, the drums often carry a piece's melody.

14. Benjamin Brinner provides a useful tripartite schema for assessing musical mixtures: contrast (how different the merged styles are), dominance (how elements are evenly or unevenly foregrounded), and blend

(how much difference is preserved or elements are integrated) (2009, 217–220). This framework has influenced my approach to analyzing Funkadesi's productions. Beyond providing a means to parse out musical dynamics, Brinner's method highlights important ways fusion artists use sound to create sociopolitical meaning. It also gives meaning to nonfusion, in that "certain aspects of a given musical practice may exert a force akin to a gravitational pull" and keep a musician from growing toward other traditions (Brinner 2009, 262). Finally, Brinner highlights how blending music can produce a shift in musicians' abilities, arguing that "producing something in a new context makes demands that differ from the culturally specific musical competences these musicians acquired" (2009, 220). In each of my cases, mixes have been the result of artists pushing beyond the techniques and forms required for a single tradition in order to appropriately respond to the other traditions present.

15. An Old Town School staff member later told me that musicians from the various ensembles at the festival jammed together backstage in the performers' green room tent. Intergroup musical dialogue was possible, but not available to the listening public.

16. Venues that present free programming, such as the Chicago Cultural Center or Chicago SummerDance, do tend to garner more economic and at times generational diversity (Peterson 2002, 260).

17. As it turns out, the HotHouse was itself forced out of this neighborhood in a dispute with its lessor. In 2007 the venue shut down and there was much turnover on its board, but the organization continued to present performances in other spaces around Chicago. As of 2013, Horberg and the original board members had reclaimed the HotHouse name with a plan to open a new venue. The organization currently presents programs in a variety of locations in the Chicago region while they work toward reopening their own space.

18. The *chekere* (or *shekere*) is a beaded gourd rattle of West African origin. The *surdo* is a Brazilian bass drum played with a mallet.

19. This was a voluntary survey administered via SurveyMonkey and I received twelve responses. Despite the small sample size, it was helpful in gaining the personal details of a few Funkadesi listeners and their thoughts on the band. Of the twelve respondents, seven self-identified as Caucasian or white, one East Indian, one Punjabi, one mixed Japanese and Irish, one Croatian, and one black. Three white respondents mentioned they sometimes talk to strangers at shows and the Japanese/Irish person claimed they "make friends" with unknown neighbors.

20. I describe here the version recorded on the group's second album, *It's About Time* (2003).

21. At one live show I attended, these same images were projected onto a large screen behind the stage as the group performed.

22. These gestures include their being featured on a variety of city-sponsored arts programs such as Chicago SummerDance, as well as their receipt of city music awards.

23. At the time of this writing, Pavithra has again become the group's lead female vocalist.

24. When the band learned about this follow-up to their performance, they wrote a letter to the company saying they found the "goddess" to be offensive.

25. A video of this statement can be viewed at https://www.youtube.com/watch?v=ll-tIbyRL6Q.

26. Sharma gave me the caveat that Obama made this statement at an "Asians for Obama" event and went on to say, as Sharma recalls, "I'm probably the only candidate who knows what a desi is." So the intent of Obama's original statement was contextual, although this is not part of how the quote currently circulates.

27. In the fall of 2008, MTV again tried to corner the Asian American market with MTV Iggy, featuring four separate "worlds": Desi, Chinese, Korean, and Global, all sharing basic content with some ethnically specific material to differentiate them.

Chapter 4

1. Some portions of this chapter have been previously published in my introduction to *Yellow Power, Yellow Soul: The Radical Art of Fred Ho* (Roberts 2013).

2. Ho passed away in April 2014, during the final stretch of my work on this book. I thus write about his legacy in the past tense, but switch to present tense when discussing musical texts.

3. I conducted multiple formal interviews and had numerous casual conversations and email exchanges with Ho, members of the Afro Asian Music Ensemble, and other artists with whom they collaborated. Quotes and paraphrased information in this chapter are from these conversations unless otherwise stated. Formal interviews were held with: Fred Ho (11/13/05), royal hartigan (4/3/06), David Bindman (3/31/06), Tsuyoshi Kaseda (4/1/06), Wes Brown (11/23/08), Art Hirahara (4/7/06), Yumi Kurosawa (2/10/09), Masaru Koga (4/7/06), and Youn Jung Kim (12/2/08).

4. There are important ways in which economic elements factor into the identity politics debate; however, this is not the focus of this chapter. Ho employs a number of tactics to mediate the disenfranchisement of artists of color, including running his own production company and not relying on nonprofit granting organizations as a sole source of funding. While I do not detail these strategies here, I hope to tease out some of the aesthetic impacts of neoliberal economics on contemporary culture. For further discussion of economics in Ho's work, see Mullen 2004 and Roberts 2013.

5. Micaela di Leonardo states: "Neoliberalism, as developed over the second half of the twentieth century, is an intellectual/political stance that presumes that capitalist trade 'liberalization'—the end of all state regulations on business, and indeed, the end of all state-run business—will lead inevitably to market growth and, *ceteris paribus*, to optimal social ends" (2008, 5).

6. The revival of white ethnic identifications in the dominant racial discourse of the early 1970s also played a role in shifting the focus of multiculturalism away from social inequalities. A co-optation of and backlash against civil rights–based politics, government and popular discourses posed formerly marginalized white communities (Jewish, Irish, Polish, Slavic, etc.) as the "forgotten" minority, contrasting them with allegedly degenerate blacks and other people of color (Jacobson 2006). Claiming a pseudo-racial identity for these dominant populations served to redirect attention from legitimate concerns of social inequity and to depict all identities—including white ones—as part of a sociopolitically equal multicultural field.

7. The Asian America Resource Workshop is an organization support-ing the empowerment of Asian Pacific Americans through programs such as arts promotion, historical documentation, and antiracist training.

8. Ho's biography has been covered extensively elsewhere. See Asai 2005, Buckley and Roberts 2013, Ho 2009, Mullen 2004, Wong 2004, and Zhang 1993/1994.

9. *P'ansori* is a Korean form of musical storytelling. *Kulintang* is a Filipino gong ensemble.

10. The *sona* is a Chinese double reed horn.

11. For more detailed description and analysis of the Monkey Orchestra and *Journey Beyond the West*, see Mullen 2004 and Zhang 1993/1994.

12. The majority of Ho's compositional efforts have been for his own projects, but he has also written and arranged music for other theater productions and groups such as experimental chamber ensemble Relâche and the Rova Saxophone Quartet.

13. See Asai 2005, Mullen 2004, and Zhang 1993/1994.

14. hartigan spells his name in all lowercase letters, a practice I preserve here.

15. hartigan continues this work in his 1995 book *West African Rhythms for Drumset*, where he seeks to "fit" West African polyrhythms onto the drum set as a way to explore links between African American and West African musical culture (hartigan, Adzenyah, and Donkor 1995).

16. Jeff Chan from Yoko Noge's Jazz Me Blues Band (Chapter 2) also performed with this group.

17. The show was produced by Peregrine Arts, Inc. and was performed at Drexel University's Mandell Theater (Philadelphia) in June 2006. I attended rehearsals over several weeks and helped out the stage crew. The production was directed by Sonoko Kawahara and choreographed by Tsuyoshi Kaseda, with lighting by Carolyn Wong and costumes by Colleen Scott. A second production ran at La MaMa (New York City) in 2013.

18. *Shakuhachi* and *fue* are Japanese flutes. The *koto* is a Japanese plucked string instrument.

19. See Lott 1995, Rogin 1998, and Roediger 1991.

20. This rhetorical question is not meant to disavow the presence of Japanese people or people who have knowledge of Japanese instruments and aesthetics in the United States. Again, I am speaking about a broader dominant cultural space in the United States, of which Japanese elements are not frequently a part. This dynamic means understanding of the details of Japanese and other Asian forms is not cultivated in mainstream consumers.

21. A good example of this type of sonic dynamic is the use of the *sitar* in the Beatle's "Norwegian Wood."

22. Ho discusses the importance of martial arts films to urban black and Latino youth in the United States in "Kickin' the White Man's Ass: Black Power, Aesthetic, and the Asian Martial Arts" in *AfroAsian Encounters: Culture, History, Politics* (Ho 2006b).

23. In fact, Ho describes being seen as an "enigma" in relation to the handful of Japanese artists working in New York when he first moved there in the early 1980s. Part of his efforts to engage with West Coast Asian American players was due to his feeling that there was not a compa-rable Asian American presence in the East Coast professional jazz scene at that time.

24. Whittington 2006, Giardullo 1996, Ouellette 1998, Takahashi 2001. All reviews accessed in the Fred Ho Papers, Archives and Special Collections at the Thomas J. Dodd Research Center, University of Connecticut Libraries.

25. See Braggs 2006, Gray 2005, McMullen 2008, and O'Meally, Edwards, and Griffin 2004.

26. This is a very cursory orientation to the history and politics of free jazz. Some scholars even counter the link between the form and black radical politics (Such 1993, 28). For more on post-1960s jazz innovations and their relationship to politics, see Kofsky 1970 and Saul 2003.

27. The first recording marked with the label "jazz" was, after all, recorded by the all-white Original Dixieland Jazz Band in 1917.

28. Ho also prefers not to call the music "jazz" as he sees this term as originating in racist depictions of black music and people as hypersexual and lacking intelligence (Ho 1995, 29).

29. Washington sometimes performed saxophone with the AAME and in other collaborations with Ho.

30. See Gallagher 2003, Leonardo 2005, Warmington 2009, and Wise 2010 for criticism of postracialism from a critical race theory perspective.

Chapter 5

1. Some portions of this chapter have been previously published in "The Elusive Truth: Intercultural Music Exchange in 'Addictive.'" *Interculturalism: Exploring Critical Issues*. Eds. Dianne Powell and Fiona Sze. Oxford: Inter-Disciplinary Press, 2004, pp. 83–86.

2. These lyrics translate to "a flower garden is then made" (Marshall and Beaster-Jones 2012, 1).

3. Beaster-Jones and Marshall point out that this is an often used sample (2012, 5). In "Addictive," it is well suited to the sono-racial space Quik conjures, as the congas also evoke the sound of *tabla*.

4. These lyrics translate to "It takes a little silk / It takes a little glass / Diamonds and pearls come together / Then such a fair-skinned body is made."

5. The particulars of the legal case are quite complicated. Lahiri attempted to sue Aftermath (along with parent companies Interscope Records and Universal and Dr. Dre, named as Andre Ramelle Young), but ultimately did not have sufficient grounds to do so because Saregama India Limited held the song's copyright. After sorting through conflicting claims to the copyright between Lahiri and Saregama, they were merged as the plaintiff in the suit. After several years, the dispute was settled out of court. Eventually, Dr. Dre's company successfully countersued Lahiri for filing a trivial suit (Conlon 2010).

6. Hankins 2011, Sharma 2010, and Zumkhawala-Cook 2008.

7. To widen the lens, this was a larger popular culture moment of Orientalist fascination with Asia and the Middle East. Two examples of nonblack artists sono-racially conjuring the Middle East in their work are Natalie Merchant's *Motherland* (2001) and Mandy Moore's self-titled third album (2001).

8. In fact, this youthful vocal profile is a large part of why Mangeshkar has experienced such lasting popularity and success (Beaster-Jones 2014, 61).

9. See de Certeau 1984, Diawara 1988, Fonarow 2006, and Small 1998.

10. Even as the racial and cultural content of the "mainstream" shifted through different eras, the consumer continued to be figured as white in journalistic address, such as in *Rolling Stone*. There are publications, such as *Vibe*, that speak to nonwhite listeners but they are explicitly marked as nonmainstream. See my "Michael Jackson's Kingdom: Music, Race, and the Sound of the Mainstream" (2011) for more on the racial definition of "mainstream."

11. See, for example, Sedgwick 1985 and Brett, Wood, and Thomas 2006.

12. I want to make clear that I am not equating queerness with antiracism. I am arguing for using the tools queer theory provides to help us to better understand race. Juana María Rodríguez defines queer as "not simply an umbrella term that encompasses lesbians, bisexuals, gay men, two-spirited people, and transsexuals; it is a challenge to constructions of heteronormativity. It need not subsume the particularities of . . . other definitions of identity; instead it creates an opportunity to call into question the systems of categorization that have served to define sexuality" (2003, 24). Afro Asian music offers challenges to racial and cultural categories and structures in similar ways to how queerness confronts systems of gender and sexuality. More specifically, by contesting body–culture determinism, Afro Asian and other interracial music disrupts biological assumptions about the existence or operation of race, resisting heteronormative figurations of race as "in the blood" and the product of heterosexual genetic reproduction. The projects I examine do not do nearly enough (or any) work to push against gender and sexual frameworks, nor are all of them even on the most radical edge of queering race. What this book's case studies do offer are spaces that raise questions about how we think about race and its fixity. I hesitate to employ queerness toward sites in which gender and sexuality are not of central concern, although I hope this theoretical gesture might, like an Afro Asian relationship, be one of solidarity rather than appropriation.

13. I use "kumbaya" here somewhat facetiously to refer to the ways in which liberal and corporate multiculturalism present on the surface and, often, obscure their deeper structures.

14. See Kenney 1999 on the impact of recording and copyright law on the repertoire and inter-artist exchange of songs within the blues.

15. See, for example, Lazar 2011.

16. Lahiri's personal style reveals a different relationship to black music, however, as his attire sometimes pays homage to hip hop fashion. This includes his frequent sporting of large gold chains around his neck, track suits, and even holding his hands in pseudo-gang signs to display his numerous gold rings.

17. It is interesting to also note Mangeshkar's statement that the U.S. artists "rapped" over her vocals, perhaps teetering on body–culture determinism (or at least lack of musical familiarity) by roping all black vocalizations into "rap." This same rhetorical gloss of the vocals on "Addictive" as soley rap is reflected in a positive 2002 *IndiaTimes* review of "Addicitive" titled "Nightingale of India Raps to New Beat."

18. Most notably the Wikipedia page for Meghna Naidu, the actor/dancer featured as the lead in the "Kaliyon" video.

19. Interestingly, a remix of "Paid in Full" includes sampled vocals by Yemeni Israeli singer Ofra Haza and served as an earlier flashpoint for debates over sampling and intellectual property (Steward 1988).

20. Lahiri reports to have forgotten "Thoda" until the "Addictive" sampling was brought to his attention. In a later interview he said, smiling: "Today, over two decades after it was composed, the song has indeed become unforgettable for me" (quoted in Bhattacharya 2002).

Conclusion

1. The "legal" and "extra-legal" killing of people of color by law enforcement officers and private citizens has a long history in the United States. In various historical moments, these homicides have served as flashpoints for larger societal discussions about race. The beating of Rodney King and subsequent acquittal of the perpetrating officers, for example, led to the eruption of the so-called Los Angeles "riots" of 1992. A more recent tipping point occurred in the fall of 2014, after a string of murders of unarmed people of color and, in most cases, light or non-existent prosecution of the perpetrators. This moment spawned numerous antiracism protests, actions, riots, and online activities, eventually uniting as the #BlackLivesMatter movement. See cofounder Alicia Garza's "A Herstory of the #BlackLivesMatter Movement" for a more detailed look at this campaign and some of the detraction and co-optation it has faced (2014).

2. The minstrel legacy is an excellent example. See Lott 1995, Roediger 1991, Rogin 1998.

3. Online journalist Zak Cheney-Rice's suggests "in a matter of years we'll have Tindered, OKCupid-ed and otherwise sexed ourselves into one giant amalgamated mega-race" (Cheney-Rice 2014).

References

Aarim-Heriot, Najia. 2003. *Chinese Immigrants, African Americans, and Racial Anxiety in the United States, 1848–82*. Champaign: University of Illinois Press.

Abu-Lughod, Janet L. 1999. *New York, Chicago, Los Angeles: America's Global Cities*. Minneapolis: University of Minnesota Press.

Alan, David C. 2009. "'A Girl Like Me': The Musical Legacy of Pat Suzuki." Paper presented at the annual meeting for the Society for American Music, Denver, CO, March 18–22.

Alexander, Michelle. 2010. *The New Jim Crow: Mass Incarceration in the Age of Colorblindness*. New York: The New Press.

Anderson, Benedict. 1983. *Imagined Communities: Reflections on the Origin and Spread of Nationalism*. London: Verso.

Anderson, Crystal S. 2013. *Beyond* The Chinese Connection: *Contemporary Afro-Asian Cultural Production*. Jackson: University Press of Mississippi.

Appadurai, Arjun. 1996. *Modernity at Large: Cultural Dimensions of Globalization*. Minneapolis: University of Minnesota Press.

Asai, Susan. 1995. "Transformations of the Tradition: Three Generations of Japanese American Music Making." *The Musical Quarterly* 79(3): 429–453.

Asai, Susan. 1997. "Sansei Voices in the Community: Japanese American Musicians in California." In *Musics of Multicultural America: A Study of Twelve Musical Communities*, edited by Kip Lornell and Anne K. Rasmussen, pp. 257–285. New York: Schirmer Books.

Asai, Susan. 2005. "Cultural Politics: The African American Connection in Asian American Jazz-based Music." *Asian Music* 36: 87–108.

Atkins, E. Taylor. 2001. *Blue Nippon: Authenticating Jazz in Japan*. Durham, NC: Duke University Press.

Attali, Jacques. 1985. *Noise: The Political Economy of Music*. Minneapolis: University of Minnesota Press.

Auslander, Philip. 2006. "Musical Personae." *The Drama Review* 50(1): 100–119.

Awkward, Michael. 2007. *Soul Covers: Rhythm and Blues Remakes and the Struggle for Artistic Identity*. Durham, NC: Duke University Press.

Bakrania, Falu. 2013. *Bhangra and Asian Underground: South Asian Music and the Politics of Belonging in Britain*. Durham, NC: Duke University Press.

Barg, Lisa. 2008. "Paul Robeson's Ballad for Americans: Race and the Cultural Politics of 'People's Music.'" *Journal of the Society for American Music* 2(1): 27–70.

Beaster-Jones, Jayson. 2014. *Bollywood Sounds: The Cosmopolitan Mediations of Hindi Film Song*. New York: Oxford University Press.

Berkman, Franya. 2007. "Appropriating Universality: The Coltranes and 1960s Spirituality." *American Studies* 48(1) (Spring): 41–62.

Berkman, Franya. 2010. *Monument Eternal: The Music of Alice Coltrane*. Middletown, CT: Wesleyan University Press.

Bhabha, Homi. 1990. "The Third Space." In *Identity: Community, Culture, Difference*, edited by Jonathan Rutherford, pp. 207–221. London: Lawrence and Wishart.

Bhaktin, Mikhail. [1965]1984. *Rabelais and His World*. Bloomington: Indiana University Press.

Bhattacharya, Roshmila. 2002. "Bappi Lahiri: Today, You Don't Have Copies, You Have Xerox Copies." *Screen*. Accessed March 6, 2015. http://archive.is/8V8Po.

Bhattacharyya, Madhumita. 2003. "After Fireworks, Dreamworks—Spielberg and *Mask* Makers at My Door, Yodels Bappi Lahiri." *The Telegraph*. Accessed March 6, 2015. http://www.telegraphindia.com/1030422/asp/calcutta/story_1895311.asp.

Bogira, Steve. 2011. "Separate, Unequal, and Ignored: Racial Segregation Remains Chicago's Most Fundamental Problem. Why Isn't It an Issue in the Mayor's Race?" *Chicago Reader*, February 10.

Braggs, Rashida K. 2006. "'American' Jazz: Traversing Race and Nation in Postwar France." Ph.D. diss., Northwestern University, Evanston, IL.

Brennan, Jonathan. 2002. "Introduction." In *Mixed Race Literature*, edited by Jonathan Brennan, 1–56. Stanford, CA: Stanford University Press.

Brennan, Timothy. 2001. "World Music Does Not Exist." *Discourse* 23(1): 44–62.

Brett, Philip, Elizabeth Wood, and Gary C. Thomas, eds. 2006. *Queering the Pitch: The New Gay and Lesbian Musicology*. 2d ed. New York: Routledge.

Brinner, Benjamin. 2009. *Playing Across a Divide: Israeli-Palestinian Musical Encounters*. New York: Oxford University Press.

Broughton, Simon, and Mark Ellingham, eds. 2000. *World Music*. Vol. 2: *Latin and North America, Caribbean, India, Asia and Pacific*. London: Penguin Books.

Brown, Leonard, ed. 2010. *John Coltrane and Black America's Quest for Freedom: Spirituality and the Music*. Oxford: Oxford University Press.

Buckley, Roger N., and Tamara Roberts, eds. 2013. *Yellow Power, Yellow Soul: The Radical Art of Fred Ho*. Urbana: University of Illinois Press.

Burns, Stewart. 1990. *Social Movements of the 1960s: Searching for Democracy*. New York: Twayne.

Butler, Judith. 1990. *Gender Trouble: Feminism and the Subversion of Identity*. New York: Routledge.

Butler, Kim D. 2001. "Defining Diaspora, Refining a Discourse." *Diaspora* 10(2): 189–219.

Cameron, Stuart, and Jon Coaffee. 2005. "Art, Gentrification and Regeneration—From Artist as Pioneer to Public Arts." *European Journal of Housing Policy* 5(1): 39–58.

Carby, Hazel V. 1992. "The Multicultural Wars." *Radical History Review* 54: 7–18.

Carby, Hazel V. 1998. *Race Men*. Cambridge, MA: Harvard University Press.

Catanese, Brandi. 2012. *The Problem of the Color[blind]: Racial Transgression and the Politics of Black Performance*. Ann Arbor: University of Michigan Press.

Chang, Edward T., and Jeannette Diaz-Veizades. 1999. *Ethnic Peace in the American City: Building Community in Los Angeles and Beyond*. New York: New York University Press.

Chang, Jeff. 2014. *Who We Be: The Colorization of America*. New York: St. Martin's Press.

Cheney-Rice, Zak. 2014. "National Geographic Determined What Americans Will Look Like in 2050, and It's Beautiful." *News.Mic*, April 10. Accessed March 8, 2015. http://www.mic.com/articles/87359/national-geographic-determined-what-americans-will-look-like-in-2050-and-it-s-beautiful.

Chi, Robert. 2007. "'The March of the Volunteers': From Movie Theme Song to National Anthem." In *Re-envisioning the Chinese Revolution: The Politics and Poetics of Collective Memories in Reform China*, edited by Ching Kwan Lee and Guobin Yang, pp. 217–244. New York: Woodrow Wilson Center Press.

Chicago Cultural Studies Group. 1994. "Critical Multiculturalism." In *Multiculturalism: A Critical Reader*, edited by David Theo Goldberg, pp. 114–139. Cambridge, MA: Blackwell.

Clifford, James. 1994. "Diasporas." *Cultural Anthropology* 9(3): 302–338.

Condry, Ian. 2006. *Hip-Hop Japan: Rap and the Paths of Cultural Globalization*. Durham, NC: Duke University Press.

Conlon, Suzanne B. 2010. *Bappi Lahiri and Saregama India Limited v. Universal Music and Video Distribution Corporation, Interscope Records, Aftermath Records, Andre Ramelle Young*. No. 09-55111. United States Court of Appeals for the Ninth Circuit, Pasadena, CA.

Contreras, Raul. 1996. "The Browning of America." *The Social Contract* 6(4): 293–294.

Cruz, Jon. 1999. *Culture on the Margins: The Black Spiritual and the Rise of American Cultural Interpretation*. Princeton, NJ: Princeton University Press.

Dagbovie-Mullins, Sika. 2013. *Crossing B(l)ack: Mixed-Race Identity in Modern American Fiction and Culture*. Knoxville: University of Tennessee Press.

Daniel, G. Reginald. 2002. *More Than Black? Multiracial Identity and the New Racial Order*. Philadelphia: Temple University Press.

Davis, Angela. 1998. *Blues Legacies and Black Feminism: Gertrude Ma Rainey, Bessie Smith, and Billie Holiday*. New York: Vintage Books.

Davis, Dedra. 2002a. "$500 Million SHOULD Hurt!" *The Law Offices of Dedra S. Davis*, July 10. Accessed June 13, 2003. http://02aa2b1.netsolhost.com/events.html.

Davis, Dedra. 2002b. "The Truth Does Hurt!" *The Law Offices of Dedra S. Davis*, September 13. Accessed June 13, 2003. http://02aa2b1.netsolhost.com/events.html.

de Certeau, Michel. 1984. *The Practice of Everyday Life*. Berkeley: University of California Press.

Demers, Joanna. 2006. *Steal This Music: How Intellectual Property Law Affects Musical Creativity*. Athens: University of Georgia Press.

Denning, Michael. 1997. *The Cultural Front: The Laboring of American Culture in the Twentieth Century*. London: Verso.

Dessen, Michael. 2006. "Asian Americans and Creative Music Legacies." *Critical Studies in Improvisation* 1(3).

di Leonardo, Micaela. 2008. "Introduction: New Global and American Landscapes of Inequality." In *New Landscapes of Inequality: Neoliberalism and the Erosion of Democracy in America*, edited by Micaela di Leonardo, Jane L. Collins, and Brett Williams, pp. 3–20. Santa Fé, NM: School for Advanced Research Press.

Diawara, Manthia. 1988. "Black Spectatorship: Problems of Identification and Resistance." *Screen* 29(4): 66–76.

Diethrich, Gregory. 1999/2000. "Desi Music Vibes: The Performance of Indian Youth Culture in Chicago." *Asian Music* 31(1): 35–61.

Dolan, Jill. 2002. "Finding Our Feet in the Shoes of One (An) Other: Multiple Character Solo Performers and Utopian Performatives." *Modern Drama* 45(4): 495–518.

Dolan, Jill. 2005. *Utopia in Performance: Finding Hope at the Theater*. Ann Arbor: University of Michigan Press.

Duberman, Martin. 1989. *Paul Robeson*. New York: Knopf.

Edwards, Brent Hayes. 2001. "The Uses of Diaspora." *Social Text* 66 (19.1): 45–73.

Edwards, Brent Hayes. 2003. *The Practice of Diaspora: Literature, Translation, and the Rise of Black Internationalism*. Cambridge, MA: Harvard University Press.

Eidsheim, Nina Sun. 2011. "Marian Anderson and 'Sonic Blackness' in American Opera." *American Quarterly* 63(3) (September): 641–671.

Eidsheim, Nina Sun. 2012. "Voice as Action: Towards a Model for Analyzing the Dynamic Construction of Racialized Voice." *Current Musicology* 93 (Spring): 9–32.

Elam, Michele. 2011. *The Souls of Mixed Folk: Race, Politics, and Aesthetics in the New Millennium*. Stanford, CA: Stanford University Press.

Erai, Michelle. 2011. "A Queer Caste: Mixing Race and Sexuality in Colonial New Zealand." In *Queer Indigenous Studies: Critical Interventions in Theory, Politics, and Literature*, edited by Qwo-Li Driskill, Chris Finley, Brian Joseph Gilley, and Scott Lauria Morgensen, pp. 66–80. Tucson: University of Arizona Press.

Farrell, Gerry. 1999. *Indian Music and the West*. Oxford: Oxford University Press.

Feld, Steven. 1996. "Pygmy POP. A Genealogy of Schizophonic Mimesis." *Yearbook for Traditional Music* 28: 1–35.

Feld, Steven. 2001. "A Sweet Lullaby for World Music." *Public Culture* 12(1): 145–171.

Fellezs, Kevin. 2011. *Birds of Fire: Jazz, Rock, Funk, and the Creation of Fusion*. Durham, NC: Duke University Press.

Fellezs, Kevin. 2012. "'This Is Who I Am': Jero, Young, Gifted, Polycultural." *Journal of Popular Music Studies* 24(3): 333–356.

Fernandes, Naresh. 2012. *Taj Mahal Foxtrot: The Story of Bombay's Jazz Age*. New Delhi: Roli Books.

Ferrao, Dominic. 2002. "Lata's Lament." *The Times of India*, September 29. Accessed June 13, 2003. http://timesofindia.indiatimes.com/entertainment/hindi/bollywood/news/Latas-Lament/articleshow/23740892.cms.

Fischer, Dawn-Elissa. 2013. "Blackness, Race, and Language Politics in Japanese Hiphop." *Transforming Anthropology* 21(2): 135–152.

Fitzpatrick, Chris. 2002. "Boom Go the Bombs, Boom Goes the Bass." *PopMatters*, June 11. Accessed June 13, 2003. http://www.popmatters.com/music/videos/t/truthhurts-addictive.shtml.

Flores, Juan. 1985. "'Que Assimilated, Brother, Yo Soy Asimilao': The Structuring of Puerto Rican Identity in the U.S." *Journal of Ethnic Studies* 13(3) (Fall): 1–16.

Flores, Juan. 2000. *From Bomba to Hip-Hop: Puerto Rican Culture and Latino Identity*. New York: Columbia University Press.

Flores, Juan. 2009. *The Diaspora Strikes Back: Caribeño Tales of Learning and Turning*. New York: Routledge.

Floyd, Samuel A. 1995. *The Power of Black Music: Interpreting Its History from African to the United States*. Oxford: Oxford University Press.

Fojas, Camilla, and Rudy P. Guevarra Jr., eds. 2012. *Transnational Crossroads: Remapping the Americas and the Pacific*. Lincoln: University of Nebraska Press.

Fonarow, Wendy. 2006. *Empire of Dirt: The Aesthetics and Rituals of British Indie Music*. Middletown, CT: Wesleyan University Press.

Fujiwara, Tomas. [accessed] 2015. "About." Accessed May 8. http://tomas-fujiwara.com.

Fulbeck, Kip. 2010. *Mixed: Portraits of Multiracial Kids*. San Francisco: Chronicle Books.

Funkadesi. [accessed] 2004a. "About Us." Accessed June 7. http://www.funkadesi.com/about.html.

Funkadesi. [accessed] 2004b. "Guestbook." Accessed June 7. http://www.funkadesi.com.

Gallagher, Charles A. 2003. "Color-Blind Privilege: The Social and Political Functions of Erasing the Color Line in Post Race America." *Race, Gender and Class* 10(4): 1–17.

Gallicchio, Marc S. 2000. *The African American Encounter with Japan and China: Black Internationalism in Asia, 1895–1945*. Chapel Hill: University of North Carolina Press.

Garofalo, Reebee. 1994. "Culture versus Commerce: The Marketing of Black Popular Music." *Public Culture* 7: 275–287.

Garrett, Charles Hiroshi. 2008. *Struggling to Define a Nation: American Music and the Twentieth Century*. Berkeley: University of California Press.

Garza, Alicia. 2014. "A Herstory of the #BlackLivesMatter Movement." *The Feminist Wire*, October 7. Accessed May 8, 2015. http://thefeminist-wire.com/2014/10/blacklivesmatter-2/.

Gaskins, Pearl Fuyo. 1999. *What Are You? Voices of Mixed-Race Young People*. New York: Henry Holt.

Giardullo, Joe. 1996. "Putting the Ming in Mingus." *Woodstock Times*, April: p. 2. Accessed in Fred Ho Papers. Archives and Special Collections at the Thomas J. Dodd Research Center, University of Connecticut Libraries.

Gilroy, Paul. 1987. *"There Ain't No Black in the Union Jack": The Cultural Politics of Race and Nation*. Chicago: University of Chicago Press.

Gitelman, Lisa. 1999. *Scripts, Grooves, and Writing Machines: Representing Technology in the Edison Era*. Stanford, CA: Stanford University Press.

Goffman, Erving. 1959. *The Presentation of Self in Everyday Life*. Garden City, NY: Doubleday.

Goldberg, David Theo, ed. 1994. *Multiculturalism: A Critical Reader*. Cambridge, MA: Blackwell.

Gray, Herman. 2005. *Cultural Moves: African Americans and the Politics of Representation*. Berkeley: University of California Press.

Grazian, David. 2003. *Blue Chicago: The Search for Authenticity in Urban Blues Clubs*. Chicago: University of Chicago Press.

Guilbault, Jocelyne. 2007. *Governing Sound: The Cultural Politics of Trinidad's Carnival Musics*. Chicago: University of Chicago Press.

Guilbault, Jocelyne. 2011. "The Question of Multiculturalism in the Arts in the Postcolonial Nation-State of Trinidad and Tobago." *Music & Politics* 5(1) (Winter): 1–21.

Hall, Stuart. [1980] 1996. "Race, Articulation, and Societies Structured in Domination." In *Black British Cultural Studies: A Reader*, edited by Houston A. Baker, Manthia Diawara, and Ruth H. Lindeborg, pp. 16–60. Chicago: University of Chicago Press. Originally published in *Sociological Theories: Race and Colonialism* (Paris: UNESCO, 1980).

Hankins, Sarah. 2011. "So Contagious: Hybridity and Subcultural Exchange in Hip-Hop's Use of Indian Samples." *Black Music Research Journal* 31(2): 193–208.

Harden, Jacalyn. 2003. *Double Cross: Japanese Americans in Black and White Chicago*. Minneapolis: University of Minnesota Press.

hartigan, royal, and Fred Ho. 2008. "The American Drum Set: Black Musicians and Chinese Opera along the Mississippi River." In *Afro Asia: Revolutionary Political and Cultural Connections Between African Americans and Asian Americans*, edited by Fred Ho and Bill V. Mullen, pp. 285–290. Durham, NC, and London: Duke University Press.

hartigan, royal, Abraham Adzenyah, and Freeman Donkor. 1995. *West African Rhythms for Drumset*, edited by Dan Thress. New York: Alfred Music.

Herd, Judith Ann. 2004. "The Cultural Politics of Japan's Modern Music: Nostalgia, Nationalism, and Identity in the Interwar Years." In *Locating East Asia in Western Art Music*, edited by Yayoi Uno Everett and Frederick Lau, pp. 40–56. Middletown, CT: Wesleyan University Press.

Hesse, Barnor, ed. 2000. *Un/settled Multiculturalisms: Diasporas, Entanglements, Transruptions*. London: Zed Books.

Ho, Fred. 1975. "Third World Understanding." Unpublished poem. Fred Ho Papers. Archives and Special Collections at the Thomas J. Dodd Research Center, University of Connecticut Libraries.

Ho, Fred. 1995. "What Makes 'Jazz' the Revolutionary Music of the 20th Century, and Will It Be Revolutionary for the 21st Century?" *African American Review* 29(2): 283–290.

Ho, Fred. 1999. "Beyond Asian American Jazz: My Musical and Political Changes in the Asian American Movement." *Leonardo Music Journal* 9: 45–51.

Ho, Fred. 2006a. *Deadly She-Wolf Assassin at Armageddon!* Program notes.

Ho, Fred. 2006b. "Kickin' the White Man's Ass: Black Power and Aesthetics and the Asian Martial Arts." In *AfroAsian Encounters: Culture, History, Politics*, edited by Heike Raphael-Hernandez and Shannon Steen, pp. 295–312. New York: New York University Press.

Ho, Fred. 2008. "Bill Cole: African American Musicians of the Asian Double Reeds." In *Afro Asia: Revolutionary Political and Cultural Connections Between African Americans and Asian Americans*, edited by Fred Ho and Bill V. Mullen, pp. 256–264. Durham, NC, and London: Duke University Press.

Ho, Fred. 2009. *Wicked Theory, Naked Practice: A Fred Ho Reader*, edited by Diane C. Fujino. Minneapolis: University of Minnesota Press.

Ho, Fred, and Bill V. Mullen, eds. 2008. *Afro Asia: Revolutionary Political and Cultural Connections Between African Americans and Asian Americans*. Durham, NC, and London: Duke University Press.

Hoeffel, Elizabeth M., Sonya Rastogi, Myoung Ouk Kim, and Hasan Shahid. 2012. "The Asian Population: 2010." *United States Census Bureau: 2010 Census Briefs*. Accessed May 30, 2014. http://www.census.gov/prod/cen2010/briefs/c2010br-11.pdf.

Hollinger, David A. 2000. *Postethnic America: Beyond Multiculturalism*. Rev. ed. New York: Basic Books, 2000.

Horkheimer, Max, and Theodor W. Adorno. 2002 [1944]. *Dialectic of Enlightenment: Philosophical Fragments*. Stanford, CA: Stanford University Press.

Horne, Gerald. 2008. *The End of Empires: Africans Americans and India*. Philadelphia: Temple University Press.

Hudson, Mark. 2010. "AfroCubism, CD Review: The Real Buena Vista Social Club Finally Get Their Moment in the Sun." *The Telegraph*, October 13. Accessed May 8, 2015. http://www.telegraph.co.uk/culture/music/cdreviews/8051798/AfroCubism-CD-review.html.

Hughes, David. 2008. *Traditional Folk Song in Modern Japan: Sources, Sentiment and Society*. Folkestone, UK: Global Oriental.

Hunger, Thurston. 2005. "Noge, Yoko & Jazz Me Bluesband—'Yoko Meets John'—[Jazz Me Blues]." *KFJC On-Line Reviews*, September 4. Accessed April 14, 2009. http://spidey.kfjc.org/index.php?p=867.

Hutnyk, John. 2000. *Critique of Exotica: Music, Politics, and the Culture Industry*. London: Pluto Press.

Ifekwunigwe, Jayne O., ed. 2004. *"Mixed Race" Studies: A Reader*. London: Routledge.

"Indian Composer Sues Rapper Dr Dre." 2002. *BBC News World Edition*, October 31. Accessed February 13, 2013. http://news.bbc.co.uk/2/hi/entertainment/2383847.stm.

Iton, Richard. 2008. *In Search of the Black Fantastic: Politics and Popular Culture in the Post-Civil rights Era*. New York: Oxford University Press.

Jacobson, Matthew Frye. 2006. *Roots Too: White Ethnic Revival in Post-Civil Rights America*. Cambridge, MA: Harvard University Press.

Jain, Sunny. [Accessed] 2015. "About." Accessed May 8. http://www.sunnyjain.com.

Janani. 2013. "What's Wrong With the Term 'Person of Color' . . . or at Least How It's Used." *Black Girl Dangerous*, March 20. Accessed March 7, 2015. http://www.blackgirldangerous.org/2013/03/2013321whats-wrong-with-the-term-person-of-color/.

Johnson, Gaye Theresa. 2013. *Spaces of Conflict, Sounds of Solidarity: Music, Race, and Spatial Entitlement in Los Angeles*. Berkeley: University of California Press.

Johnson, E. Patrick. 2003. *Appropriating Blackness: Performance and the Politics of Authenticity*. Durham, NC: Duke University Press.

Jones, Andrew F. 2001. *Yellow Music: Media, Culture and Colonial Modernity in the Chinese Jazz Age*. Durham, NC: Duke University Press.

Jones, Leroi. [1963] 2002. *Blues People: Negro Music in White America*. New York: Perennial.

Jones, Leroi. 1967. *Black Music*. New York: Quill.

Joseph, Ralina. 2013. *Transcending Blackness: From the New Millennium Mulatta to the Exceptional Multiracial*. Durham, NC: Duke University Press.

Joyce, Patrick D. 2003. *No Fire Next Time: Black-Korean Conflicts and the Future of America's Cities*. Ithaca, NY: Cornell University Press.

Jun, Helen Heran. 2011. *Race for Citizenship: Black Orientalism and Asian Uplift from Pre-Emancipation to Neoliberal America*. New York: New York University Press.

Jung, Moon-Ho. 2006. *Coolies and Cane: Race, Labor, and Sugar in the Age of Emancipation*. Baltimore: Johns Hopkins University Press.

Kato, M. T. 2007. *From Kung Fu to Hip Hop: Globalization, Revolution, and Popular Culture*. Albany, NY: State University of New York Press.

Kaufman, Gil. 2003. "Judge Rules Truth Hurts' Album Must Be Pulled or Stickered: Court Says Credit Must Be Given to Sample's Composer While Awaiting Trial." *MTV.com*, February 4. Accessed March 1, 2014. http://www.mtv.com/news/articles/1459838/truth-hurts-lp-pulled-from-shelves.jhtml.

Karp, Jonathan D. 2003. "Performing Black-Jewish Symbiosis: The 'Hassidic Chant' of Paul Robeson." *American Jewish History* 91(1): 53–81.

Kearney, Reginald. 1998. *African American Views of the Japanese: Solidarity or Sedition?* Albany: State University of New York Press.

Kelley, Robin D. G. 1999. "The People in Me." *UTNE Reader* 95: 79–81.

Kelley, Robin D. G., and Betsy Esch. 1999. "Black Like Mao: Red China and Black Revolution." *Souls* 1(4) (Fall): 6–41.

Kenney, William Howland. 1999. *Recorded Music in American Life: The Phonograph and Popular Memory, 1890–1945*. Oxford: Oxford University Press.

Kilson, Marion. 2001. *Claiming Place: Biracial Young Adults of the Post-Civil Rights Era*. Westport, CT: Bergin and Garvey.

Kim, Claire Jean. 1999. "The Racial Triangulation of Asian Americans." *Politics and Society* 27(1): 105–138.

Kim, Claire Jean. 2000. *Bitter Fruit: The Politics of Black-Korean Conflict in New York City*. New Haven, CT: Yale University Press.

Kim, Jinah. 2008. "Immigrants, Racial Citizens, and the (Multi)Cultural Politics of Neoliberal Los Angeles." *Social Justice* 35(2): 36–56.

Kim, Kwang Chung. 1999. *Koreans in the Hood: Conflict with African Americans*. Baltimore: Johns Hopkins University Press.

Kimche, David. 1973. *The Afro-Asian Movement: Ideology and Foreign Policy in the Third World*. Piscataway, NJ: Transaction.

Kofsky, Frank. 1970. *Black Nationalism and the Revolution in Music*. Atlanta: Pathfinder Press.

Kondo, Dorinne. 1997. *About Face: Performing "Race" in Fashion and Theater*. New York: Routledge.

Kopp, Ed. 2000. "Yoko Meets John." *all about jazz*, February 1. Accessed April 14, 2009. http://www.allaboutjazz.com/php/article.php?id=5084.

Krasner, David. 1997. *Resistance, Parody and Double Consciousness in African American Theatre, 1895–1910*. New York: St. Martin's Press.

Kun, Josh. 2005. *Audiotopia: Music, Race, and America*. Berkeley: University of California Press.

Kurashige, Scott. 2008. *The Shifting Grounds of Race: Black and Japanese Americans in the Making of Multiethnic Los Angeles*. Princeton, NJ: Princeton University Press.

Kusnur, Narendra. 2002a. "Melody of Errors." *Mumbai Mid-Day*, June 21. Accessed June 13, 2003. http://mid-day.com/ENTERTAINMENT/MUSIC/2002/June/25916.htm.

Kusnur, Narendra. 2002b. "Melody of Errors: The Sequel." *Mumbai Mid-Day*, June 26. Accessed June 13, 2003. https://groups.google.com/forum/#!topic/rec.music.indian.misc/i8t2hyNzcDY.

Kwan, SanSan. 2011. "Performing a Geography of Asian America: The Chop Suey Circuit." *TDR: The Drama Review* 55(1) (Spring): 120–136.

Lakoff, George. 1987. *Women, Fire, and Dangerous Things: What Categories Reveal about the Mind*. Chicago: University of Chicago Press.

Lam, Joseph S. C. 1999. "Embracing 'Asian American Music' as an Heuristic Device." *Journal of Asian American Studies* 2(1): 29–60.

Lancefield, Robert. 2004. "Hearing Orientality in (White) America, 1900–1930." Ph.D. diss., Wesleyan University, Middletown, CT.

Lazar, Zachary. 2011. "The 373-Hit Wonder." *The New York Times*, January 6. Accessed March 7, 2015. http://www.nytimes.com/2011/01/09/magazine/09GirlTalk-t.html?pagewanted=all&_r=0.

Lee, Jennifer. 2002. *Civility in the City: Blacks, Jews, and Koreans in Urban America*. Cambridge, MA: Harvard University Press.

Lee, Julia H. 2011. *Interracial Encounters: Reciprocal Representations in African and Asian American Literatures, 1896–1937*. New York: New York University Press.

Lee, Robert G. 1999. *Orientals: Asian Americans in Popular Culture*. Philadelphia: Temple University Press.

Leonardo, Zeus. 2005. "Through the Multicultural Glass: Althusser, Ideology and Race Relations in Post-Civil Rights America." *Policy Futures in Education* 3(4): 400–412.

Lewis, Earl. 1995. "To Turn as on a Pivot: Writing African Americans into a History of Overlapping Diasporas." *The American Historical Review* 100(3): 765–787.

Lewis, George E. 1996. "Improvised Music after 1950: Afrological and Eurological Perspectives." *Black Music Research Journal* 16(1): 91–122.

Lewis, George E. 2004. *"Gittin' To Know Y'all*: Improvised Music, Interculturalism, and the Racial Imagination." *Critical Studies in Improvisation* 1(1).

Lewis, Reina. 1996. *Gendering Orientalism: Race, Femininity and Representation*. London: Routledge.

Lie, John. 2004. "The Black-Asian Conflict?" In *Not Just Black and White: Historical and Contemporary Perspectives on Immigration, Race, and Ethnicity in the United States*, edited by Nancy Foner and George M. Fredrickson, pp. 301–314. New York: Russell Sage Foundation.

Lipsitz, George. 2007. *Footsteps in the Dark: The Hidden Histories of Popular Music*. Minneapolis: University of Minnesota Press.

Little, Douglas. 2002. *American Orientalism: The United States and the Middle East since 1945*. Chapel Hill: University of North Carolina Press.

Liu, Liangmo. [1950] 2006. "Paul Robeson: The People's Singer." Reprinted in *Chinese American Voices: From the Gold Rush to the Present*, edited by Judy Yung, Gordon H. Chang, and Him Mark Lai, pp. 205–207. Berkeley: University of California Press.

Longworth, R. C. 2000. "Chicago as a Global City." In *Global Chicago: Two Reports on Chicago's Assets and Opportunities as a Global City*, edited by Charles Madigan, pp. 70–93. Chicago: John D. and Katherine T. MacArthur Foundation.

Lott, Eric. 1995. *Love and Theft: Blackface Minstrelsy and the American Working Class*. New York: Oxford University Press.

Lowe, Lisa. 1996. *Immigrant Acts: On Asian American Cultural Politics*. Durham, NC: Duke University Press.

Luo, Liang. 2014. *The Avant-Garde and the Popular in China: Tian Han and the Intersection of Performance and Politics*. Ann Arbor: University of Michigan Press.

Maeda, Daryl J. 2009. *Chains of Babylon: The Rise of Asian America*. Minneapolis: University of Minnesota Press.

Mahon, Maureen. 2004. *Right to Rock: The Black Rock Coalition and the Cultural Politics of Race*. Durham, NC: Duke University Press.

Maira, Sunaina. 2002. *Desis in the House: Indian American Youth Culture in New York City*. Philadelphia: Temple University Press.

Mallapragada, Madhavi. 2014. *Virtual Homelands: Indian Immigrants and Online Cultures in the United States*. Urbana: University of Illinois Press.

Malone, Bill C., and David Stricklin. [1979] 2003. *Southern Music/ American Music*. Lexington: University Press of Kentucky.

Manuel, Peter. 2000. *East Indian Music in the West Indies: Tan-singing, Chutney, and the Making of Indo-Caribbean Culture*. Philadelphia: Temple University Press.

Márquez, John. 2013. *Black-Brown Solidarity: Racial Politics in the New Gulf South*. Austin: University of Texas Press.

Marshall, Wayne and Jayson Beaster-Jones. 2012. "It Takes a Little Lawsuit: The Flowering Garden of Bollywood Exoticism in the Age of Its Technological Reproducibility." *South Asian Popular Culture* 10(3): 1–12.

McLaren, Peter. 1994. "White Terror and Oppositional Agency: Towards a Critical Multiculturalism." In *Multiculturalism: A Critical Reader*, edited by David Theo Goldberg, pp. 45–74. Cambridge, MA: Blackwell.

McLeod, Kembrew, and Peter DiCola. 2011. *Creative License: The Law and Culture of Digital Sampling*. Durham, NC: Duke University Press.

McMullen, Tracy. 2008. "Identity for Sale: Glenn Miller, Wynton Marsalis and Cultural Replay in Music." In *Big Ears: Listening for Gender in Jazz Studies*, edited by Nichole Rustin and Sherrie Tucker, pp. 129–156. Durham, NC: Duke University Press.

Medina, Cruz. 2014. "(Who Discovered) America": Ozomatli and the Mestiz@ Rhetoric of Hip Hop." *alter/nativas* 2: 1–24.

Meintjes, Louise. 1990. "Paul Simon's *Graceland*, South African, and the Mediation of Musical Meaning." *Ethnomusicology* 34(1): 37–73.

Melamed, Jodi. 2006. "The Spirit of Neoliberalism: From Racial Liberalism to Neoliberal Multiculturalism." *Social Text* 24(4): 1–24.

Mercer, Kobena. 1994. *Welcome to the Jungle: New Positions in Black Cultural Studies*. London: Routledge.

Milian, Claudia. 2013. *Latining America: Black-Brown Passages and the Coloring of Latino/a Studies*. Athens: University of Georgia Press.

Millard, Andre. 2005. *America on Record: A History of Recorded Sound*. 2d ed. New York: Cambridge University Press.

Miller, Karl Hagstrom. 2010. *Segregating Sound: Inventing Folk and Pop Music in the Age of Jim Crow*. Durham, NC: Duke University Press.

Modirzadeh, Hafez. 2001. "Aural Archetypes and Cyclic Perspectives in the Work of John Coltrane and Ancient Chinese Music Theory." *Black Music Research Journal* 21(1) (Spring): 75–106.

Monson, Ingrid. 1998. "Oh Freedom: George Russell, John Coltrane, and Modal Jazz." In *In the Course of Performance: Studies in the World of Musical Improvisation*, edited by Bruno Nettl and Melinda Russell, pp. 149–168. Chicago: University of Chicago Press.

Monson, Ingrid. 2007. *Freedom Sounds: Civil Rights Call Out to Jazz and Africa*. Oxford: Oxford University Press.

Moon, Krystyn R. 2005. *Yellowface: Creating the Chinese in American Popular Music and Performance, 1850s–1920s*. New Brunswick, NJ: Rutgers University Press.

Moon, Krystyn R., David Krasner, and Thomas L. Riis. 2011. "Forgotten Manuscripts: A Trip to Coontown." *African American Review* 44(1–2) (Spring/Summer): 7–24.

Moore, Zena. 1995. "'Check the Box that Best Describes You.'" In *American Mixed Race: The Culture of Microdiversity*, edited by Naomi Zack, pp. 39–52. Lanham, MD: Rowman & Littlefield Publishers.

Morello, Carol. 2012. "Intermarriage Rates Soar as Stereotypes Fall." *Washington Post*, February 16. Accessed May 30, 2014. http://www.washingtonpost.com/local/intermarriage-rates-soar-as-stereotypes-fall/2012/02/15/gIQAvyByGR_story.html.

Mullen, Bill V. 2004. *Afro-orientalism*. Minneapolis: University of Minnesota Press.

Mullen, Bill V., and Cathryn Watson, eds. 2005. *W.E.B. Du Bois on Asia: Crossing the World Color Line*. Jackson: University of Mississippi Press.

Murray, Albert. 1970. *The Omni-Americans: Black Experience and American Culture*. New York: Outerbridge and Dienstfrey.

"Music: December Records." 1941. *Time*, December 22, p. 54.

Neal, Mark Anthony. 1999. *What the Music Said: Black Popular Music and Black Public Culture*. New York: Routledge.

Neal, Mark Anthony. 2002. *Soul Babies: Black Popular Culture and the Post-Soul Aesthetic*. New York: Routledge.

"Nightingale of India Raps to New Beat." 2002. *IndiaTimes: The Economic Times*, June 16. Accessed March 7, 2015. https://web.archive.org/web/20040922020943/http://economictimes.indiatimes.com/cms.dll/articleshow?art_id=13097238.

Obama, Barack. 2009. "Increasing Participation of Asian Americans and Pacific Islanders in Federal Programs." Executive Order 13515, October 14. Accessed January 29, 2013. http://www.whitehouse.gov/the-press-office/executive-order-asian-american-and-pacific-islander-community.

Obejas, Achy. 2000. "It's A Wide Musical World: Funkadesi Melds Sounds from 3 Continents." *Chicago Tribune*, April 7. Accessed May 8, 2015. http://articles.chicagotribune.com/2000-04-07/entertainment/0004070052_1_indian-classical-music-tabla-kenya.

O'Brien, Justin. 1999. Liner notes to *Yoko Meets John*. Jazz Me Blues Music. CD.

O'Meally, Robert, Brent Hayes Edwards, and Farah Jasmine Griffin. 2004. "Introductory Notes." In *Uptown Conversation: The New Jazz Studies*, edited by Robert O'Meally, Brent Hayes Edwards, and Farah Jasmine Griffin, pp. 1–8. New York: Columbia University Press.

Omi, Michael, and Howard Winant. 1994. *Racial Formation in the United States: From the 1960s to the 1990s*. 2d ed. New York: Routledge.

Ouellette, Dan. 1998. "Horn Dynasty: The Varying Sounds of Asian American Jazz." *Pulse* (March), p. 46. Accessed in Fred Ho Papers.

Archives and Special Collections at the Thomas J. Dodd Research Center, University of Connecticut Libraries.

Palumbo-Liu, David. 1999. *Asian/American: Historical Crossings of a Racial Frontier*. Stanford, CA: Stanford University Press.

Pacini Hernandez, Deborah. 2010. *Oye Como Va! Hybridity and Identity in Latino Popular Music*. Philadelphia: Temple University Press.

Paget-Clarke, Nic. 2000. "An Interview with Composers Jon Jang and James Newton: Part 1—On the Creation of 'When Sorrow Turns to Joy.'" *In Motion Magazine*, March 20. Accessed May 8, 2015. http://www.inmotionmagazine.com/jjjnint1.html.

Pecknold, Diane. 2007. *The Selling Sound: The Rise of the Country Music Industry*. Durham, NC: Duke University Press.

Peterson, Marina. 2002. "Performing the 'People's Palace': Musical Performance and the Production of Space at the Chicago Cultural Center." *Space and Culture* 5(3): 253–264.

Phinney, Kevin. 2005. *Souled American: How Black Music Transformed White Culture*. New York: Billboard Books.

Prasad, Chandra, ed. 2006. *Mixed: An Anthology of Short Fiction on the Multiracial Experience*. New York: W.W. Norton.

Prashad, Vijay. 2000. *The Karma of Brown Folk*. Minneapolis: University of Minnesota Press.

Prashad, Vijay. 2001. *Everybody Was Kung Fu Fighting: Afro-Asian Connections and the Myth of Cultural Purity*. Boston: Beacon Press.

Prashad, Vijay. 2003. "Bruce Lee and the Anti-Imperialist of Kung Fu: A Polycultural Adventure." *positions* 11(1) (Spring): 51–90.

Prashad, Vijay. 2006. "Foreword: 'Bandung Is Done'—Passages in AfroAsian Epistemology." In *AfroAsian Encounters: Culture, History, Politics*, edited by Heike Raphael-Hernandez and Shannon Steen, pp. xi–xxiii. New York: New York University Press.

Prashad, Vijay. 2007. *The Darker Nations: A People's History of the Third World*. New York: New Press.

Pulido, Laura. 2006. *Black, Brown, Yellow, and Left: Radical Activism in Los Angeles*. Berkeley: University of California Press.

Radano, Ronald. 2000. "Hot Fantasies: American Modernism and the Idea of Black Rhythm." In *Music and the Racial Imagination*, edited by Ronald Radano and Philip V. Bohlman, pp. 459–482. Chicago: University of Chicago Press.

Radano, Ronald. 2003. *Lying up a Nation: Race and Black Music*. Chicago: University of Chicago Press.

Radano, Ronald, and Philip V. Bohlman. 2000. "Introduction." In *Music and the Racial Imagination*, edited by Ronald Radano and Philip V. Bohlman, pp. 1–53. Chicago: University of Chicago Press.

Ramsey, Guthrie P. 2003. *Race Music: Black Cultures from Bebop to Hip-Hop*. Berkeley: University of California Press.

Rankin, Bill. 2009. "A Taxonomy of Transitions." *Radical Cartography*. Accessed February 27, 2014. http://www.radicalcartography.net/index.html?chicagodots.

Raphael-Hernandez, Heike, and Shannon Steen, eds. 2006. *AfroAsian Encounters: Culture, History, Politics*. New York: New York University Press.

"Ravi Shankar: Remembering a Master of the Sitar." 2012. *Fresh Air*. National Public Radio, December 13. Accessed February 26, 2014. http://www.npr.org/2012/12/14/167193821/ravi-shankar-remembering-a-master-of-the-sitar.

Red Baraat. 2012a. "About." Accessed February 28, 2014. http://www.redbaraat.com/about.html.

Red Baraat. 2012b. "Red Barock//The Whitehouse//04.02.12." Facebook page. Accessed February 28, 2014. https://www.facebook.com/media/set/?set=a.10150665058253481.387008.108467608480&type=3.

Red Baraat. 2015. "About." Accessed March 8, 2015. http://www.redbaraat.com/home/.

Reich, Howard. 2008. "It Was a Gamble, but East Thrillingly Meets West in Miyumi Project." *Chicago Tribune*. May 9. Accessed April 14, 2009. http://archives.chicagotribune.com/2008/may/09/entertainment/chi-tatsu-aoki-jazz-0509may09.

Remé. 2002. "Truth Hurts—Addictive." *ReactMag*, August 8. Accessed June 13, 2003. http://www.reactmag.com/features/truthhurts.php.

Riis, Thomas L. 1989. *Just Before Jazz: Black Musical Theater in New York, 1890–1915*. Washington, DC: Smithsonian Institution Press.

Rivera, Raquel Z. 2012. "New York Afro-Puerto Rican and Afro-Dominican Roots Music: Liberation Mythologies and Overlapping Diasporas." *Black Music Research Journal* 32(2): 3–24.

Rivera, Raquel Z., Wayne Marshall, and Deborah Pacini Hernandez, eds. 2009. *Reggaeton*. Durham, NC: Duke University Press.

Roach, Joseph. 1996. *Cities of the Dead: Circum-Atlantic Performance*. New York: Columbia University Press.

Roach, Max. 1980. "Musicians Should Choreograph the Minds of Our Youth." *Unity* 12: p. 16. Accessed in Fred Ho Papers. Archives and Special Collections at the Thomas J. Dodd Research Center, University of Connecticut Libraries.

Roberts, Tamara. 2011. "Michael Jackson's Kingdom: Music, Race, and the Sound of the Mainstream." *Journal of Popular Music Studies* 23(1): 19–39.

Roberts, Tamara. 2013. "Introduction." *Yellow Power, Yellow Soul: The Radical Art of Fred Ho*, edited by Roger Buckley and Tamara Roberts, pp. 1–31. Urbana: University of Illinois Press.

Robeson, Paul. 1978. *Paul Robeson Speaks: Writings, Speeches, Interviews, 1918–1974*, edited by Philip S. Foner. New York: Brunner/Mazel.

Robeson, Paul, and Lloyd L. Brown. [1958] 1988. *Here I Stand*. Boston: Beacon Press.

Robinson, Greg. 2006. "Internationalism and Justice: Paul Robeson, Asia, and Asian Americans." In *AfroAsian Encounters: Culture, History, Politics*, edited by Heike Raphael-Hernandez and Shannon Steen, pp. 260–276. New York: New York University Press.

Rodríguez, Juana María. 2003. *Queer Latinidad: Identity Practices, Discursive Spaces*. New York: New York University Press.

Rodriguez, Richard. 2002. *Brown: The Last Discovery of America*. New York: Penguin Books.

Roediger, David R. 1991. *The Wages of Whiteness: Race the Making of the American Working Class*. London: Verso.

Rogin, Michael. 1998. *Blackface, White Noise: Jewish Immigrants in the Hollywood Melting Pot*. Berkeley: University of California Press.

Rollefson, Griffith. 2014. "Musical (African) Americanization in the New Europe: The Case of Aggro Berlin." In *Crosscurrents: American and European Music in Interaction, 1900–2000*, edited by Felix Meyer, Carol J. Oja, Wolfgang Rathert, and Anne C. Shreffler, pp. 464–477. Woodbridge, UK: Boydell Press/Paul Sacher Stiftung.

Romulo, Carlos P. 1956. *The Meaning of Bandung*. Chapel Hill: North Carolina University Press.

Root, Maria P. P., ed. 1992. *Racially Mixed People in America*. Newbury Park, CA: SAGE.

Rose, Tricia. 1994. *Black Noise: Rap Music and Black Culture in Contemporary America*. Middletown, CT: Wesleyan University Press.

Rose, Tricia. 2008. *The Hip Hop Wars: What We Talk About When We Talk About Hip Hop—and Why It Matters*. New York: Basic Books.

Royster, Francesca T. 2012. *Sounding Like a No-No: Queer Sounds and Eccentric Acts in the Post-Soul Era*. Ann Arbor: University of Michigan Press.

Said, Edward. 1978. *Orientalism*. New York: Pantheon Books.

Said, Edward. 1993. *Culture and Imperialism*. New York: Alfred A. Knopf.

Salomon, Yves Erwin. 2003. "Dr. Dre and Truth Hurts Hit With Injunction in 'Addictive' Case." *Yahoo! Music*, February 5. Accessed February 13, 2013. http://music.yahoo.com/dj-quik/news/dr-dre-and-truth-hurts-hit-with-injunction-in-addictive-case—12048354.

Sassen, Saskia. 2001. *The Global City: New York, London, Tokyo*. Princeton, NJ: Princeton University Press.

Saul, Scott. 2003. *Freedom Is, Freedom Ain't: Jazz and the Making of the Sixties*. Cambridge, MA: Harvard University Press.

Sedgwick, Eve Kosofsky. 1985. *Between Men: English Literature and Male Homosocial Desire*. New York: Columbia University Press.

Sen, Rinku. 2007. "Are Immigrants and Refugees People of Color?" *Colorlines*, July 10. Accessed March 7, 2015. http://colorlines.com/archives/2007/07/are_immigrants_and_refugees_people_of_color.html.

Senna, Danzy. 1998. *Caucasia*. New York: Riverhead Books.

Shankarkumar, Shanthi. 2000. "Music without Borders." *Rediff*, March 28. Accessed June 7, 2004. http://www.rediff.com/us/2000/apr/28us.htm.

Sharma, Nitasha. 2010. *Hip Hop Desis: South Asian Americans, Blackness, and a Global Race Consciousness*. Durham, NC: Duke University Press.

Sharma, Sanjay, John Hutnyk, and Ashwani Sharma, eds. 1996. *Dis-Orienting Rhythms: The Politics of the New Asian Dance Music*. London: Zed Books.

Shipton, Alyn. 2007. *A New History of Jazz*. New York: Continuum.

Singhal, Manasi. [accessed] 2003. "Youth Forum: So Contagious—Truth Hurts." Accessed June 13, 2003. http://www.lokvani.com/lokvani/article.php?article_id=486.

Slobin, Mark. 2012. "The Destiny of 'Diaspora' in Ethnomusicology." In *The Cultural Study of Music: A Critical Introduction*, 2d ed., edited by Martin Clayton, Trevor Herbert, and Richard Middleton, pp. 284–296. New York: Routledge.

Slover Linett Strategies Inc. 2008. "Literature Review on Cross-Ethnic Arts Attendance: A Summary of Findings and Implications." Chicago: Slover Linett Strategies Inc.

Small, Christopher. 1998. *Musicking: The Meanings of Performing and Listening*. Middletown, CT: Wesleyan University Press.

Smith, Cherise. 2011. *Enacting Others: Politics of Identity in Eleanor Antin, Nikki S. Lee, Adrian Piper, and Anna Deavere Smith*. Durham, NC: Duke University Press.

Smith, Miyoshi. 2013. "'That's Why the Work Is What It Is': An Interview with Fred Ho." In *Yellow Power, Yellow Soul: The Radical Art of Fred*

Ho, edited by Roger Buckley and Tamara Roberts, pp. 191–213. Urbana: University of Illinois Press.

Somerville, Siobhan. 2000. *Queering the Color Line: Race and the Invention of Homosexuality in American Culture*. Durham, NC: Duke University Press.

Spickard, Paul R. 1989. *Mixed Blood: Intermarriage and Ethnic Identity in Twentieth-Century America*. Madison: University of Wisconsin Press.

Sponsler, Claire. 2000. "Introduction." In *East of West: Cross-Cultural Performance and the Staging of Difference*, edited by Claire Sponsler and Xiaomei Chen, pp. 1–12. New York: Palgrave Macmillan.

Steen, Shannon. 2010. *Racial Geometries of the Black Atlantic, Asian Pacific and American Theatre*. New York: Palgrave Macmillan.

Steingress, Gerhard, ed. 2002. *Songs of the Minotaur—Hybridity and Popular Music in the Era of Globalization: A Comparative Analysis of Rebetika, Tango, Rai, Flamenco, Sardana, and English Urban Folk*. Piscataway, NJ: Transaction Publishers.

Sterling, Marvin. 2010. *Babylon East: Performing Dancehall, Roots Reggae, and Rastafari in Japan*. Durham, NC: Duke University Press.

Steward. Sue. 1988. "Ofra Haza—Yemenite Songs." *Spin*, April: p. 27.

Stoever-Ackerman, Jennifer. 2010. "Splicing the Sonic Color-Line: Tony Schwartz Remixes Postwar Nueva York." *Social Text 102* 28(1) (Spring): 59–85.

Stokes, Martin. 2004. "Music and the Global Order." *Annual Review of Anthropology* 33: 47–72.

Stowe, David W. 2006. "'Jazz That Eats Rice': Toshiko Akiyoshi's Roots Music." In *AfroAsian Encounters: Culture, History, Politics*, edited by Heike Raphael-Hernandez and Shannon Steen, pp. 277–294. New York: New York University Press.

Stuckey, Sterling. 1976. "'I Want To Be African': Paul Robeson and the Ends of Nationalist Theory and Practice, 1914–1945." *Massachusetts Review* 17(1): 81–138.

Such, David G. 1993. *Avant-Garde Jazz Musicians: Performing "Out There."* Iowa City: University of Iowa Press.

Sundstrom, Ronald R. 2008. *The Browning of America and the Evasion of Social Justice*. Albany: State University of New York Press.

Sun Yat-Sen. 1941. Liner notes to *Chee Lai: Songs of New China*. Keynote. LP.

Takahashi, Corey. 2001. "It's a Real Kick: Composer Fred Ho Uses Martial Arts to Jab at Other Art Forms." *Newsday*, November 7, p. B3. Accessed in Fred Ho Papers. Archives and Special Collections at the Thomas J. Dodd Research Center, University of Connecticut Libraries.

Takaki, Ronald. 1989. *Strangers from a Different Shore: A History of Asian Americans*. New York: Little, Brown and Company.

Takaki, Ronald. 1993. *A Different Mirror: A History of Multicultural America*. New York: Back Bay Books.

Taubman, Howard. 1941. "Songs That Chinese People Are Singing These Days—Other Releases." *The New York Times*, November 30, p. 6X.

Taylor, Timothy D. 2007. *Beyond Exoticism: Western Music and the World*. Durham, NC: Duke University Press.

Thien-bao Thuc Phi. 2008. "Yellow Lines: Asian Americans and Hip Hop." In *Afro Asia: Revolutionary Political and Cultural Connections Between African Americans and Asian Americans*, edited by Fred Ho and Bill V. Mullen, pp. 295–320. Durham, NC, and London: Duke University Press.

Touré. 2011. *Who's Afraid of Post-Blackness? What It Means to Be Black Now*. New York: Free Press.

Tsou, Judy. 1997. "Gendering Race: Stereotypes of Chinese Americans in Popular Sheet Music." *repercussions* 6(2): 25–62.

United States Census Bureau. [accessed] 2012. "State & County QuickFacts: Chicago (city,) Illinois." Accessed June 21. http://quickfacts.census.gov/qfd/states/17/1714000.html.

United States Census Bureau. 2013. *Asians Fastest-Growing Race or Ethnic Group in 2012, Census Bureau Reports*. Accessed May 8, 2015. http://www.census.gov/newsroom/press-releases/2013/cb13-112.html.

Von Eschen, Penny M. 2004. *Satchmo Blows Up the World: Jazz Ambassadors Play the Cold War*. Cambridge, MA: Harvard University Press.

Wade, Bonnie C. 2014. *Composing Japanese Musical Modernity*. Chicago: University of Chicago Press.

Wagner, Bryan. 2009. *Disturbing the Peace: Black Culture and the Police Power after Slavery*. Cambridge, MA: Harvard University Press.

Wang, Oliver. 2006. "These Are the Breaks: Hip-Hop and AfroAsian Cultural (Dis)Connections." In *AfroAsian Encounters: Culture, History, Politics*, edited by Heike Raphael-Hernandez and Shannon Steen, pp. 146–166. New York: New York University Press.

Ward, Brian. 1998. *Just My Soul Responding: Rhythm and Blues, Black Consciousness, and Race Relations*. Berkeley: University of California Press.

Ward, Stephen. 2006. "The Third World Women's Alliance: Black Feminist Radicalism and Black Power Politics." In *The Black Power Movement: Rethinking the Civil Rights-Black Power Era*, edited by Peniel E. Joseph, pp. 119–144. New York: Routledge.

Warmington, Paul. 2009. "Taking Race Out of Scare Quotes: Race-Conscious Social Analysis in an Ostensibly Post-Racial World." *Race Ethnicity and Education* 12(3): 281–296.

Warner, Michael. 2002. "Publics and Counterpublics." *Public Culture* 14(1): 49–90.

Washington, Salim. 2004. "'All the Things You Could Be by Now': Charles Mingus Presents Charles Mingus and the Limits of Avant-Garde Jazz." In *Uptown Conversation: The New Jazz Studies*, edited by Robert G. O'Meally, Brent Hayes Edwards, and Farah Jasmine Griffin, pp. 27–49. New York: Columbia University Press.

Waterman, Christopher. 2000. "Race Music: Bo Chatmon, 'Corrine Corrina,' and the Excluded Middle." In *Music and the Racial Imagination*, edited by Ronald Radano and Philip V. Bohlman, pp. 167–205. Chicago: University of Chicago Press.

Watkins, Rychetta. 2014. *Black Power, Yellow Power, and the Making of Revolutionary Identities*. Jackson: University Press of Mississippi.

Wei, William. 1993. *The Asian American Movement*. Philadelphia: Temple University Press.

Werner, Craig. [1999] 2006. *A Change Is Gonna Come: Music, Race & the Soul of America*. New York: Plume.

Whaley, Deborah Elizabeth. 2006. "Black Bodies/Yellow Masks: The Orientalist Aesthetic in Hip-Hop and Black Visual Culture." In *AfroAsian Encounters: Culture, History, Politics*, edited by Heike Raphael-Hernandez and Shannon Steen, pp. 188–203. New York: New York University Press.

Whittington, Lewis. 2006. "An East-West Meeting of the Minds." *Broad Street Review*, July 18. Accessed in Fred Ho Papers. Archives and Special Collections at the Thomas J. Dodd Research Center, University of Connecticut Libraries.

Wilkerson, Isabel. 2010. *The Warmth of Other Suns: The Epic Story of America's Great Migration*. New York: Vintage Books.

Williams-León, Teresa, and Cynthia L. Nakashima, eds. 2001. *The Sum of Our Parts: Mixed-Heritage Asian Americans*. Philadelphia: Temple University Press.

Wise, Tim. 2010. *Colorblind: The Rise of Post-Racial Politics and the Retreat From Racial Equity*. San Francisco: City Lights.

Wong, Deborah. 2004. *Speak It Louder: Asian Americans Making Music*. New York: Routledge.

Wong, Deborah. 2006. "Asian American Improvisation in Chicago: Tatsu Aoki and the 'New' Japanese American Taiko." *Critical Studies in Improvisation* 1(3).

Yamamoto, Traise. 2002. "An Apology to Althea Connor: Private Memory, Public Racialization, and Making a Language." *Journal of Asian American Studies* 5(1): 13–29.

Yang, Jeff. 2008. "Could Obama Be the First Asian American President?" *SF Gate*, July 30. Accessed February 9, 2015. http://www.sfgate.com/entertainment/article/ASIAN-POP-Could-Obama-be-the-first-Asian-2481103.php.

"Yoko Noge." [accessed] 2006. *Centerstage Chicago*. Accessed May 15. http://centerstage.net/music/whoswho/YokoNoge.html.

Yoshida, George. 1997. *Reminiscing in Swingtime: Japanese Americans in American Popular Music, 1925–1960*. San Francisco: National Japanese American Historical Society.

Young, Cynthia A. 2006. *Soul Power: Culture, Radicalism, and the Making of a U.S. Third World Left*. Durham, NC: Duke University Press.

Zack, Naomi. 1993. *Race and Mixed Race*. Philadelphia: Temple University Press.

Zack, Naomi. 1995. "Life After Race." In *American Mixed Race: The Culture of Microdiversity*, edited by Naomi Zack, pp. 297–307. Lanham, MD: Rowman & Littlefield.

Zhang, Wei-hua. 1993/1994. "Fred Wei-han Ho: Case Study of a Chinese-American Creative Musician." *Asian Music* 25(1–2): 81–114.

Zheng, Su. 2010. *Claiming Diaspora: Music, Transnationalism, and Cultural Politics in Asian/Chinese America*. New York: Oxford University Press.

Zuberi, Nabeel. 2001. *Sounds English: Transnational Popular Music*. Urbana: University of Illinois Press.

Zukin, Sharon. 1995. *The Culture of Cities*. Malden, MA: Blackwell.

Zumkhawala-Cook, Richard. 2008. "Bollywood Gets Funky: American Hip Hop, Basement Bhangra, and the Musical Politics of Race." In *Global Bollywood: Travels of Hindi Song and Dance*, edited by Sangita Gopal and Sujata Moorti, pp. 308–330. Minneapolis: University of Minnesota Press.

Selected Discography

AfroCubism. 2010. *AfroCubism*. Nonesuch. CD.

Anand, Harry. 2002. "Kaliyon ka Chaman." *UMI 10 v.3*. Universal Music India. CD.

Eric B. and Rakim. 1987. "Paid in Full." *Paid in Full*. 4th & B'way/ Island. CD.

Fred Ho and the Afro Asian Music Ensemble. 1994. *The Underground Railroad to My Heart*. Soul Note. CD.

Fred Ho and the Afro Asian Music Ensemble. 2010a. "Momma's Song." *Deadly She-Wolf Assassin at Armageddon!/Momma's Song*. Transformation Art Publisher/Big Red Media, Inc. CD and Comic Book.

Fred Ho and the Afro Asian Music Ensemble. 2010b. "No Home to Return To." *The NYFA Collection: 25 Years of New York New Music*. Innova Recordings. CD.

Fred Ho and the Afro Asian Music Ensemble. 2011. "Gadzo." *Big Red!* Innova. CD.

Funkadesi. 2000. *Uncut Roots*. Good Intent Ahimsa Music. CD.

Funkadesi. 2003. *It's About Time*. Good Intent Ahimsa Music. CD.

Funkadesi. 2008. *Yo Baba*. Good Intent Ahimsa Music. CD.

Funkadesi. 2010. "Real Situation." *Tribute to a Reggae Legend*. Putumayo World Music. CD.

Ice Cube. 1991. "Black Korea." *Death Certificate*. Priority/EMI Records. CD.

Lahiri, Bappi. 1981. "Thoda Resham Lagta Hai." *Jyoti*. Gramaphone Company of India. CD.

Lahiri, Bappi. 2003. *Bappiwood Remixes*. Bappiwood Records. CD.

R. Kelly. 2003. "Snake." *Chocolate Factory*. Jive/Sony. CD.

Robeson, Paul, Liu Liang-Mo, and chorus. 1941. *Chee Lai: Songs of New China*. Keynote. LP.

Shepp, Archie. 1969. "Blasé." *Blasé*. BYG Actuel. LP.

Timbaland and Magoo. 2003. "Indian Flute." *Under Construction, Part II*. Blackground/Universal. CD.

Truth Hurts. 2002. *Truthfully Speaking*. Aftermath/Interscope. CD.

Yoko Noge and the Jazz Me Blues Band. 1999. "I Want a Little Girl." *Yoko Meets John*. Jazz Me Blues Music. CD.

Yoko Noge and the Jazz Me Blues Band. 2001. "I Confess." *Struttin' With Yoko*. Jazz Me Blues Music. CD.

Yoko Noge and the Jazz Me Blues Band. 2002. "Georgia/Osaka On My Mind." *Yoko's Blue Monday Jam at Hothouse*. Jazz Me Blues Music. CD.

Selected Filmography

Dall, Christine, dir. 1989. *Wild Women Don't Have the Blues*. Calliope Films. Film.

Dong, Arthur, dir. 1989. *Forbidden City, U.S.A.* DeepFocus Productions, Inc. Film.

Chakravorty, Pramod, dir. 1981. *Jyoti*. Music Directed by Bappi Lahiri. Pramod Films. Film.

Figueora, Jose, dir. 2003. *All Power to the People! The Black Panther Suite*. Music Directed by Fred Ho. Innova and Big Red Media, Inc. DVD.

Index

marginalization of
  blackness, 118
no-places, 101
race and sound, 92–100
race as determinant of cultural
  taste, 119
racially diverse audiences,
  103–104, 195
representing interracial music in
  the culture industry, 110–111
sono-racial articulation, 95, 109
sono-racial categories, 93
sound to space transition, 101
spatial dynamics of the culture
  industry, 110
theater of diversity, 110–120
unity through diversity, 116
utopia, 120–121
utopian performative, 101,
  107, 109
venues, 101–104, 195
visible diversity, 111
articulation, definition, 92, 93
Asian, definition, 185
Asian American Art Ensemble, 130
Asian/American artists
  vs. Asian immigrant artists, 184
  definition, 184
Asian American music,
  definition, 10
Asian American Resource
  Workshop, founding of,
  127, 197
Asian Americans and Pacific
  Islanders (AAPI), 1
Asian-black enmity, 4
Asian Crisis, 55
Asian exclusion laws, 31–32, 188
Asian immigrant artists *vs*. Asian
  American artists, 184
Asian Improv aRts, 66
Asian music, 35–37. *See also*
  Afro-Asianization.
Asian population in the U.S.,
  growth rate, 1
Asian sounds
  merged with black sounds. *See*
    "Addictive"; Afro Asian.
  Oriental. *See* Orientalism.
assessing musical mixtures,
  194–195
Atkins, E. Taylor, 64

Attali, Jacques, 100
Atwell, Philip G., 154
audience interactions,
  107–109, 195
audiotopias, 91

Bakrania, Falu, 18
Balkan Beat Box, 3
Ballad for Americans, 45
"Bambaya," 128
Bando, Takumi, 138
bands. *See specific bands*.
Bandung Afro-Asian Solidarity
  Conference, 51–52, 190–191
Bappiwood Remixes, 168
Barg, Lisa, 45
Barron, Bill, 131
Basati, Navraaz, 92, 95, 117
Basie, Count, 49
Beaster-Jones, Jayson, 156
Beatles, 39
Bell, Lurie, 63
Bhabha, Homi, 11
bhangra music, 1, 37, 96, 98–99,
  101–102, 111, 117–119
Bindman, David, 130, 131–132,
  148, 150
black, definition, 185. *See
  also* Afro.
Black Arts Movement, 127–128,
  130, 145, 163
black-Asian enmity, 4
black Chinese impersonators, 29, 188
black music
  vs. Chinese music. *See* Afro
    Asian roots.
  as only true world genre, 119–120
  popular music, and world
    music, 119
  racialization, 37–40
  visibility and audibility in world
    music, 120–121
a black musical comedy, 29
black musicians,
  Afro-Asianization, 66
blackness
  and Asianness/Indianness.
    See "Addictive."
  definition, 14
  marginalization, 118
black Orientalism, 32, 171. *See also*
  Afro-Orientalism.